TWAYNE'S WORLD LEADERS SERIES

EDITORS OF THIS VOLUME

Samuel Smith, Ph.D.
Robert Riemann, Ph.D.

American Writers on Education after 1865

TWLS 54

Robert Frost: The Writer as Teacher

American Writers on Education after 1865

By ABRAHAM BLINDERMAN
State University of New York at Farmingdale

TWAYNE PUBLISHERS
A DIVISION OF G. K. HALL & CO., BOSTON

Library of Congress Cataloging in Publication Data
Blinderman, Abraham, 1916-
   American writers on education after 1865.

   (Twayne's world leaders series ; 54)
   A continuation of the author's American writers on
education before 1865.
   Bibliography: p. 263 - 71.
   Includes index.
   1.   Educational literature—United States—History.
2.   Educators—United States—History.   I.   Title.
LA205.B66   370'.973   75-43528
ISBN 0-8057-7654-0

To Adolphe E. Meyer,
friend, mentor, and belletrist of the textbook

Contents

About the Author

A "G.I." student at Brooklyn College and New York University, Abraham Blinderman earned his B.A. in English in 1948 and his M.A. in 1950. From 1950 to 1963 he worked as a high school teacher and studied intermittently for his doctorate at New York University. Finally, in 1963, he was awarded the Ph.D. degree at New York University.

In his quarter of a century of teaching, Dr. Blinderman has taught in junior high schools, vocational, technical, and academic high schools, two- and four-year colleges, evening departments of high schools and colleges.

Since 1966, when the *University Review* of the State University of New York carried his first article, Dr. Blinderman has written about fifty articles for academic and general publications, including *College Composition and Communication, U.S. Camera, The Christian Century, The Teachers College Record, The Water Skier, The History of Education Quarterly, The National Jewish Monthly, The New York State Journal of Medicine, Newsday*, and *The American Journal of Psychoanalysis*. In addition, he has published teaching manuals for Prentice-Hall and Glencoe, a chapter "Shamans, Witchdoctors, Medicine Men, and Poetry," for *Poetry the Healer*, edited by Jack Leedy, M.D. The University of Miami Press will publish his forthcoming edited work on criticism of Upton Sinclair.

Since 1970, Dr. Blinderman has won these academic honors: a Research Fellowship granted by the Research Foundation of The University of the State of New York; a National Endowment for the Humanities Fellowship for a year's study; and the Chancellor's Award for Excellence in Teaching. In 1974 he was nominated by the college as its candidate for one of the eight Distinguished Teaching Professorships named by the State University of New York.

Preface

In this volume I have continued my studies of the fictional and biographical views of American writers on education that I had recorded in *American Writers on Education before 1865*. Since I could not cite the educational references in the works of many writers because of space limitations, I have tried to emphasize the meaningful controversial motifs that our writers have dwelled on, hoping that they realistically reflect educational conflicts recognizable to both laymen and teachers.

Fictional and biographical educational narrations are not generally included in educational histories. I believe that educators should pay more attention to the "undisciplinables" who fictionalize their school and college experience, because many college novels are undoubtedly the cathartic outpourings — written in later periods of tranquility — of aggrieved students with long memories. For example, Upton Sinclair, denied a fellowship in writing when he was a senior at the College of the City of New York, recalls in his autobiography that he was the only potential writer of note in his graduating class. At Columbia University he was told by Professor William Henry Carpenter that he could not write, a belief entertained by many American critics; yet Sinclair wrote more than one hundred books, among them *The Jungle, Boston, Oil*, and the ubiquitous Lanny Budd novels. Sinclair avenged himself upon his college dons in his educational muckraking; *Love's Pilgrimage, The Jungle, Oil, Boston, Samuel the Seeker, Mountain City*, and *The Goose-Step* point accusing fingers at the trustees and administrators of colleges, charging them with molding education to fit the needs of a business civilization. For reasons other than Sinclair's, Thorstein Veblen, H. L. Mencken, John Jay Chapman, Sinclair Lewis, Theodore Dreiser, Jack London, James Thurber, Elmer Rice, Albert J. Nock, George Santayana, Clarence Darrow, Vardis Fisher, Thomas Wolfe, and scores of other writers examined the schools and found them wanting in every category of the educational experience.

One hundred years of belletrist thought on education includes fictional and biographical commentary on academic freedom, administrative malpractice, political and industrial indoctrination, timid teaching, racial segregation, useless curriculums, female education, promotional backbiting, and financing of schools. But not all of the commentary is negative; many critics of education attest to the influence of one teacher who more than compensated for the otherwise vapid schooldays they encountered.

I wish to extend my gratitude for their help and encouragement to friends and colleagues whom I named in the preface to *American Writers on Education before 1865*. Dr. Adolphe E. Meyer, Dean Hyman Lichtenstein of Hofstra University, Dr. Louise Rosenblatt, Gertrude Langsam of Adelphi University, Professor Raynor Wallace and Parker Van Hoogenstyn of the State University of New York at Framingdale, Prescott Harmon of the Levittown Public Library, and my son, Mark, have all contributed to the making of this book.

I wish, especially, to acknowledge my debt to Dr. Samuel Smith, editor of Twayne's World Leader Series, for his unfailing optimism as he guided me through these volumes. A man who has edited hundreds of books in forty-five years is a remarkable person to be apprenticed to. And for Robert Riemann, editor of this volume, I have unbounded admiration. Perhaps the highest praise that I can accord him is to recommend that a major university seek his services as a teacher of English teachers. He is a unique wordsmith whose excisions, transpositions, and accretions transform hesitant passages into assertive formulations.

In his review of *American Writers on Education before 1865* for *The Library Journal*, Philip A. Kalish wrote ". . . it effectively does its job and should serve to whet the reader's appetite for more detailed study." As a teacher, I seek no higher praise. Let those younger take up the torch.

Chronology

Date of Birth		*Date of Birth*	
1893	Joseph Wood Krutch		Phillip Duffield Stong
	John Phillips Marquand	1900	Thomas Wolfe
1894	Brooks Atkinson	1902	Langston Hughes
	Katherine Anne Porter		Max Lerner
	Mark Van Doren		Ogden Nash
1895	Louis Bromfield	1903	James Gould Cozzens
	John Roderigo Dos Passos	1904	James T. Farrell
	F. Scott Fitzgerald	1905	Robert Penn Warren
1897	William Faulkner		
1898	Stephen Vincent Benét	1907	Jesse Hilton Stuart
1899	Robert Maynard Hutchins	1908	William Saroyan

CHAPTER 1

From Johnson to Wilson:
The United States a World Power

The belief is common in America that the day is at hand when corporations far greater than the Erie — swaying power such as has never in the world's history been trusted in the hands of private citizens, controlled by single men like Vanderbilt, or by combinations of men like Fisk, Gould, and Lane, after having created a system of quiet but irresistible corruption — will ultimately succeed in directing government itself.[1] — Henry Adams

I Some Problems Facing the Nation After 1865

THE military settlement of the Civil War ended the bloodshed between the Blues and the Grays, but it did not end the ideological warfare that had brought the North and South into costly conflict.

The Civil War was a bloody industrial catalyst. Never before had the growing nation needed such gargantuan tonnage of food, clothing, machinery, armaments, and construction materials. The subsidies to capital accelerated the multiplication of tentacled corporations that in turn subsidized the politicians who opened the nation's treasury to them.

Looking about the land, captains of industry lamented the limited national trade that they controlled. Why not venture into the Pacific?

Railroads spanned the nation. Factories belched pollution into sky and river. Immigrants toiled in mill and mine, on railroad and steamship. Vast cities arose and with them hordes of humanity. Labor organized, politicized, and became mighty in its own right. The freed black soon learned that fetters of the soul are perhaps more damaging than fetters of the foot. For his part in the building of the nation he received but a pittance — and even that begrudgingly given by his overlords. And the original Americans were driven from their lands, defrauded of their inherent resources,

13

and humiliated by being forced to live in a state of quasi-serfish dependency on what were euphemistically called reservations. Reservations for oblivion!

Possessed with the dogma of Darwinism, leaders of industry, state, religion, education, and the media adapted Darwin's biological theories to their respective disciplines. Social Darwinism supplanted the Sermon on the Mount as a way of life. In the eyes of William Graham Sumner, for example, charity was a sin because it perpetuated shiftlessness and dependency among the poor. But the assumptions of the social Darwinists did not reign without challenge. Protesting the financial and political domination of the nation by the rich and the super-rich was a host of reformers, dissenters, and dreamers who sought places at the nation's great barbecue. Populists, utopians, Farmer-Laborites, unionists, social Gospelers, socialists, and scores of ephemeral messiahs exposed the injustices of the social order. Muckrakers arose like Hebraic prophets; in militant rhetoric they denounced the trespasses of the rich and mighty but their fires were soon banked by the countervailing orations of the plutocracy's skilled penmen.

But the nation that had homespun philosophers like Franklin to inspire commoners to obtain wealth through thrift, hard work, and investment had no need to fear leveling tendencies in its constituents. The workingman's dream was to become a foreman or a partner in his plant. The farmer dreamed of independent holdings, not of the socialistic dreams of John Ball and Wat Tyler.

II *Political Parties Reflect the Nation's Problems*

Although the Republican and Democratic parties persisted as the major parties after the Civil War, numerous smaller ones challenged them. When hostilities ceased both North and South lacked the greatness of heart to regard the emancipated black with the humanitarianism implicit in the Judeo-Christian tradition. Earlier, in 1860, proslavery Democrats and Southerners had given the prefix "Black" to the Republican party, a reference which lasted until 1870. Another faction of the Republican party, the Black and Tans, opened its rolls to both blacks and whites in Texas and South Carolina. A militant branch of the Republican party, the Bloody Shirts, fought the excesses of the Ku Klux Klan and continually raised the late war issues to maintain its political momentum. But the Lily Whites in Texas, the Lincoln League in Florida, and the White Liners in Louisiana fought vigorously to deny the blacks enfranchisement.[2]

The nation's economic problems inspired special interest parties. Gold Bugs, Free Silverites, Greenbacks, and National Silverites battled the gold and silver issue until 1896, when gold triumphed conclusively. The parties of the poor popped up frequently to assert their demands for a larger share of the swelling cornucopia, but they rarely dismayed the confident leaders of the major parties, who were loath to dispense significant portions of their holdings to commoners.

There were anti-immigrant and anti-Catholic parties. The American party, the American Protective Association, the Know-Nothing party, and the Anti-Mongolian party were essentially patriotic associations that feared the influx of immigrants, especially Catholics, who they believed would remain dedicated to the Vatican. Fearing educational parochialism, these bigoted parties supported free public education. Conveniently forgetting that their own ancestors were immigrants, the anti-immigrant parties tried to extend the naturalization period for prospective citizens to fourteen years, a policy reminiscent of the Federalist Alien and Sedition Acts of 1798. An earlier party of infamy belongs in this grouping — the notorious Ku Klux Klan. The Klan intimidated America's black population — the nation's only major block of involuntary immigrants.

Imperialism was denounced by the Anti-Imperialist League and by the Anti-Imperialists, but their efforts could hardly affect a nation schooled to believe in manifest destiny. Spain's weakness provided an excellent opportunity for the nation to demonstrate its strength.

Republican or Democrat, the United States continued to advance industrialization after the Civil War. High protective tariffs, lavish grants of land and money to railroads, cheap contract labor from Europe, legislation favorable to creditors, and business domination of the new public lands were some of the manifestations of Washington's good will to the industrial and commercial establishment. The major triumph of capitalism in the nineteenth century was the nation's formal adoption of the gold standard. American political life was at its lowest ebb in the years from 1865 to 1890. Dull, mediocre men sat in the White House faithfully endorsing the legislative fiats of the lobby-led legislators.[3]

III   *Big Business After 1865*

Wendell Phillips stormed against the arrogance of big business: "Of what good is equality of suffrage if corporations can buy legislators?" he asked.[4] Henry Adams' equally pessimistic brother, Brooks, charged that the autocratic power uses its police power to deter revolt; the ruling class has one major problem — "Whether it is cheaper to coerce or bribe."[5] Perhaps Mark Twain overindulged in hyperbole when he quipped that the only criminal class left in the nation was the congressional class, but affairs such as the Crédit Mobilier that involved a vice-president, a future presidential candidate, and highly influential congressmen soured the public on public virtue. Senator Chandler rationalized his $3,000 bribe of reporters on the questionable premise that his seemingly criminal deeds were justified since he was undermining rascally Democrats intent upon halting the nation's progress.[6]

To dignify its patently aggressive role, big business sought intellectual acolytes to justify its ways to mankind. The genteel churchmen whose churches were built with the dollars of businessmen overlooked many of their questionable business practices. The Astors, Vanderbilts, Rockefellers, Wanamakers, Armours, Pullmans, and Mellons contributed handsomely to the churches,[7] but men worked seventy-two-hour weeks in the steel mills, and children labored in sweatshops as the spires soared heavenward from hundreds of new churches. Prominent ministers wrote wealth-through-virtue books which were nothing more than spiritualized versions of Horatio Alger themes. The titles betray the ministerial approbation of materialistic goals: *Successful Folks* (1878), *Acres of Diamonds* (1875), *Our Business Boys* (1884), *Successful Men of Today* (1883), *How to Succeed* (1882), *What They Say of Success* (1883).[8]

Typical of the attitude of many leading clergymen is this excerpt from Dr. Lyman Abbott's baccalaureate sermon at Harvard: "I do not attack the millionaire. It is better to be a millionaire than to wish you were one without the ability to get the wealth."[9]

But what of the poor? How would they sublimate their longings peacefully and fruitfully? Scott Nearing pondered these questions when Billy Sunday, the leading evangelist of the age, came to preach in Philadelphia. In a letter to the *North American* of February 2, 1915, Nearing described the conditions of the poor in Philadelphia and contrasted them with the "well-fed people, whose ease and luxury are built upon this poverty, child labor, and exploitation." Why pray only for those "who sit in your congregation, contribute to your campaign funds, entertain you socially, and invite you to hold prayer meetings in their homes?" He challenged Billy: "Turn your oratorical brilliance for a moment against low wages, overwork, unemployment, monopoly, special privilege and the other forces which grind the faces of the poor and watch them show their fangs. Before you leave Philadelphia, will you speak these truths? Dare you preach them from the pulpit? Will you champion the cause of the poverty stricken, the underpaid, and the exploited? . . . While exploitation and injustice remain, the Kingdom of God can never come on earth and never will."[10]

But Billy Sunday was not persuaded to preach Nearing's gospel. To the newspapers he said: "I am here to preach religion. I am familiar with social conditions, but I hold these problems will solve themselves, if capital and labor come to God and accept Jesus Christ as their savior from sin. That's what I am here for, to preach the atoning blood of Jesus. And I won't permit anyone to get me off that purpose."[11]

But there were sensitive churchmen who were truly "familiar with social conditions" and earnestly desired to better them. To Richard Hofstadter, the social gospel movement was a compromise among Protestant leaders who were sincerely appalled by the wretched plight of the slum dwellers who had been neglected by their churches. But fearful of the socialistic and anarchist movements in Europe, they proposed a peaceful program to meliorate the condition of the poor.[12] The movement, however, attracted socialists and other types of radicals. William Dwight Porter founded *Dawn* in 1897, a journal dedicated to Christian Socialism. Clergymen and professors contributed to *Dawn*, among them Daniel De Leon, George D. Herron, Edward W. Bemis, and Albion W. Small.[13]

Professor Walter Rauschenbusch won the leadership of the social gospel movement after the publication of his *Christianity and the Social Crisis* in 1907.[14] A student of church history and the radical economics of Henry George and Edward Bellamy, Rauschenbusch found delight in the teachings of European writers as well. He read the works of Sidney and Beatrice Webb, John Ruskin, and the rational historians of Germany. Influenced by his studies at home and abroad, Rauschenbusch developed an evolutionary religious philosophy which proclaimed: "Translate the evolutionary themes into religious faith, and you have the doctrine of the Kingdom of God."[15] But too often the church is static: "It identifies itself with the social conditions of an age and then clings to them when they are passing away."[16]

The social gospel movement did not appeal much to Catholic Americans whose church was based on a conservative Irish population.[17] But in the person of Father John Augustine Ryan, the social gospel cause had a Catholic voice of formidable amplification; Ryan found in Pope Leo XIII's encyclical *Rerum Novarum* a social message which declared that "a small number of very rich men had been able to lay upon the masses of the poor a yoke little better than slavery itself" and that "no practical solution of this question will ever be found without the assistance of religion and the church." Armed with this sanction, Ryan constantly fought conservatism in and out of the church.[18]

Mark Twain in *The Gilded Age* and Henry Adams in *Democracy* depict the American senator as a self-seeking booster of venal institutions. It is tempting to caricature the senator and to expose his lapses of judgment. In illustration, it probably salved the consciences of bankers whom he addressed when Senator Elkins uttered this brilliant platitude: "Very rich men never whistle; poor men always do. Bird-songs are in the heart of every poor man."[19]

Not all statesmen and politicians were deaf to the cries of the poor. The elections of 1892 raised the number of the nation's Populist senators to five, the number of Populist congressmen to ten. Three Populist governers were seated, and about 1,500 local Populist candidates elected.[20] The Populist tide receded in 1900, never again to threaten the established parties, but its slogans and shibboleths were adopted by liberal Democrats and Republicans.

One of the titanic figures of the age, John D. Rockefeller, was not satisfied with the decline of physical attacks upon capital; he deplored, in 1906, the muckraking attacks upon the integrity of business. Probably irritated by Upton Sinclair, the Ralph Nader of his day, Rockefeller asked the nation to disregard the flamboyant nonsense of industry's detractors: "Is it common sense to tell our young men, on whom the future must depend, that they can hope for no other award for carrying our commercial flag forward than frenzied attacks at home, and all the handicaps their own government can pile upon their business to satisfy the violent prejudices excited against them?"[21]

In the Final Report of the Commission on Industrial Relations, 1915, Senator Thomas J. Walsh's investigators reported that wealth was passing into fewer hands, namely, those of rulers of corporations; that U.S. Steel was dominated by 1.5 percent of its stockholders; that corporations were violently antiunion and that they employed labor spies to keep tabs on union organizers; that the Morgan First National Bank controlled corporations employing 785,-499 workers; that the sad state of laboring conditions was a menace to the welfare of the state; that foundations subsidized teachers and writers who influenced the public and the government; and that teachers who had testified before the commission were losing their jobs.[22]

IV *Manifest Destiny*

Were distant lands, colonies, and protectorates necessary for the nation's well-being? Were foreign markets vital to the economic growth of an already expanded industrial establishment? Captain Alfred Thayer Mahan's heralded *Influence of Seapower on History, 1660 - 1783* was a scholarly boon to imperialists who agreed with Mahan's thesis that a major maritime power must maintain a vast merchant fleet shepherded by an alert navy to insure its dominance in trade.[23]

The scholar gave the militarist and the businessman a moral boost in colonial undertakings. The eminent political economist, Professor John W. Burgess of Columbia University, wrote in 1890 that the Teutonic and Anglo-Saxon nations have a mission to politically civilize the world. Only the Teutons had developed a truly national state worthy of emulation.[24] Furthermore, since there is no "human right to the status of barbarism," civilized states have a duty to impose organization upon barbarians by any means necessary.[25] Interestingly, Burgess opposed imperialism in the Spanish-American War because he thought that America would lose by subjugating and ruling other nations.[26] The notion that Americans were God's chosen race had many advocates. In 1900 Senator Beveridge avowed that "of all of our race He has marked the American people to finally lead in the regeneration of the world."[27] Before the Spanish-American War, religious journals had contested the shibboleth, "America the Chosen." Although Protestant journals clamored for war with Spain in God's name, the wrathful editor of the Catholic *Ave Maria* accused clerical militants of favoring war over arbitration.[28] But when war finally came, all the churches save the Quaker and the Unitarian chorused hosannahs for the government's action.[29] The pipings of the American Anti-Imperialist League were drowned out by the collective war cries of the hawks,[30] including the raucous jingoism of gun-itching Theodore Roosevelt who wrote to his friend Henry Cabot Lodge that, although the country needed a war, it was not on the horizon because William McKinley "had no more backbone than a chocolate éclair."[31]

Whitman had foreseen the imperialistic trend in 1871. In

Democratic Vistas he wrote that imperialism had perverted the nation, for an expanding nation loses its spirit and falters in its art.[32] In 1900 Senator George Frisbie Hoar tried in vain to halt our expansion into the Pacific. The nation was in no mood to be told that it had no right to govern the Philippines against their will nor did his colleagues care for the dictum that a nation must not impose freedom on another nation from without.[33]

Fifteen years after our Philippine adventure, the nation appeared to be drifting into the First World War. Not all of President Woodrow Wilson's followers believed implicitly that he would keep America out of the war. After the German submarine war intensified in 1917, Walter Hines Page sent this painful telegram to the tortured Wilson: "Perhaps our going to war is the only way in which our preeminent trade position can be maintained and a crash averted. The submarine has added the last item to the danger of a financial world crash."[34] The telegram is an admission that none of the great capitalistic powers had learned to order their affairs; the war was between two sets of capitalistic powers, and Page's telegram stressed cash, not human values.

From the ashes of this indecisive war fearsome progeny arose — communism in Russia, fascism in Italy, nazism in Germany, and military autocracy in Japan. Lesser states in the Balkans, in Asia, and in the Western Hemisphere assumed stances imitative of the major martinets. Old slogans became meaningless. The rumblings of another war dealt the deathblow to Henry Adams's wistful hope at the end of his *Education* that his friends Clarence King and John Hay and he might return to earth in 1938, their centenary, "to see the mistakes of their own lives made clear in the light of their successors; and perhaps then, for the first time since man began his education among the carnivores, they would find a world that timid and sensitive natures could regard without a shudder."[35]

V   The Business Mind and Education

Before 1870, wrote Richard Hofstadter, American academic men had little influence. Business leaders questioned the value of a college education. However, even though self-made millionaires such as Andrew Carnegie, Horace Greeley, and Edward Bok minimized the value of a college education, they found it expedient to underwrite colleges and send their sons to them for "finishing." Carnegie himself helped higher education liberally and his monied associates validated his truism that "it is to the businessmen following business careers that we chiefly owe our universities, libraries, and educational institutions."[36]

With this influx of funds, the expansion of the university after 1870 was chaotic. Brooks Adams attacked capital's control of the universities. He despised the commercialized education of the universities, their tendency to specialize, and their lowering of standards in all fields but science and mechanics. The ownership of the universities by right of purchase was an academic travesty that would debase education.[37]

Brooks Adams thought that the elective system fallaciously sought to teach everything. Its methodology lacked coordination, and the duplication of courses, the lack of guidance, and the bad administration that it encouraged nullified its limited gains.[38]

Professors hired by college presidents who subscribed to the doctrines of social Darwinism generally accepted the philosophical mandates of their superiors. Most were more concerned with extending their tenures than they were with programs to rid man of his carnivorous instincts. The schools and colleges rarely opposed the social policies of a business-oriented government,[39] and those aesthetes of the genteel tradition who could not sanction the grossness of the industrial mind, escaped to the more refined intellectual milieu of British conservatism, engaging in literary and social excursions that had little to do with American thought and tradition.[40]

The conservative domination of school, press, and clergy created a climate of opinion hostile to labor unions and social reform. In *Wealth Against Commonwealth*, Henry Demarest Lloyd accused big business of ruining the spiritual and artistic aspirations of the people, a charge that Thorstein Veblen would develop fully in *The Higher Learning in America* and that Upton Sinclair would try to document in *Mammonart*, *The Goose-Step*, *The Goslings*, *The Profits of Religion*, and *The Brass Check*. Lloyd's indictment of plutocratic Philistinism is a lay sermon that those who have thoughts to sell might profitably ponder: "Art, literature, culture, religion, in America, are already beginning to feel the restrictive pressure which results from the domination of a selfish, self-indulged, luxurious, and anti-social power. . . . When churches, political campaigns, the expounding of the law, maintenance of schools and colleges, and finally life itself all depend on money, they must become servile to the money power."[41]

There were, of course, academic philosophers who sincerely believed in conservative educational and social principles. The idealism of Josiah Royce included educational precepts based on order, obedience, and loyalty. Rules, he wrote, are the basis of education and to thwart them is to be rebellious. The teacher must profess loyalty to his country and to his calling. By inspiring his students with patriotism, the teacher can insure that disloyal immigrants and selfish labor unions will be restrained from excesses inimical to the nation's well-being.[42] At Yale, William Graham Sumner preached the gospel of Herbert Spencer; since evolution is a tediously slow process, man can hardly hope to affect the stream of history. His doctrine is fatalistic: "Everyone of us is a child of his age and cannot get out of it. Change is wrought by great inventions and discoveries, "new reactions inside the social organism," and cosmic changes. We are carried along with these changes. All we can do is note and observe, but to plan a social world with a pencil is folly."[43]

But to manage a trust, to influence legislators, to control the media are attributes of the efficient, industrial manager. Is success a random happening of an immutable evolutionary process or is it true that in this process of natural selection the most efficient are chosen? There are overtones of Calvinism in Sumner's social thought, for he is actually telling men to accept the order of things, since one cannot fight the inscrutable cosmos. But even a great anthropologist and political economist can be humorous — unwittingly perhaps, but still humorous. Sumner denied that the rich oppressed the poor; if so, the newspapers would denounce them![44]

Somewhat akin to Royce in his conservatism, W. T. Harris, a powerful force in public education, taught that civilized life is contingent upon order, self-discipline, civic loyalty, and respect for private property.[45] From kindergarten to college, the schoolboy must be taught self-discipline, a mastery of the fundamentals in all the educational steps, and those precepts that will enable him to exercise "freedom in the terms of his civilization."[46] Opposed to socialism, determinism, and epicureanism, Harris discouraged teachers from joining labor unions.[47]

Many of the academic dissenters were young men who had studied abroad. Those who sought superior learning in England were subjected to the anti-Spencerianism in the universities there, and those who journeyed to Germany were affected by the German preoccupation with social reform. Back in America, the young reformers discovered that their older colleagues were apathetic to reform and followed the edicts of the boards of trustees unquestioningly. Academic freedom was almost nonexistent in this hectic age; perhaps only at Johns Hopkins, Columbia, Washington, Chicago, and Wisconsin universities were there havens for dissenting professors.[48] Although irked and harried intermittently by politicians, administrators, and fellow teachers, John R. Commons, Richard T. Ely, E. R. Seligman, Thorstein Veblen, Charles A. Beard, Arthur F. Bentley, J. Allen Smith, E. A. Ross, Lester Ward, John Dewey, and Roscoe Pound managed to teach in their respective schools for reasonable periods without harassment.[49] When Charles A. Beard could no longer teach under the alleged despotism of Nicholas Murray Butler, he resigned. But before leaving, he wrote a manifesto of belief that occasioned Butler to write an unsigned editorial in *The New York Times* uncharitably entitled "Columbia's Deliverance." Beard's famed defense of his resignation appeared in *The Dial*, April 11, 1918. It should be read at the commencement of all teachers:

Men who love the smooth and easy will turn to teaching. As long as they keep silent on living issues, their salaries will be secure. It will not be important that they should arouse and inspire students in the classroom. They need not be teachers. They are asked only to be the purveyors of the safe and insignificant. Afraid of taking risks, they will shrink into timid pusillanimity. Risking nothing, they will accomplish nothing. . . . Men of will, initiative, and inventiveness, not afraid of falling into error in search for truth, will shun such a life of futile lucibrity as the free woman avoids the harem. Undoubtedly, it will be possible to fill all the vacant chairs and keep the "learned" publications up-to-date; but to what purpose? That the belly might be full, the mind slothful with paid and pensioned ease? Those who have the great passion to create, to mold, to lead, to find new paths will look upon the university as an unclean thing, or at best, no thing to challenge their hope and courage.[50]

VI   *The Reformers and Dissenters React to Big Business*

With industry entrenched in government and much of the significant media sympathetic to the business ideology, the small farmer, the laborer, and the salaried professional classes could do little to better themselves. Labor associations were unpopular because of the intenseness of the American dream of success. But in the early 1870s the farmers began to protest Eastern industrial practices.[51]

The farmers revolted against the deflationary policies of the government, the high rates charged them for shipping and storage by railroads and bankers, and the low, competing prices of foreign agricultural products.[52] Before farmers and laborers united to form the Populist party, the farmers formed their own party, the Granger Movement, and formalized it at a convention held in Springfield, Illinois, on April 2, 1873. Here they lustily denounced the malevolent derring-do of the "arbitrary and extortionate" railroad moguls, including their trickster games with watered stock and their questionable generosity with railroad passes to legislators.[53] Five years later, The Knights of Labor announced to capital and to the government that labor was unhappy with its lot. In brief, the Knights asked for a greater share of the wealth they produced, health and safety laws in the major industries, prohibition of child labor in hazardous occupations, reduction of the workday to eight hours, equal pay for equal work — to satisfy female workers — and the substitution of arbitration for strikes.[54]

The platform of the Populist party in 1892 was even more critical of the establishment. Corrupt balloting, silencing of newspapers, impoverishment of labor, mortgaged homes, importation of job-usurping aliens, and violent militiamen were some of the evils cited.[55] But the Populist party committed suicide in 1896 by endorsing William Jennings Bryan, a betrayal of Populist canon to traditional Populists. Though dead in name, the Populist creed was perpetuated in the liberal laws passed within twenty years of its demise — in railroad regulation, income tax legislation, direct election of senators, initiative and reform, postal savings banks, and expanded currency and credit facilities.

Richard Hofstadter points out interesting parallels between the Populists and members of the imperialist elite, namely, their common interest in militancy, nationalism, apocalyptic forebodings, hatred of businessmen and trusts, fear of immigrants and workmen, and "toying with anti-Semitic rhetoric."[56]

The Populist movement was followed by the Progressive movement, a liberal reform movement of middle-class urbanites,[57] mostly of native Protestant stock, including many college men and professionals.[58]

In the election of 1912, an "egg-head" defeated two powerful opponents for the presidency. William Howard Taft on the Republican ticket and Theodore Roosevelt on the Progressive, were the victims of the split Republican vote.[59] The mild-mannered Democrat, Woodrow Wilson, kept good his promise to liberalize the laws; his administrations enacted bills to reduce tariffs, the Federal Reserve Act, The Clayton Act, an eight-hour day for railroad workers, and bills to control banks.[60] Social evolution had accelerated inordinately, undoubtedly to the chagrin of William Graham Sumner.

Associated with the quest for social justice in the United States were scores of dreamers and visionaries of whom few, according to Stewart H. Holbrook, "are found in textbooks." Eccentric, flamboyant, and erratic, they were nevertheless "enormously effective in making the United States a better place to live than it otherwise would have been and is. They were a daft, earnest, honest, and all-but-incredible lot of men and women. I think of them as a sort of national conscience."[61]

It is unfortunate that schoolbook authors have slighted the contributions made by the off-beats in our history. What schoolboy or college man would pass a test in American history that requested information on Ignatius Donnelly, idealist, congressman, writer, Populist, and author of *Atlantis*, an imaginative work that sold a million copies? In which texts would the student read of the amazing adventures of Dr. Dioclesian Lewis, bearer of an honorary degree from a homeopathic medical school, who organized legions of women in twelve states to march in a crusade against saloons and breweries? What textbook of history would acquaint the nation's youth with the spirited doings of Populists Mary Elizabeth Lease, Sockless Jerry Simpson, Pitchfork Ben Tillman? What student historian of the Civil War is aware that James B. Weaver, a Northern general, was the Populist candidate for the presidency in 1892 — that his running mate, James G. Field, was a Confederate general? And how many testtakers would score on Coxey's army, Eugene Debs, Bill Haywood, the Wobblies, the Molly Maguires, Susan Anthony, Lucy Stone, Carrie Nation, Dorothea Dix? Where would they place Margaret Sanger, Carrie Chapman Catt, the Knights of Labor, and the Pinkertons? How would they deal wth Oneida Community and the amazing family Noyes that shocked America for several decades? Perhaps schoolboys have enough "basic" studies to master without making peripheral historical excursions to the haunts of ephemera. But they would discover grass roots America in the idealistic eccentricities of the legions of Americans who perform in Holbrook's *Dreamers of the American Dream*.

VII   *Schools and Educators*

The concern of the Founding Fathers for a "general diffusion of knowledge" was not given first priority. Property was synonymous with happiness; therefore, if it could be acquired without learning, why fiddle-faddle with books? Besides, the schoolmaster himself was a poor example of the bookish way to wealth. The noted sociologist Pitrim A. Sorokin's study proved that education in the nineteenth century was not a significant cause of affluence. Of all American millionaires rising from poverty 88.3 percent had no more than a high school education; and 71.7 percent had only an elementary education or none at all.[62] Later, when millionaires began to endow universities liberally, some of them, notably Andrew Carnegie and Andrew Mellon, preferred technical education to classical studies in the institutions they favored because, as Mellon said, classical learning "is difficult to acquire, easy to lose."[63]

How were the public schools of America faring after the Civil War? Ten years after war's end, an English traveler, Francis Adams, wrote that Americans were proud of their schools and recognized the importance of the continued excellence of education.[64] He approved of the decentralization of the American school system, favored its policy of compulsory education, and also praised the refusal of Americans to subsidize parochial schools. Unfortunately, the shortness of the school term and the low salaries tended to lower the level of education, but teachers were ranked high socially. This last observation was not generally supported by educational critics of the period. For example, in Hall County, Nebraska, 1871, classes were held in a rude log or sod building. The teacher boarded with the poorest families, frequently dining on corn bread and molasses. Paid from twenty to thirty dollars a month, the poor teacher served also as a janitor without additional remuneration.[65] The teacher who lacked brawn rarely survived. Learning was not revered; property was the sign of success, and many of the county's rich were illiterate. Since good teachers would not come to the prairies, educated homesteaders did the teaching. They had little to fear from the district superintendents who sometimes knew less than the novice teachers.[66]

The major city public schools also had problems. In December, 1880, *The North American Review* carried an article by Richard Grant White, "The Public School Failure," charging that the School Board of New York City was a tool of corrupt politicians, wasteful in its expenditures of $4,000,000 annually, one-fourth of which was allotted to primary teaching.[67] And for this vast investment what could the schools boast of? The children could not read intelligently, spell correctly, or do anything that reasonably well-educated children should do with ease. Most of their learning was painfully memorized, and their ability to apply rules was pitifully deficient.

Nor did knowledge appreciably raise the well-being of the masses. In the large towns idle lads without any obvious means of support loitered aimlessly, and rural areas were infested with young tramps lacking ambition. Education had not prevented legislative corruption, purchase of politicians' souls by businessmen, and betrayal in the judiciary. Divorces were becoming commonplace, crime and vice were rampant, and young men and women had fallen in virtue. Schools did not prepare the young for life. Furthermore, White wrote that where more public schools exist, more crime, immorality, and insanity exist. In the Southern states where there was more illiteracy than in the North, there was less crime and immorality, an argument that did not fairly assess the reasons for this apparent paradox. White thought that children should only be taught reading, writing, and arithmetic at public expense — all other educational costs should be borne by parents. For most children, assignment to public farms and public workshops would be more advantageous, for there they would learn how to earn an honest living.[68]

Richard Grant White was answered by John D. Philbrick in the March issue of *The North American Review* in an article called "The Success of the Free School System." Philbrick charged White with slanting percentages in several instances by omitting important data that were damaging to his thesis.[69] But the critics of public education continued to damn the alleged malpractices in education. When the pediatrician turned pedagogue, Joseph Mayer Rice, returned from his tour of thirty-six cities in which he interviewed 1,200 teachers, he published his findings in the *Forum*, and later, in a still valuable book, *The Public School System of the United States*. Basically, Dr. Rice was critical of public apathy, political cynicism, and professional indecision regarding public education. Newspapers reacted favorably to Rice's study, but educational journals considered the muckraking physician unfit to comment on education.[70]

Dr. Rice wrote in 1893. Ten years later, Adele Marie Shaw made a similar study and found little change for the better. Poor administration, political corruption, and antiquated methodologies limited the school's usefulness. But she thought a school in Manominie, Wisconsin, funded by James Huff Stout, a lumberman, educated its patrons well. In addition to offering the basic curriculums, Stout's school was fitted with workshops, a gymnasium, and a swimming pool. The physical education teachers worked with all of the students, not just athletes. In time the school became a civic center as well, a model of what a well-planned school can do for students and adults alike.

The number of high schools grew from 500 in 1865 to more than 6,000 by the turn of the century, and enrollments rose in that same period from 80,000 to over 500,000. A landmark decision of the Supreme Court in 1874 — the famed Kalamazoo Case — gave local communities the right to levy taxes for high school education, a right that directly led to the growth of American colleges because of the increasing numbers of high school graduates. But were these high schools fulfilling their goals? In 1892, the celebrated Committee of Ten chaired by Charles W. Eliot, Harvard's illustrious president, dutifully recognized the needs of the vast majority of the high school's terminal students, but the committee was not successful in luring away secondary school administrators from inordinate flirtation with the college mystique. Consequently, high schools became standardized college preparatory schools which catered to their policy-making overlords in higher education.[71]

VIII *Vocational Education*

Before 1905 vocational training was not urgently needed. The immigrants who fled Europe provided a plentiful supply of skilled labor. But after 1910, American trade expanded enormously, and skilled hands were needed in production and management. In 1914, The National Commission on Vocational Education reported that only 1 percent of the nation's 12,500,000 agricultural workers had received any training and that less than 1 percent of the nation's 14,-500,000 mechanical and manufacturing workers had attended a vocational school. Bavaria had more trade schools than all of the United States. But worse yet, the commission revealed that of 7,222,-298 young people between the ages of fourteen and eighteen, only 1,032,461 had enrolled in some kind of high school.[72] Industry now wanted more trained men, especially technicians. In 1917 Congress enacted laws that subsidized vocational training in the public schools. Programs in agriculture, the trades, commerce, and home economics were established as well as research programs to insure sound vocational training.

IX *The Progressive Movement in Education*

Twenty years before Dr. Rice wrote his public school exposé, Francis W. Parker, called "the father of the progressive school" by John Dewey, introduced a unique school at Quincy, Massachusetts. Bronson Alcott and George Bancroft had experimented in progressive education earlier in the nineteenth century, but their

ideas were too advanced for their age. Colonel Parker — he had
served in the Civil War and retained his title — astonished
traditional educators with his innovations at Quincy: field trips, in-
ductive approach to arithmetic, abandonment of formal textbooks
for maps and newspapers, teacher-prepared materials, and inter-
disciplinary studies.[73] He taught that nothing can be understood out
of context. For example, a tree should be studied in the context of its
ecological significance. Arithmetic in isolation is meaningless, but if
employed as a measuring tool in all disciplines by the child its beauty
and practicality become apparent.[74] Flogging defective and
backward children is useless and cruel. Instead, they should be
treated with love, care, and interest to motivate them to achieve
their potentials. A child should not be forced to learn. The parent
and teacher must learn to respect the child without pampering him.
To encourage the development of good minds Colonel Parker
recommended physical exercise, noting that physically strong
children are frequently among the brightest.[75]

X   *John Dewey and the Function of the Schools*

John Dewey admired Colonel Parker's progressivism but went
beyond the colonel's expectations for education by naming education as "the fundamental method of social progress and reform."[76]
When most of the academic world looked with disfavor upon unions,
Dewey joined the American Federation of Teachers. To some of his
philosophical brethren this was heresy, but to a pragmatic
philosopher the union was a practical instrument for improving the
welfare of the underpaid and intimidated teacher. How could underpaid and servile teachers inspire children with truth, courage, and
altruism?

Dewey undertook a dangerous mission when he set out to steer the
child's natural impulses into desirable social behavior. If school is a
part of life, not a mere preparation for life,[77] how could the child's
school experiences be grounded on his experiences at home and at
play?[78] Is the school equipped to cope with the multiplicity of experiences that students bring to class? How will the teacher steer the
drunkard's child, the sadist's child, the bigot's child, and the
criminal's child into socially desirable behavior? Perhaps at the
laboratory schools where class size is limited and teachers are
dedicated, children can realize their optimum mental and moral
development, but before such schools become commonplace the
opinions of taxpayers will have to undergo a radical revision.

Professor George Sylvester Counts's question, "Dare the Schools Change the Social Order?" seems naïve today. The schools represent the present social order. Dewey's pragmatism, his scientific attitude toward change, his opposition to dogmatism in religion, his stress on a student-oriented curriculum, his belief in liberal reformism, and his antimetaphysical philosophy alienated millions of Americans. Unfortunately for Dewey, his exposition of his views was too complex for lay and academic readers. Perhaps much of the criticism of his educational ideas came from careless readers who confused his advocacy of gentleness toward children with pampering; his progressive curriculum with a denial of the value of fundamentals; his participation in reform movements with un-Americanism; and his relativism in religion with atheism.[79] Dewey had angry words for the cult of self-expression whose students exhibited "deplorable egotism, cockiness,. impertinence, and disregard for others."[80]

Can the schools teach the gospel of peace in a world of conflict? Obviously not, for only rarely — as at Dowling College in 1973 — will schools and colleges institute courses to wage peace. But President Faunce of Brown spoke prophetlike in 1907 on peace in education: "In time of peace we must prepare to make wars impossible." His appeal to mankind to educate children for peace is a noble call to reason, one that the United Nations might well publicize to the world: "We can teach in our schools that peace hath her victories no less renowned than war. We are learning to exalt a new kind of heroism — the heroism of the city missionary, of the men and women who are devoting their lives to the uplifting of social conditions in the heart of our great cities. This newer heroism must be taught in our public schools."[81]

XI   *The Normal School*

The expansion of public schools highlighted the lack of trained teachers. Normal schools were established to train teachers. The first such school opened its doors to three female students at Lexington, Massachusetts, in 1839.[82] At first, normal schools offered a modest, one-year program; later, another year of fundamentals and discourses on piety was added. Subjected to political sniping and legislative miserliness, ignored by "scholars," and despised by practical educators, the schools graduated into degree-granting colleges, and some affiliated themselves with universities.[83] In 1899, 32 percent of New York City's high school teachers had college degrees, 39 percent were normal school graduates, and the remaining teachers were hired because of their scholarly talents or success in teaching.[84] Today, as then, the value of teacher-training programs is under attack. The liberal arts schools with some justification attack the intellectual shallowness of many educational courses.

XII   *Attitudes toward Blacks and Education*

In the concluding paragraphs to his *History of Education* (1920) Ellwood Cubberley assigns education the task of making democracy a safe form of government for the world."[85] He sees it as the mission of the progressive nations to lead the backward peoples of the world to a democratic Eden, even as England and France have "civilized" their inferior wards — even as the United States has uplifted the peoples of Cuba, Puerto Rico, and the Philippines.[86] But of the black American Cubberley says nothing. And one hundred years after the Civil War, black Americans have not yet been accorded those self-same democratic rights that Cubberley envisioned as the divine gift of the democracies to those aching for them.

Laws, constitutional amendments, sermons, white liberalism, and common participation of blacks with whites in America's wars have not created a mood of brotherliness. The heritage of the Civil War has been continued polarization of the races, unwritten warfare, and growing despair. The hostility of whites toward blacks from the infamous Draft Riots of 1863 in New York City to the obstructive tactics of whites in halting the construction of apartment buildings for blacks in Newark, 1973, is a painful record of man's retreat from the universal brotherhood of man.

President Andrew Johnson addressed himself to the race problem in America in his annual message to Congress on December 3, 1867. What he said about the black race probably expresses the consensus of Americans today. Johnson's statement is direct, candid, and shorn of hypocritical apologies for his stand: "The great differences between the two races in physical, mental, and moral characteristics will prevent an amalgamation or fusion of them together in one homogeneous mass. If the inferior attains the ascendancy over the other, it will govern with reference only to its own interests . . . and create such a tyranny as this continent has never yet witnessed."[87]

In 1865, the United States had to deal with four million blacks who were without homes, clothing, jobs, and names.[88] In the South the freed black had to deal with two classes of whites — those who returned to ruined homes and refused to participate in rehabilitation and those who wanted to heal the nation's wounds. A third class of whites — the unreconciled — left for new destinies in Cuba, Australia, Egypt, and Europe.[89] But for the most part, Southerners believed that the black held a middle ground between man and beast, that he would work only under compulsion, and that his labor should be restricted to raising cotton, rice, and sugar for the whites.[90] As late as 1890, an Alabama school superintentent addressing the national Education Association reiterated President Johnson's views on the black race. But, he added, the best Southern people have a kind regard for the black who in turn honors and respects his white friends.[91] The "best Southern people," meaning of course the old aristocratic line, may have been paternalistic to their old hands, but the poor whites feared the blacks' emancipation as a threat to their livelihood.[92] The homecoming veteran eyed the freedman suspiciously. Would the former slave become arrogant? Would he use Northern military power to assume political power?[93] Would public education train him for the skilled trades?

Ill-used by the native white Republicans who generally had no education, social position, and wealth, the Scalawags, and the Northern opportunists who came South to exploit them, the blacks lived in a fearful world of broken promises, dashed hopes, and sordid poverty.[94] Almost immediately after the war's end, Southern states tried to impose Black Codes. For example, in 1865 the General Assembly of Louisiana enacted a labor act that compelled the laborer to sign a work contract with his employer in January for a full year. This act prohibited the worker from changing his place of employment during the contract year, decreed a ten-hour workday in summer months, and held the worker responsible for damage to machinery, injury to livestock, and shoddy workmanship.[95] The Black Codes of Mississippi were even harsher; they forbade blacks to wed whites, held them subject to arrest for leaving an employer before contract expiration, and declared as vagrants unemployed blacks or those who assembled night or day without permission.[96] These unfortunates were forced to work for employers who were authorized to deduct taxes from the pitiful wages of their legalized slaves — a subterfuge that created a new form of peonage in the South.[97] In the North, Samuel Jones Tilden, a Democrat, warned that the Republican party was trying to exploit black naiveté by creating black governments subservient to Republican kingpins; his fears were similar to those of Andrew Johnson, namely, that three million blacks in the South would control the destinies of four and a half million whites. It was conceivable, he said, that the South might be represented by twenty black Senators and fifty black Congress-men.[98]

In response to the Black Codes the Northern Military govern-ments in the South issued orders to their commands to prohibit dis-crimination on public conveyances, on navigable waters, and in the streets. In Georgia, Alabama, and Florida, chain gangs were abolished and indentures of minors contracted since 1865 were revoked. Pauper relief was made nondiscriminatory and blacks were given the same privileges in prisons as whites.[99] But Wendell Phillips in Boston complained that of the three aims abolitionists sought for the blacks only the ballot was achieved — and that insecurely. The other two — land and education — were only promised.[100]

According to John R. Lynch, a prominent black statesman and historian of Reconstruction times, eminent Southern Republicans sincerely hoped that they could work harmoniously with the en-franchised blacks.[101] But George W. Williams, another black historian, minimized the role of the Southern white Republican because he had almost disappeared from the political scene before 1875. The army had to protect black leaders from angry mobs, but the show of strength merely antagonized militant Southerners. Williams attributes the failure of North-South relations in this period to the foolish Northern policy of entrusting leadership to in-competents and to the refusal of the Southern leaders to participate in finding paths to reunion with the North.[102] Meanwhile, those critical of blacks exulted in what they cited as examples of black im-morality. In view of the national turmoil, the general fear and dislike of the black, and the greedy opportunists who hovered hawklike over the distressed earth for booty, it is not unlikely that blacks, like their white critics, indulged in crime and immorality. But ignorant of the law, exiled from their homes, subject to the dubious justice of bigoted judges, unable to purchase the services of lawyers, un-ceremoniously sentenced to chain gangs and forced labor camps,[103] is it any wonder that the black man hated the white man's law and took the law into his own hands at times? There was biblical prece-dent; had not Moses slain an Egyptian overseer who had beaten an Israelite slave? And was exodus better? Escape to the city brought similar evils — unsanitary living conditions, unemployment, and physical attacks by immigrants who resented competitors for their jobs.[104]

The return of white power to the South after the departure of military governments was a deadly blow to the freedman. Local governments appropriated his property on the pretext that he owed "delinquent taxes." Laws were enacted to prohibit white men from selling property to blacks. Landless and penniless, the black had to migrate or sell himself for life as a sharecropper. Now he was at the mercy of his former employer who paid him in script and cheated him at the plantation store. Disenfranchised by poll taxes and literacy tests, the black farmers were helpless. Those who still were permitted to vote were intimidated to vote Democratic. Intimidation frequently was fatal; General Sheridan reported in 1875 that at least 1,200 blacks were killed for political reasons in Louisiana since 1866. Of 47,932 registered Republican voters in Louisiana, only 5,360 cast their ballots in the 1868 elections.[105] Law and order rode rampant — with rope and shotgun as reasoning agents.

XIII   *Education for Blacks in the South*

A society that was defeated militarily, dominated politically by its conquerors, and frustrated psychologically by its enforced servility would hardly behave benignly toward the alleged cause of its downfall. The unfortunate black, brought in chains to the New World and enslaved by his purchaser, ultimately became the scapegoat of all factions in the land. The departure of Northern troops and politicians from the South signaled the end of proper education for the black citizens of the South, the philanthropy of many Northern and Southern educational benefactors notwithstanding.

The large numbers of slaves who escaped to Fort Monroe, Virginia, in 1861, were probably the first freedmen to be educated before the end of the Civil War. Reverend Lewis C. Lockwood, representing the American Missionary Association, arrived at Fort Monroe on September 3, 1861. Impressed with the desire of the escaped slaves to read, Lockwood wrote to his associates in New York City for additional missionaries to help him and literate black "brothers" to teach the illiterate freedmen and their children. His call was heeded; the recruited missionaries started schools at Fort Monroe, at Camp Hamilton, at the Chesapeake Female College, and in the home of ex-President Tyler. Day classes were held for the children, night classes for adults. An outstanding black teacher, Mary S. Peake, worked valiantly to advance education for her people until she died of tuberculosis in 1862.[106]

In 1863, General Benjamin Franklin Butler used government funds to found a school for black children. The government turned the school over to the American Missionary Association in 1865.

Later, the Butler School became the property of the Hampton Institute which had been built in 1868 when Brevet Brigadier Samuel Chapman Armstrong had a school built for black children with the salvaged lumber of the demolished Hampton Military Hospital. Today, Hampton Institute is a well-known college, attracting people of all races to its diversified curricula.[107]

After the Civil War, the problem of educating the emancipated slaves was a major test of the nation's sincerity. An anonymous Northerner warned legislators that "to set the slaves free will be a doubtful blessing to them if we do no more. American society has little patience with the weak and thriftless."[108] Here indeed was a challenge, and many men of good will committed themselves to readying the illiterate and unskilled ex-slaves for vocational competition in a society that worshiped individualism. Missionaries opened schools to train the new citizens in the vocations, and, with God's help, to convert the perplexed black to their respective faiths. The army sponsored schools under the Reconstruction governments, but private philanthropy and missions assumed a large role. For example, the Peabody Fund of $2,384,000 for educational development of the South included sizable grants for black education,[109] but the Peabody practice of providing matching funds only aided large towns that had money. In addition, since the Peabody Fund would not aid mixed schools, it encouraged segregation and retarded the growth of integrated education for seventy-five years.[110] For a time, freedmen contributed large sums to pay for their own schools and teachers; in 1869 they raised $200,000 for education. But in Georgia, their efforts were partly nullified, because the hundreds of thousands of dollars they paid for rent brought them no educational benefits, whereas taxes for the education of whites were deducted from taxes on rented property.[111]

In 1869, there were 9,503 white and black teachers in the South, most of them Yankee women, who were disliked by Southerners.[112] What offended many Southerners was the Northern double standard for the schools — integration in the South, segregation in the North.[113] General Oliver Otis Howard, commissioner of the Freedmen's Bureau and Howard University's first president, found white Southern teachers incompetent and apathetic to the needs of their black students.[114] The certification bills gave white teachers double the salaries of their black colleagues.[115] Carpetbaggers like ex-Governor Daniel H. Chamberlain of South Carolina sometimes became enamored of their erstwhile enemies; Chamberlain reversed himself on Reconstruction, asserting that blacks did not need higher education. The three Rs and vocational and manual training would benefit them more than a wasteful four-year stay at a black college. Self-help, thrift, prudence, acquisition of property, and loyalty were the virtues that the black should diligently aspire to.[116]

The South resisted the imposition of integrated schools. In 1874, federal troops had to quell an uprising in New Orleans by White Line Leagues,[117] but not all Southerners felt this way. In 1875, Thomas Nelson Page protested to two of the city's newspapers against the opposition to mixed schools in the city. Why fear mulatto teachers? Were not thousands of white children breast-fed by black wet nurses?[118] But such occasional protestations were unheeded.

Many respectable Southerners opposed Negro education because they feared that blacks would give up manual labor for teaching, preaching, and politics.[119] Besides, would not educated blacks organize their people, and stir them up to mischief?[120] Not all educated blacks would be like Richard Theodore Greener, Harvard's first black graduate, who praised Harvard's liberalism, teachers, and traditions. But, notes historian George Williams, Greener himself was a racist.[121] Why should this apostle of liberalism support Chinese-Exclusion Acts?

Until quite recently, the black community itself was divided on the issue of gradualism versus immediacy. Booker T. Washington, in his famous Atlanta speech of 1895, advocated that his people accept social inequality for the right to advance politically and educationally.[122] But by 1900, Booker T. Washington's gradualism was repudiated by more militant blacks. Quiescence had brought them to second-class citizenship in the South. In the North they were greeted with race riots and segregation. There was no place to go. A new leader arose — W. E. B. Du Bois. A militant scholar, he opposed Washington's compromising ways. There had been too much delay already in granting to blacks the rights enjoyed by whites. There had been too much servility; educated blacks were Pullman porters, waiters, or even ordinary laborers. There was no more sense in waiting. The black man would have to fight for equality.[123]

David Tyack attributes the failure of black education to the failure of American society to make emancipation real.[124] Both the North and the South were responsible for the plight of blacks in America.

XIV *Female Education*

Until 1900, not much national regard had been shown for female education above the elementary level. The monied classes sent their daughters to female academies or had them taught by private tutors. Most of the colleges were closed to women; to most Americans the role of the woman was to master the domestic arts, marry, bear children, and supervise the developing family. But as industrialism swept the nation after the Civil War, women began to infiltrate shop, mill, and office.[125] After 1880, female normal school graduates began to replace men as school teachers. These young ladies, schooled in the latest theories of child development,[126] probably inspired their pupils with greater enthusiasm than the more tradition-bound males who were loyal to the ferrule and birch rod.

Colleges reluctantly admitted women. From 1870 to 1892, Michigan, Wisconsin, Cornell, M.I.T., and Chicago successively became coeducatioal colleges. Columbia and Harvard were adamant in their stand against mixing the sexes in their schools, but they relented somewhat by sponsoring the female "sister" colleges Barnard and Radcliffe. Most of the female students majored in teaching, arts, or letters. The professions were securely closed to them, and the few doctors or lawyers who managed to graduate from professional schools found that their male colleagues made it almost impossible for them to practice.[127]

Although many of the taboos against professional education of women were lifted by 1900,[128] the popular sentiment against higher education for women did not wane appreciably until women had won enfranchisement. In *Hungry Hearts*, a feminist novel by David Graham Phillips, a scornful husband disparages his wife's college education: "A few more years'll wash away the smatter she got at college, and this restlessness of hers will yield to nature. . . . As grandfather often said, it's a dreadful mistake, educating women beyond their sphere."[129] Two weeks before he was slain by a lunatic, Phillips mailed the manuscript of *Susan Lenox: Her Fall and Rise* to Appleton and Company, but Joseph Sears, the publisher, told Phillips that the novel was terrible. The book was set aside for six years before Appleton risked publishing it. When the book appeared in 1917, it was an immediate success, and it became the Bible of feminists. In a sense, Phillips made fine use of the Pygmalion theme. In turn a prostitute, fashion model, sweatshop worker, and heiress, Susan is saved from the usual dismal fate of the streetwalker by the generosity of a murdered dramatist who had willed his fortune to her. Now rid of poverty and ignominious whoredom, Susan rises to stardom in the theater, a matchless paragon of morality and decorum.[130] But what of the poor factory girls who will never inherit fortunes? The diseased harlots who are destined to bed forever in

Potter's Field? Phillips does not neglect them. His Hollywood ending highlights the miseries of the poor by contrasting the undeserved wealth of Susan through fortuitous inheritance with the doomed destinies of the hapless and hopeless poor.

XV Conclusions

A twenty-two-year-old soldier at Appomattox would have been seventy-five on November 11, 1918, when the Central Powers surrendered to the Allied Powers in France. Had he been politically active he would have participated in the great debates and movements from which was distilled the power that shaped the nation's destinies for decades to come. The young veteran had his choice to embrace the freed black and to sincerely guide him to equal citizenship or to return the black to a legalized type of servitude and qualified citizenship; to follow the agrarian shibboleths or to submit to an advancing predatory capitalism; to fight for the right of the Indian to his land or to gaze enviously at the millions of acres seized from the helpless Indian tribes; to join the corrupt politicians in office or to support the muckrakers who opposed them; to endorse free public education or to usurp the state's right to educate the young; to favor isolation or to wave the flag with ardent advocates of manifest destiny; to fight for social reforms or to allow prisons, hospitals, and factories to operate inhumanly; and to grant women equal rights with men or to degrade them as in the past by limiting their roles to the domestic arts.

Agrarian, Silverite, Gold Bug, Populist, capitalist, social Darwinian, social Gospelist, imperialist, muckraker, Progressive, Molly Maguire, Pinkerton, Perfectionist, isolationist, racist, clansman, Socialist, Greenback, nativist, prohibitionist, single-taxer, utopian, evangelist, speculator, banker, broker, lobbyist, feminist, and militarist appealed to the youth after peaceful Appomattox for allegiance. Those who clamored for his vote, his loyalty, and his dollar were America's true educators. Compared to the dull learning of the schools, the dramatic learning of the universities of life was immeasurably more meaningful. But as schools improved in pedagogy, the gap between school and life narrowed. To John Dewey and his followers school and life were inseparable, but Dewey's advanced educational theories were not particularly liked by traditionalists.

Since most of the schools were supervised by conservative boards of education, administered by men who were allied to the trustees in political and educational philosophy, and taught by timid teachers, students were denied an education that would offer them a full spectrum of thought on debatable topics. Later, the progressive educational ideas of Colonel Parker, John Dewey, and William James brought some relief to the subject-oriented classes in American schools, but the willful or unwitting perversion of Dewey's theories by educators and teachers sparked antiprogressive movements.

The backlash against blacks and their supporters continues to impede meaningful education for blacks and other minorities all over the land. The white population since the end of the Civil War has resisted total integration of the schools and today's busing problem has intensified the friction among the nation's races. In principle, Du Bois has won over Bookter T. Washington; blacks no longer want euphemistically named courses that lead to quasi-professional positions.

When nationalism becomes the major preoccupation of a people, the schools will support the governmental projects advanced by the nation's leaders. Teachers who oppose policies leading to war or to erosion of the people's rights are suspect; those who cannot teach in good conscience what they deem untruthful or harmful have brief careers as schoolmasters. Until 1917 at least, there is no evidence of any concerted academic opposition to the imperialistic programs of the successive administrations.

It is ironic that a former professor of history, initially opposed to American entry into World War I, yielded to what he thought were justifiable provocations by the Germans, took his nation into a costly war, and vainly attempted to apply his learning, his humanitarianism, and his repentance to the building of a brave, new world. History presented a schoolmaster with an opportunity to remedy the ills of a wounded world, but the balm he used was rejected by those who were his true masters. They rejected salve and they rubbed in salt — and the world still smarts from the cruel bite.

CHAPTER 2

Lower, Female, Black, Adult, and Utopian Education, 1865 - 1918

Her teacher's certainty it must be Mabel
Made Maple first take notice of her name.
She asked her father and he told her "Maple —
Maple is right."
    "But teacher told the school
There's no such name."
    "Teachers don't know as much
As father about children, you tell teacher.
You tell her its M-A-P-L-E.
. . . Well you were named after a maple tree.
Your mother named you."[1] — "Maple," by Robert Frost

I Some Fictional Educational Attitudes

THE sons and daughters of the poor went willingly or coercedly to the rural, district, and city public schools. The sons and daughters of the affluent classes went to private schools generally selected for them by their parents. In Santayana's *The Last Puritan*, Oliver Alden's parents debate his educational future. Peter Alden rejects the public schools as too common for a gentleman's education, but his wife Harriet objects to boarding schools since they tend to deaden the student's mind and stereotype his character.[2]

Farmers in fiction are represented as opponents of public school consolidation. Fearing town domination of the schools, farmers were formidable foes of public education. The new-fangled schools would keep their children away from the fields in critical seasons, a strong economic reason for the farmer's tepid support of schooling.[3] In *So Big* by Edna Ferber, Pervus advises his wife Selina that their son Sobig had no need of learning beyond reading, writing, and "figgering."[4]

The fictional aristocrats regard public schools as a menace to their political independence. Monsignor Darcy in *This Side of Paradise* applauds young Amory's humanistic tendencies; a convert to Catholicism, Darcy admires St. Regis and recommends that Amory matriculate there "because it's a gentleman's school and democracy won't hit you so early. You'll find plenty of that in college."[5]

But the public high school has its supporters. Martin Eden is advised to attend high school by Ruth, his pretty gadfly. "You must get a thorough education," she urges, "whether or not you ultimately become a writer. This education is indispensable for whatever career you select, and it must not be slipshod or sketchy. You must go to high school."[6]

Education, however, begins long before a child's first class. The speech, attitudes, and general culture of his parents, relatives, and friends all influence the child. Peter Alden is very circumspect in choosing a nursemaid for his son Oliver. She must not stress ghost stories or fairy tales, but she must speak perfect English to insure that "all the abominable speech he will have to hear will seem to him absurd and amusing." In addition, the ideal governess will inspire good manners and good feelings in Oliver, wake up his wits, and teach him literature that is as important to his development as biblical tales.[7]

Clarence Darrow thought that most of public school was a waste, especially the study of grammar. He wrote that "the correct use of words can only come from environment and habit, and all of this must be learned in childhood from family or associates."[8] Unfortunately, a child's family or associates are not always worthy of emulation. The children of the poor are not tutored or guided by governesses endowed with cultural and intellectual graces.

II   *Administration of the Lower Schools*

The attitudes of the public toward education are best illustrated at board of education meetings where the people criticize educational policies. As history, literature, and the newspapers have reported, board meetings are sometimes violently disrupted by militant parents who in the name of education negate its spirit. The better debates sometimes divide the town, and board members are not innocent of fanning civic discord. Mark Twain hyperbolized when he said: "First God made idiots. That was for practice. Then he made school boards." Fortunately, some school boards have members who have no political axes to grind, who sincerely believe in education, and who exemplify the finest ethical traits.

In *His Family* by Ernest Poole, Deborah Gale, principal of an elementary school located in one of New York City's tenement districts, has a hectic time administering her school. Assisted by two vice-principals, Deborah is in constant touch with her teachers. After school hours, Italian mothers seek her advice. One has a disobedient son who steals, another has a daughter who runs out to dance halls, and still another wants Deborah to send her eight children to the country. Even mothers of graduates come to her. How can they get their daughters away from rotten sweatshops owned by lecherous bosses? Deborah is sincere, but what can she do to help these unfortunate immigrants? Almost nothing.[9]

Fictional administrators have their living counterparts. Robert Frost admired Ernest R. Silver, principal of Pinkerton Academy where Frost taught. Silver was socially informal, cordial with the faculty, and friendly with the students. He won the loyalty of the football team by cooking them a victory dinner.[10] Theodore Dreiser was inspired by a superintendent of schools who spoke to him of art, culture, and history. This man was devoted to the development of youthful potential,[11] an unusual administrative virtue.

Frank Dobie charged that the Texas State Teachers Association was dominated by superintendents whose major concerns were plant extension, new equipment, winning athletic teams, and patriotic palaver. In addition, they were a bigoted lot who questioned a teaching applicant about his church affiliation, ancestry, and other personal matters. At Alpine, Texas, however, he was hired to teach at $100 per month without benefit of questionnaire. To his delight the superintendent was a man of common sense, imagination, and unimpaired mentality who had sensibly refrained from electing useless education courses in college.[12]

Principals are sometimes portrayed as hardhearted bigots. In Dorothy Canfield Fisher's novel, *Seasoned Timber*, Mr. Wheaton has no qualms about cutting teachers' salaries. "Oh, a teacher's a teacher," he remarks. "Anybody can teach Latin about as well as anybody else. There's no competition in Latin. It's not like football." As for admitting Jews to the school, Wheaton has a neat objection. "Admit just one and the ghetto pushes in after him."[13]

While he was a pupil at Chicago's Seventh Ward School, Carl Sandburg witnessed Superintendent W. L. Steele punishing a boy, ruler on hand, in full view of his peers. This episode troubled Sandburg: "Maybe the boy had it coming to him. But if the boy had done something terribly wrong to be hit and shamed that way before the

whole room Mr. Steele should have let the forty boys and girls looking on know what it was for."[14]

Owen McMahon Johnson's famed *Lawrenceville Stories* should
be required reading for all education majors — and liberal arts majors intending to teach — because of its sensible and entertaining
tales of adolescent glories and mishaps in the college preparatory
school. To one of the school's celebrities who protests the poor estate
of "sinkers" in the dining hall, the uncompromising headmaster
responds: "Don't you dare young man to come to me again with
such a complaint. You get your work up to where it ought to be, or
down you go, and there isn't a power in this country that can prevent
it."[15] But the martinet has his soft moments, even when he is compelled to expel the "prodigious Hickey," the school's famed master
of student derring-do. After Hickey has outlived his usefulness at the
school, the headmaster tells him: "We're parting with you, Hicks,
because we feel we no longer have anything to teach you. . . . Hicks,
we part in sorrow, but we have the greatest faith in your career. We
expect in a few years to claim you as one of our foremost alumni.
Perhaps some day you will give us a library which we will name after
you."[16]

In Timothy O'Shea, Myra Kelly's fictional associate superintendent of New York City's schools, we have an educational administrator who dislikes immigrant children and terrifies the young
teachers whose certification depends upon his approval.[17] He visits
their classes unannounced. In eight days he had dismissed five
teachers and had caused nine cases of nervous exhaustion among
those accepted. Although Miss Bailey, a sensitive and dedicated
teacher, has been notified by a colleague that Mr. O'Shea was planning to visit her class, she is tense when the despotic superintendent
walks into her classroom. Her anxiety is aggravated when Morris
Mogilewsky, a Jewish boy who adores her, presents the startled
O'Shea with a gift of conciliation — a disfigured sleeve link of brass
— to protect Miss Bailey from the overseer's alleged tyranny.
O'Shea doesn't like the lower East Side Jews who had displaced the
Irish inhabitants of the neighborhood. He becomes irritated when
Morris raises his hand repeatedly but fails to respond to Miss Bailey's
recognition. How is Miss Bailey or Mr. O'Shea to know that poor
Morris was trying to alert Miss Bailey that her clothing was in dis-
array? O'Shea is now convinced that Miss Bailey coddles her young
Jewish pets, but when Morris finally reveals his chivalric intent, both
O'Shea and the principal smile sympathetically. O'Shea commends

the class, praises Miss Bailey, and shakes hands with heroic Morris before leaving the room. And so are reasonably humane administrators developed from the mouths of babes.[17]

III *In Praise of the Public School*

Theodore Dreiser, usually an inveterate foe of American institutions, has praise for the public school teachers who encouraged him to study at a time when he was disillusioned with schooling. Of his female teachers he writes compassionately: "It is true . . . perhaps, that vain, ignorant, prejudiced, yearningly and selfishly ambitious and sex hungry young women have too often taught the young — today more so than ever I hear — but, as frequently, they teach them very well. In so far as I could see at that time, they inspired as well as suggested ways and means for the future that were of great value and import, and that is all that any educational system can do, is it not?"[18]

Teaching forty-nine children ranging in age from five to sixteen was no easy task for Mary Ellen Chase, but she respected the rural school as a training center for teachers. [19] Dreiser, unhappy with his educational experiences at St. Joseph's German Catholic School in Terre Haute, Indiana, found relief in a nearby free public school "where an at least fairly liberal and honest brand of information concerning life was being dispensed."[20] The district schools as described in Louis Bromfield's *The Farm* are democratic; poor students living in the Western Reserve sat beside their wealthier schoolmates.[21] Du Bois wrote in praise of the schools of Great Barrington where the fundamentals were taught simply and effectively;[22] and Randolph Bourne wrote glowingly of the experiments in the Gary, Indiana, schools where "most of the current educational problems, the books and ideas on pedagogy, educational psychology, administration, teaching methods, classroom management, discipline, etc., which fill the attention of the current educational world, are here as if they were not. It is a school built up outside the influence of the professors of education, the teachers' colleges, and the normal schools of the land."[23]

The friendly and competent teachers at Dozier School in St. Louis taught Orrick Johns little, but they gave him a sense of democratic and civilizing ethics.[24] At Central High School, Johns mingled with the French, German, Jewish and old-line Southern students, and discovered at least one inspiring teacher in Will Schuyler, the assistant principal.[25] William Allen White found the schools of Eldorado, Kansas, worthy of their name. The two-story stone building was well equipped with good seats and blackboards. Young William had to sing Gospel hymns and listen attentively to Bible readings, but he fondly recalled the playground and fights that made life exciting.[26] And before the coming of the twentieth century, precocious Mary Antin, a child in love with her adopted land, attended the Girls Latin School in Boston. To her delight, she found her aristocratic classmates were cordial and unaffected.[27] Having escaped from Czarist oppression, she could view her new land only with reverence. If Mary Antin was unduly saccharine in her testimonial to America in *The Promised Land,* she had reason to be, considering the terrifying world of bigotry and pogroms she had escaped.

IV   *In Praise of Private Schools*

The literature in praise of private schools is not extensive. But some of those who studied at small boarding schools under strict but fair-minded masters, enjoyed their classical training. Albert J. Nock respected one teacher in particular — a New Englander who was a paragon of culture and manners, crippled though he was.[28] Ezra Pound enjoyed everything but military drill at Cheltenham Academy, a school that offered him courses in Latin and Greek when he was twelve.[29] Milton Academy in 1905 was good to Robert Sherwood: "I don't believe there are many boys at school," he wrote, "who received so much in the way of tolerance, understanding, and superhuman forgiveness as I did at Milton."[30] Even sorely tried Eugene O'Neill could write warmly of his preparatory school. In 1923 he recalled that his memories of Betts are all delightful ones — "which, speaking for myself, is more than one can say of most memories."[31] Edmund Wilson was almost ecstatic about Hill School. Run by John Meigs, the school was efficient, employed the best available staff, and boasted the best equipment. Despite its formalism and strict discipline, its teachers taught so well that each student easily passed the college-entrance examinations.[32] Another type of private school, the seminary, was admired by Ida Tarbell. Antecedent to the high school and college, the seminary did the work of both for a time, but it vanished as the high school assumed college preparatory functions and the colleges themselves introduced preparatory departments.[33]

V   *The Pains of Early Schooling*

Romantic adults who yearned for the "good old days" of the little red schoolhouse must have found E. W. Howe's *The Story of a Country Town* hard reading. The novel debunks the folklore of rural schooling.[34] The school is in a church, and the playground is the graveyard. In winter, rural school children fought to sit around the stove; those who won choice spots around the stove roasted, and those near the window froze.[35] Frank Dobie was unhappy in the ranch school he attended in Texas. Little was taught — some poetry and a smattering of geography. The children of Mexican parents who came timidly to the school were ostracized by their English-speaking counterparts.[36] The chief values of district schools, said Clarence Darrow, were the games and sports.[37]

Denominational schools also had their problems. Selina Peake in *So Big* taught in 1885 at a Dutch school near Chicago for $30 a month and board. In Edgar Lee Master's novel, *Skeeters Kirby*, the children at a German school read aloud in German, chew licorice as they recite, and receive thumpings on their backs from the raucous, insulting teachers.[38] Dreiser detested the parochial school which he said alienated him from the church. The school taught him nothing, and he especially hated his teacher who knuckled him for reading instead of doing sums. He questioned the entire basis of parochial education: "Hasn't the world had enough of unsubstantiated dogma by now? Why should an unwitting child be dosed with all of the impossible vagaries of religious and social folderol when there are masses of exact data at hand?"[39] Eugene O'Neill felt similarly about his boyhood education at the Academy of St. Vincent in Riverdale, New York. He experienced waves of hysterical loneliness there and the "life of fantasy and religion" made him unable to belong to reality.[40].

To Randolph Bourne school was an enormous joke. Unable to take his spinster teacher seriously, he mimicked her without apparent consequence to his school standing.[41] Of his schooldays in Knoxville, Tennessee, Joseph Wood Krutch writes that the system was bad, but it did teach him to write. Unhappily, the principal function of the schools was to provide a livelihood for otherwise improvident teachers,[42] a bit of sarcasm matched by Clarence Darrow's witticism that "schools became popular because people didn't want children about the house all day."[43]

Meanwhile, the urban schools struggled to bring a little light to the underprivileged children of sweatshop-ridden parents. Idealistic Deborah Gale tries heroically to engender in her teachers and students a love of learning, but she senses her losing battle against powers beyond her scope to subdue. "A school is nothing nowadays," she observes. "It's only a part of a city's life, which for most tenement children is either very dull and hard, or cheap and false and overexciting."[44]

VI *Sorrows at the Boarding School*

The unhappy recollections of boarding school life by writers are painful reading and, perhaps, overly severe. Undoubtedly, the individualism of the writer manifests itself in his student life. John Jay Chapman, a social critic in later life, hated St. Paul's which, he said, ruined his love of institutions.[45] John Tunis described his education at Stone's Academy as "pallid" instruction, hardly suitable for college preparation;[46] Stephen Crane said of Claverack College that in 1888 it was a mere boarding school which taught him nothing;[47] and Sinclair Lewis wrote in his unpublished autobiography that six months at Oberlin Academy gave him a model for the small, pious Midwestern college that he satirizes in several of his novels.[48] Stephen Vincent Benét's traumatic experiences in the years 1910 - 1911 at Hitchcock Military Academy are bitterly memorialized in his poem "Going Back to School," which he wrote at the age of nineteen. A "timid, fattish, and very spectacled youth," Benét wrote that Hitchcock was the educational slum of private education, manned by a poorly trained faculty of neurotic, miserable, and sluggish teachers. This dark moment of his life was "an agonizing caricature of what every sensitive, overcherished Anglo-Saxon boy endures in the first term at boarding school."[49]

In his renunciation of the schoolboy's worldly life for the graver world of intellectualism at Mercersburg Academy in 1898, Max Eastman succinctly defines schoolboy athletics as "the state of wordly grace — under which term I mean to include toilet articles, clothes, spending money, social ease and humor, loafing gracefully in pool rooms, familiar talk about sex and defecation, and all the rest that goes to make up a boy - of - the - world."[50] To a sensitive Jewish boy, preparatory school in Port Deposit, Maryland, was a veritable hell. Badgered constantly by the sons of reactionary, anti-Semitic Southern families, George Oppenheimer was not accepted by the future "Grand Wizards and Kleagles" who scorned his lack of athletic, social, and pugilistic graces.[51]

VII *The Preparatory School in Fiction*

Fictional criticisms of the private boarding school are similar. In *The Magnificent Ambersons*, young George Amberson is sent at the age of twelve to a private school in town where in his own words he "acquired some rudiments of a liberal education and learned nothing whatsoever about himself."[52] Densmore Academy, a Midwestern school created by Winston Churchill in the *Far Country*, is a hideous building in which a seven-year course could have been reduced to three had the faculty understood adolescent psychology. Rote learning, futile map-drawing, and stupid translating from the Latin discouraged Densmoreians from diligent study. Hugh Paret, a graduate, recalled "that knowledge was presented to us as a corpse, which bit by bit we painfully dissected."[53] St. Andrews in the seventies is another Densmore; Louis Auchincloss draws a sorry picture of the life that is contained within the school's quaint Gothic gingerbread buildings. The weak were hazed, the students rarely bathed, and the rooms were cold and dirty. The faculty lived their own lives, removed from the students. Dr. Howell, the headmaster, was a cleric who hated boys, ruled despotically, and threatened Unitarians and Baptists with damnation.[54] H. M. Pulham cannot quite fathom the social thinking of his rebel roommate, Bill King, who is not impressed with the artificial world at St. Swithens, where one was never taught anything about the poor or any other segments of the nonrich 99 percent of the population.[55] Young Lanny Budd in *World's End* is unhappy at St. Thomas; his classmates mock his fluent French, and they also resent the tendency of the masters to rely on Lanny because of his wide knowledge of literature and history. Lanny, of course, is Sinclair in his youth, a voracious reader bored with the slow pace set by his teachers.[56]

Self-conscious American aristocrats were unhappy with the American academies for another reason. Henry James, Henry Adams, and T. S. Eliot, for example, longed for cathedrals, universities, and schools that would rival England's. In *The Last Puritan*, Peter Alden tries to fathom Eton's greatness. "How do students taught by sheltered priests and pedants," he asked, "acquire a maximum of those qualities requisite in one having breeding and a knowledge of the world?"[57] F. Scott Fitzgerald, in *This Side of Paradise*, praises Eton for creating "the self-consciousness of a governing class. St. Regis, like all other American preparatory schools," is crushed under the heel of the universities, "and remains a representative, clean, flaccid, and innocuous" private school.[58]

VIII   *The Good Teacher*

In the Talmud it is written that he who saves one life has in essence saved the world, an exaggeration to be sure, but if each human being would be kind to but one person a cumulative effect would result. The teacher who "saves" one student has not saved the world, but he has initiated a wondering child into the world of the mind. In recent years student evaluation of teachers has provided scholars with some measurement of student reaction to their masters, but literature and biography are still the most useful sources for learning the attitudes of successful people toward their teachers.

The roll call of honored American teachers is long, and only a handful may be cited here. Barrett Wendell praised his tutor John Adams for teaching more than he really knew. Adams made Latin interesting and avoided assigning wearisome copying of the classics.[59] Max Eastman wrote happily of four of his teachers at Mercersburg Academy: "They all stand in my inner mind; and they command my reverent feelings, for where intelligence replaces superstition, teachers replace priests."[60] Mary Antin remembered her teachers gratefully in *The Promised Land*, especially Miss Nixon, an inspiring elementary schoolteacher; Miss Carrol, her kind and efficient second grade teacher; and her third grade teacher, Miss Dillingham, who was aware of Mary's talents and promoted her as soon as she showed accomplishment.[61] Carl Sandburg credits his grade school teacher, Miss Hogue, with giving him what little education he obtained from formal schooling;[62] Frank Dobie, although critical of his meaningless education in Alice, Texas, nevertheless respected "Professor" Nat Benton, an easygoing instructor who asked the class to write a theme, the only written assignment Dobie had before college.[63] Louis Untermeyer, although fond of his geometry teacher who tried to show him the relationship between good music and mathematics, was unable to transform his interest into mastery of geometry, and he left school forever.[64]

Willa Cather attributed her ability to rise above the moral and intellectual flaws in the society of Red Cloud, Nebraska, to her English teacher, Eva Case. A great teacher, Miss Case expanded Miss Cather's cultural horizons and undoubtedly helped inspire her to become a writer.[65] Not overly fond of the teaching profession, H. L. Mencken softened his criticisms in his recollections of his teachers at Baltimore Polytechnic. An eccentric lot of tobacco chewers and beer drinkers, his humanities teachers "had in common an ardent and an almost pious delight in good writing, and in their catch-as-can way they managed to convey it to such of the boys as were susceptible to such infections."[66] Evidently, Mr. Hunt who taught Robert Sherwood at Milton Academy impressed the writer for life, since he wrote to his teacher for ten years after he left the school and inscribed many of his books to Mr. Hunt.[67] An admirer of Dr. Coit, headmaster of St. Paul's, characterized the noted educator as an in-spirer of burgeoning intellects whom he set on the right road to learning and living and a master teacher of English usage.[68] To Ed-mund Wilson, the only unpleasantness manifested by his Greek teacher at the Hill School was his irritability with students who dis-liked his beloved Greek. Mr. Rolfe was not content with having his students get through examinations; he demanded that they read widely and broaden their interests, and in Wilson's case he succeeded.[69] The Stone School in Boston was not elegant, but John Tunis found compensation in the teaching of the school's head-master, Charles Wellington Stone, whose old-fashioned techniques in Greek, Latin, and English classes were unlike those of modern teachers who prate like salesmen in IBM computer jargon.[70] And Horatio Alger, whose self-help novels were read by millions of America's lowly, was impressed with his teacher, Mr. Albee, a man who allowed whispering, group study, and advancement of in-dividual tastes.[71]

IX   Fictional Examples of the Good Teacher

The fictional teacher is the counterpart of the teacher who left his impression for good or evil upon the student that later damned or praised him. Santayana's gentle Irma who tutors young Oliver Alden in *The Last Puritan* inspires the boy to love music, language, and art.[72] But the children of the poor are not blessed with private tutors. Yet, bright and radiant schoolmistresses occasionally appear in these neglected schools. In Howe's *The Story of A Country Town*, Agnes Deming brightens the day for her students by singing for them, tutoring them, and befriending them when she boards at their homes. Life in the country town is severe, but Agnes helps the children forget for a time how poor they are.[73] The plight of the poor student in a New England high school is realistically etched by Mary E. Wilkins in *The Portion of Labor*. On her first day at school only the teacher is kind to Ellen Brewster — the students scorn and tease her.[74] Norman Lloyd, her teacher, is charmed by Ellen's beauty and grace and admires her remarkable mind. He urges Ellen to go on to college, but Mr. Risley, one of the town's merchants, argues against the idea. First, a factory hand's daughter has no business seeking a college education; second, a workingman's daughter should not aspire to rise in class; and third, the textbooks in school do not prepare girls for their true roles in life. Master Lloyd reasons that the children of the poor should be given a chance to better their conditions. If all the children go to school who will make shoes? Risley asks. Happily, Risley is more progressive than his words signify. He assures the startled schoolmaster that he really believes in higher education.

The dedicated teacher of slum or ghetto pupils deserves more praise than his colleague in a suburban community. In *The Father*, Charles Calitri almost sanctifies Deborah Bruno, an idealistic young Jewish public school teacher in New York City. Deborah visits her ailing Italian students in unpleasant neighborhoods and battles to have playgrounds built in the middle of the Bowery to spare her children injury from the horse traffic as she marches them from school to distant playgrounds.[75]

Another schoolmistress, Kate Smith, in Sherwood Anderson's "The Teacher," sublimated her frustrated sexual passion in attempting to spark the genius of young George Willard. "Don't be a peddler of words," she told him. "The thing to learn is to know what people are thinking about, not what they say."[76]

Stern words from a fair-minded teacher are not taken amiss by students. Professor Roman of Lawrenceville upbraids his class after suffering through a painful lesson with them: "I have, in the course of my experience as a teacher, had to deal with mere idiots; but for sheer, determined, monumental asininity I have never met the equal of this aggregation. I trust this morning's painful, disgraceful, disheartening experience may never, never be repeated."[77] To Dink, one of his students who admitted that he didn't understand him, Roman confides: "It is a truth which it is, perhaps, unwise to publish abroad, and I shall have to swear you to its secret. It is the boy whose energy must explode periodically and disastrously, it is the boy who gives us the most trouble, who wears down our patience and tries our souls, who is really the most worthwhile."[78]

X   *Teachers Who Inspire Students*

Charles Townsend Copeland of Harvard is the most celebrated teacher of American writers, but he must share his fame with other teachers. Edmund Wilson praised Alfred Rolfe who taught him at the Hill School in Pottstown, Pennsylvania, as a radiant teacher who introduced him to Thoreau, Emerson, Shaw, and Chesterton and delighted in seeing his students' literary work in the *Hill School Record*. Rolfe was a great formative influence, a reasonable disciplinarian, and a lover of the noble and beautiful.[79] Santayana was grateful to Mr. Grace, his English teacher, who taught him "to distinguish the musical and expressive charm of poetry from its moral appeal."[80] At the High School of Commerce in New York City, Elmer Rice loved his English teacher, John B. Opdycke, who guided him through dictional logic. But Rice hated school games and assemblies and left high school at the age of fifteen to help his needy family.[81] Willa Cather was encouraged to write by Professor Ebenezer Hunt of the Latin School in Lincoln, Nebraska. Hunt found originality in the girl's themes and had several published in the *State Journal,* March 1, 1891.[82] In like fashion, Gertrude Atherton was urged to write by Miss Haight, her composition teacher;[83] Edgar Lee Masters' themes were lauded by his rhetoric teacher, Mary Fisher,[84] and Mary Antin's essays were published in a school journal through the intervention of her teacher, Miss Dillingham.[85]

Theodore Dreiser was told by his English teacher, Miss Mildred Fielding, to "go on for your mind will find its way,"[86] and another English teacher, Miss Calvert, showed excellent judgment in passing him in grammar even though he had failed the course. Her rationalization of her kindness to the deficient grammarian is an admirable statement of reasoned denial of the claims of formalism: " 'You have done well in everything else, Theodore,' she said to me one afternoon, 'but you don't know anything about grammar. Yet because I know you you don't need to, I'm going to pass you just the same. You're too bright to be held back for that. Grammar isn't everything.' "[87]

XI   *In Censure of Teachers*

Adults rarely forget the hurts inflicted upon them in childhood by incompetent teachers. Southerners, impoverished by their defeat, were unable to support public education generously. Private schools would hire Confederate veterans who had some education, but teaching was dull to many of them. They preferred to tell their students stories of the war.[88]

Things were not much better in other rural areas; teachers in the 1890s were paid seven dollars a week for teaching fifty children.[89] Robert Frost, who succeeded his mother as teacher of the Second Grammar School in Methuen, Connecticut, was soon exhausted in his efforts to discipline a band of malicious schoolboys.[90] Joseph Wood Krutch attributed the exhaustion of teachers to their lack of training. Science, for example, was "taught by an elderly spinster who could not demonstrate one scientific principle."[91] John Tunis denounced the schools of Boston, charging that they were in the hands of Irish politicians who "milked the schools and underpaid the teachers."[92] Even Boston Latin School teachers were not always praised. George Santayana wrote:

But were the teachers of the Latin School, perhaps the best of American schools, happy? Or were the boys? Ah, perhaps we should not ask whether they were happy, for they were not rich, but whether they were not enthusiastically conscious of a great work, and endless glorious struggle and perpetual victory. And I reply, not for myself, since I don't count, being an alien, but in their name, that they decidedly were conscious of no such thing. They had heard of it, but in their daily lives they were conscious only of hard facts, meagerness, routine, petty commitments, and ideals too distant and too vague to be worth mentioning.[93]

XII   *Fictional Criticism of Teachers*

Novelists sometimes criticize teachers because they acquiesce in the political expediencies. In *His Family*, Deborah Gale strives valiantly to provide meaningful education for the elementary school that she supervises in New York City's lower East Side. She tells her father that 800,000 pupils attend the city's schools, a number that staggers Mr. Gale's imagination. He asks: "With the mad city growing so fast, and the people of the tenements breeding, breeding, breeding, breeding, and packing the schools to bursting, what could any teacher be but a mere cog in a machine, ponderous, impersonal, blind, grinding out future New Yorkers?"[94]

But who volunteers to be "a mere cog in a machine?" Can a resolute, idealistic, and courageous teacher submit to inane directives without losing his soul? Santayana has Oliver Alden respond to this question in *The Last Puritan*. "Most schoolmasters," says Oliver, "were people who had failed in the world or were afraid to fail in it."[95] Willa Cather's Agatha Graves in "The Professor's Commencement" berates her brother Emerson for teaching in high school where "failures in every trade drift to teach the businesses they cannot make a living by."[96] Sinclair Lewis, whose teachers are limned meanly in most cases, epitomizes his criticisms in the rebuke by Carl Ericson. Carl, a junior at Joralemon High School in Minnesota, complains that his teachers "were almost perfectly calculated to make any lad of the slightest independence hate culture for the rest of his life."[97]

It is sad when teachers teach poorly, but it is even sadder when teachers do not attempt to understand their students. In "Paul's

Case," Willa Cather describes the downfall of a young student whose theatrical ambitions were so distasteful to his teachers that they were blinded to his needs.[98] When he asked for reinstatement to Pittsburgh High School, Paul was greeted with rancor and antagonism by his teachers. Only his drawing teacher asked the committee to understand Paul. One of his teachers left the meeting "humiliated to have felt so vindictive toward a mere boy, to have uttered this feeling in cutting terms, and to have set each other on, as it were, in the gruesome game of intemperate reproach."[99] Paul's crime was that, obsessed with the theater, he found the "schoolroom more than ever repulsive," especially "the bare floors and naked walls; the prosy men who never wore frock coats, or violets in their buttonholes; the women with their dull gowns, shrill voices, and pitiful seriousness about prepositions that govern the dative."[100] Unfortunately, Paul's dismissal from school led to his loss of his usher's job at Carnegie Hall, and adding to his discomfiture was the opinion of the stock actresses that his teachers were correct in their repudiation of him because he was "floridly inventive." Today, a boy like Paul might be saved by a guidance counsellor who would suggest that he participate in the school play as writer, actor, or director. Perhaps. But "Paul's Case" should be read by teachers. If truth is stranger than fiction, why not read fiction to explicate truth?

XIII   Some Notes on the Curriculum

What shall we teach our youth? From ancient times this question has troubled parents, politicians, and philosophers. Until the revolutionary movements of the twentieth century rocked the societies of the world, many of them in semifeudal condition, the concept of the great chain of being suppressed the aspirations of the lowly. In Moses Maimonides' commentary from the *Mishna*, "Why All Men Cannot be Intellectuals," we have a medieval rationalization of aristocratic education: "If all men were students of philosophy, the social order would be destroyed and the human race quickly exterminated, for man is very helpless and needs many things. It is necessary for him to learn plowing, reaping, threshing, grinding, baking, and how to fashion implements for these tasks, in order to secure his food. Similarly, he must learn spinning and weaving to clothe himself, the building art to provide a shelter, and craftsmanship to provide tools for all these works."[101] Obviously, continues Maimonides, no man can learn all of these occupations in a lifetime. Since it is necessary for gifted men to study and acquire wisdom, Maimonides recommends that the majority of men should follow the productive occupations.

Maimonides' theme was restated by Wendell Phillips in an article carried by *The New York Tribune,* on December 7, 1876. Phillips wrote in defense of technical education, charging that "our schools ignore the fact that seven tenths of their scholars must earn their daily bread. They teach without reference to that. . . . They should be trained with constant reference to affairs — toward and not away from the farm, the shop, the counting room. The instruction ought to be technical."[102]

Perhaps Phillips was right. Few of the high school students in his age were college bound. And bright students were unchallenged by the so-called academic curriculum. H. L. Mencken was able to "wolf" a subject that had engaged the class a year in desperate study; after his "tutorials" in algebra with Mr. Uhrbrock he won the highest grades on the examination for the gold medal.[103] Similarly, Jack London passed the entrance examinations at the University of California after cramming two years of high school in three months.[104] Self-education is the best education wrote Louis Bromfield in his novel, *The Farm.* Jamie Ferguson, a good man of the soil, "never saw that within himself lay the greatest and surest means of acquiring an education," and he never saw that "his own passionate curiosity about everything in the world and his own hunger for knowledge was a better means than all the sorts of professors and academies."[105]

High school was meaningless to Randolph Bourne; he hated the emphasis upon building plants and the unreal curriculum.[106] Clarence Darrow questioned the value of teaching Latin and Greek in high school. The attempt of educators to retain these studies was an effort to preserve ignorance at the expense of knowledge. Darrow had barbs for history teachers also; they never taught relationships between events, but instead resorted to memorization.[107] Louis Bromfield was even more critical of history teaching in *The Farm.* Johnny Ferguson was taught lies in the school he attended on the Western Reserve: The Indians and the British were cruel, Roosevelt and Lodge were Christian gentlemen, all Southerners were evil, and the president's will was sacred.[108]

Grammar classes were odious to Clarence Darrow,[109] an opinion shared by Max Eastman, who saw no value in parsing and diagraming.[110] School textbooks in general alienated Louis Untermeyer. Their inane questions and exercises kept him from the literature he yearned to read.[111] Fortunately, he read voraciously after school, a practice that undoubtedly helped him in his literary career.

XIV   *A Look at Innovation*

Had Clarence Darrow studied Latin with Florence Rafter, the Latin teacher of Mary Ellen Chase at the Blue Hill School, he might have enjoyed the classics. Anticipating the methodology of the progressives, Miss Rafter taught Latin inspiringly.[112] Later, she praised the Hillside Home School in Spring Green, Wisconsin, for its superb use of progressive techniques. Hillside Home School in 1909 combined the best features of farm, school, and home life. Students learned to ride, to garden, and to study nature in the field and went on bird study and nut gathering expeditions on horseback.[113] Young students sat with older students at the dining table; students cooperated with one another in the best Froebelian tradition; few rules distracted them from study, most of which was informal; and curiosity and relevancy were stressed.[114] But at the Hill School under Alfred Rolfe, Edmund Wilson learned to dislike the slackness allegedly implicit in progressive methodology. The only way Homer could be studied, unless outlines are surreptitiously used as substitutes, is by digging in the Greek lexicon and grammar.[115]

A progressive student government plan was instituted by members of the faculty in Owen Johnson's fictional Lawrenceville Prep. The boys formed two parties, the Feds and Anti-Feds, who fought each other on the issue of faculty or student control of athletic finances. This basic issue soon became enlarged to include a program for more and better food, cushioned seats in the chapel, and elimination of compulsory baths. The campaign grew in intensity. Zealous combatants splashed the buildings with eggs and posted banners bearing vitriolic slogans. But before the school erupted into civil war, the alert headmaster stopped the conflict. Examinations were announced for the next day and peace came to Lawrenceville by fiat.[116]

An innovator, Robert Frost taught English composition his own way. He never assigned subjects for themes and graded papers only if students wanted him to read them.[117] Contrary to the procedure of many of his colleagues, Frost had his students read minor authors in class, advising them to read the great writers leisurely at home or elsewhere.[118]

The kindergarten was slowly gaining favor in the United States. Richard Watson Gilder gave much of his time to advancing the cause of nursery school education, and as president of the New York Kindergarten Association he argued enthusiastically for establishment of kindergartens everywhere. "Plant a few kindergartens in any quarter of the crowded metropolis," he said, "and you have begun then and there the work of making better lives, better homes, better citizens, and a better city."[119] Deborah Gale, the heroine of Poole's *His Family,* also thought kindergarten was a blessing for the children in her crowded tenement district.[120] But Mr. Dooley, Finley Peter Dunne's skeptical bartender, ridicules the kindergarten where children paint and dance in wild abandon as the teacher placidly watches an ingrate pull out a child's long hair.[121]

XV   Student Wastefulness and Cruelty

Even in the best schools, concludes Santayana, almost all of the school time is wasted. Schools exist primarily to give boys time to grow up and avoid mischief.[122] Mary Ellen Chase learned to teach the hard way at the Irving School. The students were decent but lazy; they hated grammar and were perplexed by poetry. In the study hall, sixty apathetic boys and girls sat pointlessly, watching the clock or gossiping.[123] The one aim of the pupils in Professor Ludwig von Volkenburg's classes attended by Theodore Dreiser was to get out of the classroom to play, fight, and loaf. Why try to master the meaningless curriculum — a "mixed gibberish of minor arithmetic, beginner's grammar, reading, Bible history, spelling, and catechism?" In Volkenburg's classes students never learned anything of United States history, science, or art. After the three R's, the children went to workshops — full-fledged and solidly-believing Catholics."[124]

In the private boarding school, sports maintained an uneasy truce between faculty and students. Owen Johnson describes this temporary condition in "The Varmint," one of his famed Lawrenceville stories: "A school of four hundred fellows is a good deal like a shaky monarchy; the football and baseball seasons akin to foreign wars; as long as they last the tranquility of the state is secure, but with the return of peace a state of fermentation and unrest is due."[125] Hazing is one of the signs of the onset of fermentation; at Lawrenceville, John Smeed is hazed because he is too thin for football and does not seem to fit in anywhere. But Smeed is made of finer mettle — and finer intestinal fortitude — than his peers credit him with. At Conover's eatery, the amazing Mr. Smeed breaks the pancake-eating record, a feat that means free pancakes for all.[126]

To achieve popularity in school, students try to excel in sports.[127]

The high school girls talk of football, fudge, clothes, and boys. They cut classes whenever possible and are turned out by the hundreds like the sausages in a meat factory.[128] And to a child of minority parents life in high school could be hellish. In Ludwig Lewisohn's *The Island Within* the classmates of a Jewish high school student force him to strip in the gymnasium to reveal his badge of Jewishness, circumcision — ignorant in their ridicule that Christ, too, was circumcised.[129]

XVI *Discipline and Moral Education*

Ideally, schools should be administered without corporal punishment, but biographical and fictional stories of school life include many instances of birch-wielding, knuckle-rapping, and thumb-pressing schoolmasters. At the better preparatory schools masters were more circumspect, probably because the affluent parents would brook no sadistic harm to their children. Owen Johnson explains the tacit communion between student and faculty that insures justice at Lawrenceville in his introduction to the *Lawrenceville Stories:* "Between masters and students there was an armed and exceedingly wary neutrality. Nothing was taken for granted on either side. It was a battle of wits and the rule of the master was sternness tempered with Justice."[130]

H. L. Mencken denounced the progressive teacher in his journalistic diatribes. The old-fashioned teacher who taught fact-mastery was better than his lenient counterpart. Those who learned well received apples; those who did not or were mischievous were fanned.[131] One of his teachers, Professor Knight, used the rattan freely.[132] In William Faulkner's *The Hamlet,* schoolmaster Labove had to prove himself to his class of pupils who ranged in age from six to nineteen by subduing the "toughs" with his fists. Once dominant, he forced the older boys to stay in after school to do chores.[133]

Clarence Darrow denounced the absurd whippings in district schools.[134] Santayana wrote disparagingly of the Brimmer School, a poor boy's free school, where students were frequently whipped for poor learning and for fighting.[135] In her recollections, Mary Ellen Chase, only a sophomore in 1909 when she taught at Buck's Harbor, Maine, narrates how she used the razor strop to instill obedience in her first class.[136]

Mr. Dooley has his fun with the progressive philosophy on whipping. He is curious to know how Mary Ellen, a school teacher, feels on the subject. Their dialogue is amusing, and Mary Ellen's last words are especially significant:

> "But whisper, Mary Ellen," says I. "Don't ye niver feel like bastin' the seeraphims?"
> "The teachins iv Freebul and Petzotly is contrary to that," she says." But I'm going to be maried an' lave the school on Choosdah, the twenty-second iv Janooary," she says, "an' on Mondah, the twenty-first I'm goin' to ask a few iv the little darlins to th' house an," she says, "stew them over a slow fire. . . . "[137]

The immigrant father, told by his son that his teacher had whipped him, shouts, "Good, now I beat you too!" This story, repeated too frequently to be apocryphal, illustrates the immigrant's respect for education in a land that made learning available to all. But Boston blue bloods, at least in John Phillips Marquand's *The Late George Apley*, resented any kind of physical discipline. George is a freshman at Hobson's School in Marlborough, a district in Boston. He taunts meek Mr. Treete who cannot control the class. Desperately, Mr. Treete boxes George's ears publicly, and he is fired by Mr. Hobson.[138]

It has never been demonstrated that the moral precepts swarming ubiquitously in the early American schoolbooks appreciably diminished the wrongdoing of their readers. In composition textbooks, all vices were condemned and all virtues extolled. The almshouse or jail was the destination of the girl or boy who did not do his lessons diligently, who did not revere his parents and teachers, who loved riches and ambition, and who did not love to work.[139] In addition to moral training in literature, students were subjected to daily chapel sermons in private schools and Bible readings in public schools. Edmund Wilson hated the chapel sermons at Hill School.[140] Cynical Ambrose Bierce wrote scathingly of prayer in public schools, especially the Lord's Prayer which "has been brought into disrepute about long enough by being snarled through dirty noses of a hundred bad boys and preposterous girls. . . . Down with the Lord's Prayer — in schools."[141]

XVII   *On the Education of Females*

And how should "preposterous girls" be educated, especially after leaving public school or private elementary school? The well-to-do child might enter a finishing school like St. Stephen's Seminary for Ladies, described by Hjalmar Boyesen in his story, "A Candidate for Divorce," which appeared in *Cosmopolitan Magazine* in 1890. The school's founder, Miss Van Pelt, thought of education as "the filling of a bog." Boyesen believed that girls should be trained for wifehood and motherhood, but he objected to Miss Pelt's saccharine teaching which avoided the "crude and contaminating facts of life." Miss Hammond, their English teacher, spared her students the purple passages in the Bible and Shakespeare, fearing that they might confront her with embarrassing questions.[142]

Agnes Repplier, a fair-minded critic, offered a balanced set of arguments for and against female college education. At college, she wrote, girls rarely read for delight and therefore lose the power "of rapturous reading and the power of secret thinking which make for personal distinction."[143] Furthermore the college girl is less mature than the girl who has left school at eleven to work. A strong opponent of coeducation at Harvard, Barrett Wendell saw the college girl as a threat to manly education. Radcliffe was drawing away talented young scholars from Harvard by paying them better salaries. At Radcliffe, these enticed dons forgot about research and became mere schoolmasters. Besides, argued Wendell, women offer men little scholarly competition.[144]

But Charlotte Perkins Gilman disputed Wendell's thesis that desire and combat, two manly virtues, have spurred on American education. American education, she said, has made only a few happy; to the rest it has been a weary and dreary institution. Only when women will "consciously dedicate themselves to the teaching of the young child" will the race advance in "strides hitherto unthought of."[145] But men refuse to accord women equal educational privileges. Even when women struggled through professional schools for degrees, "grave professors and grinning students used obscene language and played cruel tricks to drive them out."[146]

Not all men objected to the higher education of women. For example, Matthew Vassar wrote to the trustees of the college he founded: "It occurred to me that woman, having received from her Creator the same intellectual constitution as man, has the same right as man to intellectual culture and development."[147] In his address commemorating Vassar's twenty-fifth academic year, George William Curtis praised the schools founded by Emma Willard, Catharine Esther Beecher, and Mary Lyons for showering "the seeds of higher education all over the country."[148]

Agnes Repplier, who had some misgivings about higher education for girls, pointed out some of the benefits too. The campus taught students tolerance for people of other backgrounds. College life instilled a serious view of life in some students; in others it engendered a healthy sense of humor.[149] Pearl Buck was grateful for the sound curriculum at Randolph-Macon in Virginia. No frilly subjects were taught, and when the students petitioned for a course in home economics the faculty told the students that cookbooks can be read at home.[150] Ida Tarbell was one of four girls admitted to Allegheny College in 1876. She enjoyed the teaching of Professor Jeremiah Tingley, a science teacher and friend of Louis Agassiz. Tingley taught with enthusiasm; from him she learned that work can be pleasurable.[151] To her good fortune she studied with another outstanding teacher, George Haskins, professor of Latin, who taught her "to cherish her contempts." Like Tingley, Haskins was a foe of indifference, carelessness, and neglect, and he inspired young Miss Tarbell to make good use of time, to finish projects, and to study in her courses, whether or not they were pleasurable. It is obvious that Ida Tarbell's industrious undertaking, the writing of *The History of the Standard Oil Company*, was influenced to some extent by the disciplined teaching she received at Allegheny from Professors Haskins and Tingley.

XVIII   *Female Education in Fiction*

A traditional attitude of the rural mother toward the education of her daughters is strongly depicted in Faulkner's *The Hamlet*. Mrs. Varner argues against sending her daughter Eula to school. Of what value would reading, writing, and arithmetic be to a girl who was destined to be a housewife?[152]

Ellen Glasgow criticized the value of genteel finishing schools in Virginia. She writes that such schooling is

. . . founded upon the simple theory that the less a girl knew about life, the better prepared she would be to contend with it. Knowledge of any sort (except the rudiments of reading and writing, the geography of countries she would never visit, and the dates of battles she would never mention) was kept from her as vigorously as if it contained the germs of a contagious disease. And this ignorance of anything that could possibly be useful to her was supposed in some mysterious way to add to her value as a woman and to make her a more desirable companion to a man. . . .[153]

In the nineteen thirties Edith Crandall, dean of women at Eureka University, wrote to Professor Clavercin, a Harvard-bred man entertaining Barrett Wendell's antipathies for female college education.

"Only get over that Harvard idea that women are not for higher education," she tells him. "They are for everything, the same as men! The segregation rule is over, in this world, my man!"[154] To the Clavercins of the latter half of the twentieth century, Edith Crandall's words have become prophetically but painfully true. Other women's colleges are now following Vassar's surrender to the modern temper and admitting men.

For Smith College, Mary Ellen Chase had nothing but praise. Smith educated the whole personality. Guided by a tolerant faculty, the students developed good taste, read intelligently, and participated eagerly in the school's life.[155] A fictional student, Elizabeth Stockton, persuades her mother to let her attend Smith in lieu of going to a finishing school, which ultimately meant French, music, a trip abroad, and marriage.[156] But Mrs. Stockton is not impressed with Smith; the Saunders' daughters who were at the college showed no obvious improvement. Elizabeth's teacher, Miss Hunter, complains that her papers, like those of the other students, are becoming stupider and stupider. Finally, Elizabeth leaves Smith, convinced that there are better things than grades — life abroad, for example, and marriage. Actually, Elizabeth's uncle had conspired with Miss Hunter to send Elizabeth home to marry Arnold, her fiancé, before he leaves for business. Elizabeth is a victim of middle-class values. Her talk of independence and liberation is mere prattle. Smith College was unable to wean her away from the strong bonds of her mothering family.

Sinclair Lewis chooses to educate Ann Vickers, in the novel of the same name, at Point Royal College in Connecticut.[157] In 1910 Vassar College regarded Point Royal as "on a level with agricultural schools, Catholic academies, and institutions for instruction in embalming."[158] Professor Glen Hargis is disdainful of the female students. Socially, the college is in the dark ages. The girls were regarded by their keepers as nuns in a convent for "in this cloister even the girls who had been wholesomely brought up with noisy brothers, were so overwhelmed in the faint-scented mist of femininity that they became as abnormal as the hysterical wrens in a boarding-school."[159]

XIX   On the Education of Blacks

The struggle of American blacks to attain more than "separate but equal" schooling in the land that they have labored in since the

Jamestown landings goes on as lawsuits and counterlawsuits engage the nation's courts. Even today the tragedy of Giles Johnson is repeated in the lives of many American blacks:

Giles Johnson, Ph.D.

Giles Johnson
had four college degrees
knew the whyfore of this
the wherefore of that
could orate in Latin
or cuss in Greek
and, having learned such things,
he died of starvation
because he wouldn't teach
and he couldn't porter.[160]

Giles Johnson's sad plight is the culmination of decades of distrust of universal suffrage. Wendell Phillips addressed himself to the fear of black enfranchisement in his oration, "The Scholar in A Republic," which startled sedate Harvardians in 1881. Phillips charged that "the white South hates universal suffrage; the so-called cultivated North distrusts it. Journal and college, social-science convention and the pulpit, discuss the propriety of restraining it. Timid scholars tell their dread of it."[161] But universal suffrage required universal education. Therefore, said Comfort Servasse in Albion W. Tourgee's Reconstruction novel, *A Fool's Errand*, "make the spelling-book the scepter of national power. Let the nation educate the colored man and the poor white man because the nation held them in bondage, and is responsible for their education; educate the voter because the nation cannot afford that he should be ignorant."[162]

Comfort Servasse is a Northern Reconstruction officer who sincerely believes that the federal government has a mandate to educate all its citizens. But another character, Dr. Martin, asks, "But how shall the citizens of the States be educated by the Government without infringement of the rights of the States?"[163]

Thomas Dixon's novel, *The Leopard's Spots*, presents a classical argument against the education of blacks. Mrs. Durham, the novel's heroine, reasons that, since education will inspire the black man to rise from menial to more profitable employment which society will deny him, it is a crime to educate blacks. The black must be kept in his place; education will serve only to disturb him.[164] A preacher agrees with Mrs. Durham; the more you try to elevate the mind of a black, the more you increase his problems. The spelling book will not change the black's mystique, since "he is a human donkey." And it is wrong to call the Southern attitude toward blacks race prejudice; it is "simply God's first law of Nature — the instinct of self-preservation."[165] Mark Twain and Dudley Warner satirize this viewpoint in *The Gilded Age*. Go-getting Colonel Sellers engages Senator Dilworthy in a discussion on the black mind. Colonel Seller's beliefs on the intellect of blacks are still heard today:

"You can't do much with 'em. They are a speculating race, sir, disinclined to work for white folks without security, planning to live only by working for themselves. . . ."

"There's some truth in your observation, Colonel, but you must educate them."

"You educate the niggro and you make for more speculating than he was before. . . ."

"But Colonel, the Negro when educated will be more able to make his speculations fruitful."

"Never, sir, never. He would only have a wider scope to injure himself. A niggro has no grasp, sir."[166]

Mark Twain had little faith in the Reconstruction Congress's intentions of granting aid for the education of freedmen. Eventually, he charged, this money found its way into the coffers of scheming investors and landowners.[167] Dudley Warner lampoons the ostentatious Northern philanthropist who sets out on a train journey to dedicate a building which he had donated to a college for blacks. He travels on a special train "the cost of which . . . would have built or furnished an industrial school and workshop for a hundred Negroes."[168]

The plight of the dedicated New England teacher who volunteered to teach freedmen in the hostile South was pitiful. Metta Servasse has six young female teachers of the Missionary Association for dinner. They are refined and cultivated ladies, but they are despised and insulted by the white Southerners in the community.[169] Squire Hyman, for example, thought that Northern teachers who came South to teach could not be of much account, nor was he overly impressed with Servasse's rejoinder that he would prefer the society of Northern teachers to the esteem of white aristocrats.[170]

Especially hateful to the Southerner were Northern female abolitionists like Miss Sally Walker, whose life and fortune were devoted to the education of blacks.[171] Held up to ridicule by Thomas Dixon in *The Leopard's Spots*, Miss Walker aims to set up Negro schools and colleges in the South and to send promising blacks to Northern universities where in an atmosphere of cordial democracy they will become creative.[172] The book portrays the Northern do-gooders as either naive idealists or malicious, corrupt, and vindictive parasites.

The black writer had strong misgivings about the value of Negro schools. In Charles W. Chesnutt's "The Sheriff's Children," Sheriff Campbell is pained to see his mulatto son a prisoner in the Troy, North Carolina jail. "What went wrong?" he asks his son. "There are schools. You have been to school." His son is laconic in response. "Yes, there are schools, but all they teach a Negro is that his skin will never change by learning and that he will always wear a badge of shame."[173] Children in Southern schools were acutely aware of racial differences. A white child who associates with blacks is made aware that he is different. In *Stringtown on the Pike*, little Susie who was raised by Cupe, an old Negro, is greeted in class by her sadistic classmates with a frightening chant, "Only Susie, Nigger Susie, Nigger Susie!" Overcome by this unexpected omen of ostracism, the poor child faints.[174] Charles W. Chesnutt's story of the hardships of the rural teacher of black children in Sampson County, North Carolina, is especially poignant because Rena, the unfortunate heroine of the novel, is almost white in appearance. Mr. Wain, a school trustee, offers Rena a position in his school because "a lady in her color kin keep a lot er little niggers straighter'n a darker lady could."[175] Although Rena was not allowed to sit with white candidates who were being examined for the job, she excels on the examination and receives a first-class certificate to teach. Her school is a one-room log cabin in which she teaches docile children the alphabet from Webster's famed *Blue-Backed Red Speller*, "the palladium of Southern education at this time." Mr. Chesnutt extols the virtues of this best-selling primer and compliments the much abused carpetbagger who "had put the spelling book within reach of every child of school age in North Carolina — a fact which is often overlooked when the carpetbaggers are held up to public odium."[176] Here in this barely furnished school, surrounded by adoring children, Rena felt "that to sacrifice her life to open the door of opportunity for these children of ex-slaves was an imperative duty."[177]

A novel written by Cyrus Townsend Brady in 1903, although excessively melodramatic in places, delineates the ironic tragedy of the daughter of an octoroon who passionately defends the rights of blacks to equality. Later, learning of her true parentage, she disowns her father and marries a mulatto. But, unable to respond to his love, she kills herself. Before her fatal recognition scene, however, she is a happy candidate for the doctoral degree at Brookford College in Philadelphia, proud of the faculty and of President Whyot, an educator who treated blacks impartially and kindly, although he really disliked them.[178] Mr. Brady writes that Philadelphians at the turn of the twentieth century had a tendency "not only to consider the Negro as a man and a brother, but almost as a man and a superior, although temporarily in reduced circumstances and humble condition."[179] Alicia believed in this gospel implicitly. In her thesis, which was awarded *summa cum laude* honors, she detailed a program for uplifting the black race.[180]

The problems of fair-skinned blacks in fiction are experienced by their living counterparts. Young Wendell Johnson never thought of himself as a black until he attended a public school in Connecticut. When a group of black boys attacked a white boy, he joined the white boys in assaulting the "niggers," a word that his mother warned him never to use again.[181] Later in the term he learned of his ancestry in a scene that he never forgot. The principal says,

> "I wish all of the white scholars to stand for a moment."
> I rose with the others.
> "You sit down now and rise with the others."
> I sat down dazed.[182]

Humiliated and heartsick, Wendell asked his mother to verify the principal's insinuations. She did so, reluctantly: "No, I am not white, but your father is one of the greatest men in the country — the best blood of the South is in you."[183] In his turn, every immigrant lad learned in school, neighborhood, and society what epithet applies to him; the mental and physical scars inflicted upon those called dago, mick, kike, kraut, hunk, spick, and shine are immeasurable. Of his more genteel initiation to bigotry, Wendell Johnson wrote that "perhaps it had to be done, but I have never forgiven the woman who did it so cruelly. It may be that she never knew that she gave me a sword-thrust that day in school which was years in healing."[184]

Langston Hughes recalls both good and bad experiences at Central High in Cleveland. His English teacher, Ethel Weimer, interested him in Carl Sandburg and scores of other eminent poets. She encouraged him to develop his own style because "there are beautiful ways to do things that aren't customary."[185]

XX *The Educational Experiences of W. E. B. Du Bois*

The bibliography in the 1968 edition of W. E. B. Du Bois' *Autobiography* lists twenty books and ninety-nine articles written by him; yet the 1968 edition of the *Literary History of the United States* by Spiller et al. cites him only once, on page 1314. The bibliographical volume of the same work, 1948 edition, does not even mention this prolific and influential black writer, a neglect which is difficult to understand. Du Bois began to plan carefully for the liberation of the black race while he attended Fisk University; there he was able to study all kinds of Southerners. He enjoyed the teaching of the excellent and earnest faculty, the small classes, and the absence of social and athletic distractions, qualities which Abraham Flexner and Albert J. Nock also admired. After graduating from Fisk, he enrolled for teacher-training courses at the Teacher's Institute in Nashville. Here novices were introduced into the mysteries of teaching fractions and spelling; white teachers were taught by day, black teachers at night. Du Bois then accepted a position in Watertown. This philanthropic town paid the young teacher $30 per month, and for his stipend he taught thirty eager students to read, write, and spell. To amuse them he told them stories and took them on flower-picking expeditions.[186]

Not satisfied, Du Bois applied for admission to Harvard. He was accepted, but for all of its liberal persuasion Harvard was not yet ready to accept a black student socially. The glee club declined to hear him, although he had a fine voice.[187] Happily, William James and other teachers befriended him, but he would have preferred the friendship of his peers. However, they ostracized Irish, Jewish, and black students. When Clement Morgan, a black, was chosen class orator in 1890, social Harvard was astounded. Leading newspaper editorials, especially Southern, opposed Morgan's election to academic fame.

Henry Adams noted in his autobiography that Marx and Comte were not even mentioned when he studied at Harvard. Du Bois observed the same avoidance of revolutionary thinking in 1890; he attributed this to Harvard's subservience to wealth and capital. Karl Marx was hardly mentioned, all radical movements were regarded as evil, and labor was seen as too grasping. In retrospect, Du Bois charged that "the same community that mobbed Garrison, easily hanged Sacco and Vanzetti."[188] Yet, Professor Shaler, a Southerner, asked a student to leave the classroom because he refused to sit in class with Du Bois. William James introduced him to Santayana and Royce at the Philosophy Club, and Barrett Wendell praised his themes. Of his teachers at Harvard, Du Bois wrote: "I revelled in the keen analysis of William James, Josiah Royce, and young George Santayana. But it was James with his pragmatism and Albert Bushnell Hart with his research method that turned me back from the lovely but sterile land of philosophical speculation to the social sciences as the field for gathering and interpreting that body of fact which would apply to my program for the Negro."[189]

A graduate *cum laude* of Harvard, Du Bois again turned to teaching, accepting a position at Wilberforce University, a small denominational school tolerated by the state as a lure to keep blacks out of other schools. Most of the students were of high school caliber and little could be done for the handful of brilliant students.[190] From Wilberforce, Du Bois moved to the University of Pennsylvania, where he was an assistant instructor in sociology. He was invisible to the administration for he had no status, no studies, and no listing in the catalog. But he began a study of the problems of the Philadelphia slum dwellers, a work opposed by both blacks and whites. Nevertheless, to this day *The Philadelphia Negro: A Social Study*, published in 1909, has withstood the hostility of its critics. Du Bois bitterly observed that his inferior white classmates were sporting full professorships at his school and at the University of Chicago. Was it because big business controlled the colleges? Was not his college president a high official of the Sugar Trust?[191] Finally, at Atlanta University, Du Bois was able to commit himself fully to his study of blacks in America. In thirteen years he compiled 2,172 pages of research which became the basic resource for the study of race problems between 1896 and 1920.[192] Especially significant to Du Bois was the "uprising of the black man and the pouring of himself into organized efforts for education in those years between 1861 - 1871, . . . one of the marvelous occurrences of the modern world. . . ."[193] William Cullen Bryant in a letter to Miss Janet Gibson dated April 13, 1873, wrote favorably of education in the South in that troubled period. St. Augustine had excellent schools for both black and white children, and a school for the poor whites (a degraded race) at Wilmington, North Carolina, was wonderfully successful. The school at Hampton, Virginia, for the preparation of black teachers was also commended by Bryant.[194] But in his summarizing statement in *An Educational History of the American People* on the educational contributions to education in the postwar South, Adolphe E. Meyer is less flattering about the Freedmen's Bureau's work than Bryant. True, the Freedmen's Bureau spent $6,000,000 in five years to establish 2,550 schools for the initial education of 150,000 children, but its partisanship was too ideologically related to the aims of the victorious wing of the Republican party. Many Southern families — and even some anti-Southern scalawags — could not tolerate the sight of black and white children sitting side by side in classrooms. Unfortunately, history vindicates Thomas Dixon's charge in *The Leopard's Spots* that the Northern teachers recruited to teach in the South included large numbers of altruistic men who were zealously "ablaze with moral self-ascendancy." Failing to understand the psychology of the defeated Southerner, they disparaged the Southern white mercilessly and deified the Northern soldier as the liberator of blacks. It was inevitable, therefore, that they would be socially detested and, occasionally, physically assaulted.[195]

Booker T. Washington and Du Bois both agreed that rural education in the South was superficial; poor teachers, poor schools, and poor apparatus were retarding the mental development of children. In many districts schools were open for only three months of the year.[196] But Washington was fearful of having his people take "a great leap forward." His gradualism was based on sociological premises stemming from the condition of servitude that blacks had suffered. Of slavery's principal harm to blacks, he wrote: "Perhaps the worst feature of slavery was that it prevented the development of a family life, with all its far-reaching significance. . . . No race starting in absolute poverty could be expected, in the brief period of thirty-five years, to purchase homes and build up a family life and influence that would have a very marked impression upon the life of the masses.[197]

The black man should strive for economic well-being, Washington advised. The freedman had little time for professional and cultural studies. The vocational, industrial, or technical school was the black man's salvation.[198] Washington realized his educational dreams when he founded Tuskegee Institute in 1880, an industrial school which was generously subsidized by wealthy Northern and Southern patrons. An optimist, Washington believed that as the white man developed culturally his prejudice would diminish, and he would assist in uplifting the former slave.[199]

Du Bois hated Washington's gradualism. An excellent scholar himself, he resented Tuskegee's opposition to a request which he had made to study the blacks scientifically. He regarded Washington's strong influence on the philosophy of the Southern Educational Board and the General Education Board as a major impediment to advancing college training for blacks.[200] What good had Washington's conservatism brought to his people, asked Du Bois. From 1890 to 1910, the black witnessed his disenfranchisement, the victory of "jim-crowism, and the intensification of racial segregation." By 1911, a legal caste system based on race and color had been "openly engrafted on the democratic institutions of the United States."[201] Du Bois was appalled; the Tuskegee machine, backed by Northern capital, was opposing his people's desire to liberate themselves from agricultural and industrial peonage and from developing their artistic and professional aspirations.[202] Embittered, Du Bois grew increasingly militant in his struggle to wrest the leadership of black destiny from Washington.

XXI On Adult Education

The American lyceum brought enlightenment and cheer to millions of Americans, mainly adult, who had neither the inclination, the time, nor the money for a formal education. Since 1826, when Josiah Holbrook opened the doors of the Millbury Lyceum No. 1, curious adults have listened to touring Ciceros lecturing on an almost endless range of themes, from the sun to the honeybee, and from Mohammed to the legal rights of women.[203] Evening schools have provided instruction for workers since about 1833, when the first one was opened in New York City. The first evening high school was opened in Cincinnati in 1856, and by 1870 there were sixty public evening high schools in the United States.[204] Although these schools were not primarily designed for adults, they often included cultural and self-improvement courses. William Cullen Bryant visited a female evening school in 1874 and was impressed with the four hundred workers who eagerly tried to master the rudiments of learning after a hard day's work.[205] In addition to his literary career, Sidney Lanier occupied himself with educational planning. He designed a plan for adult education in literature, art, science, and home-life improvement, but his plan was not adopted.[206] Lanier was unhappy with the traditional modes of adult education; even graduates of colleges require further schooling, since they leave school at a time when they are about ready for purposeful study.[207] Another Southern writer, George Washington Cable, introduced a system of adult education known as the Home Study Club. Catering to the educational needs of people of humble origin, the teachers of the clubs, recruited from the more educated classes, including college students, visited groups of club members in their homes and helped them study history, music, and science.[208] In *Equality*, his sequel to *Looking Backward*, Edward Bellamy strongly supports a continuing system of education for retired adults.[209] If organized sensibly, the adult program can become a People's College,[210] but even if it does not flower into a Cooper Union or a New School, adult education can provide basic education, vocational training, social clubs, and cultural courses for the worker who seeks more than bread to grace his life.[211]

"As distinctively American as baseball and banana splits is the correspondence school," writes Adolphe E. Meyer. A child of the nineteenth century, the correspondence school has "prospered steadily, growing in scope and worldly goods, until in the days of the lush twenties, with more than 2,000,000 subscribers on its lists, it had become the *garde du corps* of American adult education."[212] As is the case with all good things, quacks exploited correspondence schools, a tendency illustrated in George Babbitt's droll speech to his son Ted: "I knew this correspondence school business had become a mighty profitable game — makes suburban real-estate look like two cents! — but I didn't realize it'd got to such a reg'lar key industry. Must rank right up with groceries and movies. Always figured somebody'd come along with the brains to not leave education to a lot of bookworms and impractical theorists but make a big thing out of it."[213]

George Babbitt is alert to the practical possibilities of innovation. Educational institutions such as the Empire State College have correspondence curricula leading to degrees, and The United States Armed Forces Institute has been granting college approved credits for correspondence courses since World War II. Unfortunately, Babbitt's concern with correspondence courses is mainly mercenary. In his continuing oration on education to Ted, he reveals his educational philosophy.

I can see what an influence these courses might have on the whole educational works. Course I'd never admit it publicly — fellow like myself, a

State U. graduate, it's only decent and patriotic for him to blow his horn and boost the *alma mater* — matter of fact, there's a whole lot of valuable time lost even at the U., studying poetry and French and subjects that never brought in anybody a cent. I don't know but what maybe these correspondence courses might prove to be one of the most important American inventions.[214]

XXII   *Utopian Thought in American Education*

That the most economically advanced nation in the world, heir to the intellectual riches of the world, should produce shallow, materialistic, and pompous beings like Babbitt, fretted utopian reformers. Their dilemma has never been solved. Since society can be reformed only by properly educating the masses, how might one institute "proper education" in a society whose schools are dominated by the wealthy classes, who sensibly will not sponsor leveling educational studies? Several years after the end of World War I, James Harvey Robinson addressed himself to this question in his still relevant *The Mind in the Making:*

But how can we ever expect to cultivate the judgment of the young in matters of fundamental social, economic, and political readjustment when we consider the really dominating forces in education? But even if these restraints were weakened or removed, the task would remain a very delicate one. Even with teachers free and far better informed than they are, it would be no easy thing to cultivate in the young a justifiable admiration for the achievements and traditional ideals of mankind and at the same time develop the requisite knowledge of the prevailing abuses, culpable stupidity, common dishonesty, and empty political buncombe which too often passes for statesmanship.[215]

Cognizant of this difficulty, Edward Bellamy undauntedly preached the gospel of cooperation in his two utopian novels, *Looking Backward* and *Equality*. The books had sensational sales, and a million Americans joined the Nationalist Clubs that proliferated soon afterward to advance Bellamy's social aims. Bellamy, like most utopian writers since Plato, gave education a prime role in the life of his projected state. The aims of education, he wrote, are threefold. "First, the right of every man to the completest education the nation can give him on his own account, as necessary to his enjoyment of himself; second, the right of his fellow citizens to have him educated, as necessary to their enjoyment of his society; third, the right of the unborn to be guaranteed an intelligent and refined parentage."[216] Included in the state's program of education is a strong physical education regimen for "the faculty of education is held to the same responsibility for the bodies as for the minds of its charges."[217]

After graduating from high school, all young people are required to serve the state for three years, a kind of Peace Corps. Since wars are not expected, the young are to participate in civic services of benefit to society. Those who complete the service requirement may apply for matriculation at professional schools which are centers for serious study. Those who seek escape from the labor force to dally at the university are soon found out and swiftly dismissed. Students are given until thirty to select a profession; after thirty they must either become part of the labor force or stay with the profession of their last choice.[218] To a question put to him concerning educational priorities, Dr. Leete offers a Jeffersonian reply: "If indeed, we could not afford to educate everybody, we should choose the coarsest and dullest by nature. . . . The naturally refined and intellectual can better dispense with aids to culture than those less fortunate in natural endowments."[219] Vocational guidance is an ongoing process in Bellamy's utopia; parents and teachers carefully study the child's development for clues to his vocational propensities. Students are introduced to the National Industrial System: they study each trade carefully; and they visit workshops and industries.[220]

In *Equality*, Bellamy proposes community colleges. Since all students are guaranteed a college education, each community will have its own university and it will have "more students from the vicinage than one of your great [nineteenth-century] universities could collect with its dragnet from the ends of the earth."[221] For the utopian student, the curriculum at twenty-one is only a beginning. After completing their professional educations, the graduates may continue to elect postgraduate courses for as long as they care to. Serious work starts after college, because the young cannot fully do justice to serious study until twenty-one,[222] a theory frequently sustained by the achievements of adult student returnees.

William Dean Howells anticipated some of Bellamy's educational criticisms in his utopian novel, *A Traveler from Altruria*. In a discussion on education, the banker sees little value in the three R's since they will not improve the quality of mechanics who will lack time to utilize the little culture their schooling gives them. College education renders business life unpalatable; the high ideals engendered in college are in opposition to the tooth and fang law of business.

Ideally, a college education is for the aristocrat who has leisure time
to develop his tastes, but in America, where the work ethic prevails,
no one leads a life of leisure, invalidating the advertised ethical and
cultural aims of higher education.[223]

Mark Twain's contribution to utopian fiction, "The Curious
Republic of Goncour," incorporates Platonic and Jeffersonian
themes in its educational philosophy. The Republic's constitution
features this unusual scheme for voting privileges:

Requisites for Voting[224]

Class of Citizen	Number of Votes
Poor or ignorant	1
Common school graduate	2
High school graduate	4
Propertied high school graduate	5
Propertied high school graduate owning 50,000 sacos	Additional vote for each 50,000 sacos
University graduate	9

Twain's society is paternalistic since the learned voters who will
possess the balance of power tend to be upright, tolerant, and compassionate; thus they will serve as "the vigilant and efficient protec-
tion of the great lower rank of society." Officialdom is a high-
minded class of "men of property, character, and intellect who took
competitive examinations for the posts."[225] Goncour seems to be
Twain's answer to the tarnished gold of the gilded age. Compassionate as he was for the helpless victims of the "robber barons,"
imperialists, and corrupt statesmen, Twain was curiously drawn to
tycoons and knew many intimately. He admired Carnegie. Vexed
perhaps because of his inability to penetrate the iron curtain of New
England literary Brahmanism, he sought compensation in the com-
panionship of unlettered moguls whose derring-do, although frequently tainted, nevertheless was stirringly romantic.

Unhappy with academia as he found it, Ezra Pound formulated a
plan for an aesthetic utopian college of arts. His college was un-
concerned with social movements, but it was revolutionary in its
curricula and aims. Pound announced his prospective college in
"Preliminary Announcement of a College of Arts," an article carried
by the *Egoist* in its edition of November 2, 1914. The college never
took root, but Pound's notions are interesting. Because of the
facilities of the British Museum for scholarly research, the college
was to be based in London. To insure that its students would have a

unique faculty, the college would invite established artists who had suffered for art, especially in the literary disciplines. Inter-disciplinary teaching would be encouraged, an educational practice now widely accepted. At least one more idea proposed by Pound is in wide use today — the setting up of chairs of artists and writers in residency to familiarize the student with the creative idea in progress.[226]

XXIII *Conclusions*

From kindergarten to graduate school, education made remark-able advances from 1865 to 1918. The industrialization of the nation, its geographical expansion, and its increased population and wealth created great educational problems. As late as 1911 only one of ten students graduated from high school. Sid Caesar dramatized this statistic cleverly in one of his television skits. A young lady presents her boyfriend to her awed parents. In a proud voice, she proclaims, "Father and Mother, I wish to introduce you to the high school graduate." They all but swoon in ecstasy. Their daughter has snared the town's only graduate.

Interestingly, of the forty-eight teachers discussed in this chapter, twenty-nine are singled out for praise in fictional and biographical works, and of these, twenty-one are biographical characters. Ed-mund Wilson, George Santayana, Elmer Rice, Gertrude Atherton, Edgar Lee Masters, Theodore Dreiser, and Willa Cather all wrote highly of their teachers who inspired them to write, but at least thir-teen fictional writers created teachers in the image of Ichabod Crane. Private schools and public schools fare about the same in the estimation of writers. Of twenty-six private schools cited, seventeen are censured, and of twenty-five public schools discussed, sixteen are rated poorly.

The problems of black education in the Reconstruction period are depicted from two different viewpoints in the fiction of Tourgée and Dixon. But the major issues of black education were fought dramatically in the battle of the books between Booker T. Washington and W. E. B. Du Bois.

Bellamy's community college idea has become an integral part of American educational planning and policy. Even his "electroscope," a device mentioned in *Equality* that would bring the sound and form of professors thousands of miles distant to each community college, has become a reality.

Many of the lads graduating from high school in 1916 were destined to die on foreign soil a few years later; many of the girls who graduated with them were destined for widowhood. A schoolman who allegedly hated war soberly cautioned a cheering Congress to diminish their applause for our entry into the war since the declaration of war meant death to thousands of American and foreign youths. Whether another kind of education would have spared them cannot now be more than conjecture, but Senator George Norris and Congressman Charles Augustus Lindbergh, the father of the aviator, looked upon the cheering politicians and wondered. Were they wrong in voting against our entry into the war? Was education ultimately an education for death? Could war make the world safe for democracy?

They had their answer soon after the war's end. Communism in Russia, fascism in Italy, and Nazism in Germany made Wilson's words puerile. Practical statesmen could now point to his handiwork and announce self-righteously, "A schoolman may birch a classroom into order, but he cannot wield the ferrule effectively in the university of the world."

CHAPTER 3

Writers on the Higher Learning, 1865 - 1918

Few important American writers have distinguished themselves in school or have attempted to prolong the educational process; their real school is the wider world and their way of learning is more intuitive than formal; they are born dropouts.[1]
Richard O'Connor, *Ambrose Bierce*

AFTER decades of meditating, teaching, and writing, William James sadly informed the Harvard graduating class of 1903 that "the old notion that book learning can be a panacea for the vices of society lies pretty well shattered today."[2] Three years later, Upton Sinclair, in his novel *The Jungle*, denounced the educated classes for their apathetic acquiescence in the plutocratic perversions of learning. Sinclair's socialist orator tells his ragged listeners: "We have schools and colleges, newspapers and books; we have searched the heavens and earth, we have weighed and probed and reasoned — and all to equip men to destroy each other."[3] Perhaps Sinclair's panacea, world socialism, would be as impotent as any other society, past and present, has been in leading men to sanity and grace, but the hypothetical denials of his premises do not exculpate these societies for their intermittent negation of education.

I Some Educational Attitudes

In his dialogues with the worldly Peter Dooley, Father Kelly offers a simple philosophy of education that many educators secretly believe in. "Childer shuddn't be sent to larn," says Dooley's friend, "but to larn how to larn. I don't care what ye larn them so long as 'tis onplesant to them."[4] American writers and scholars were saddened by the commercial tone of the nation. How could education fare meaningfully in a milieu of strife, competition, and gilded age values? John Jay Chapman shook his head and despaired of an

America "beset by influences inimical to development of deep thought."[5] George William Curtis warned the graduating class of Union College in 1877 that the nation disparages intellect; jealous of the college man, the public praises instead the self-made man and condemns higher learning.[6]

Education should begin at the mother's knee, urged John Jay Chapman. "The whole future of civilization," wrote Chapman, "depends upon what is read to children before they can read to themselves."[7] The premise is difficult to assail, but it leaves many questions unanswered. What should the preschool legions be trained for? What books should be read to them and who should select them? How competent are parents to read the "proper" books? Even if Edward Bellamy's utopian dream were fulfilled — the right of every unborn child to have educated parents — there would still be the problem of defining education. Before he adopted a more pessimistic view of education, William James saw in America's well-organized educational institutions a multiplicity of types for the world to emulate, but he recognized that it would take a generation or two of superior teachers to elevate American pedagogy to world leadership in education.[8]

Education must be more than a rational instrument for uncovering knowledge, endowing the young with practical skills, and providing the state with political technicians. The poet Stephen Vincent Benét valued character in the teacher more than erudition. First, the teacher must have character, but an English teacher, for example, will not acquire character by writing "the most scholarly thesis on the minor works of Hannah More, or the rhyme endings of Wordsworth's 'Ecclesiastical Sonnets.' "[9] Although Mark Twain's skepticism later developed into cynicism, he advocated education as a powerful force in society: "Inestimably valuable is training, influence, education, in right directions — training one's self-approbation to elevate its ideals."[10] Obviously, if each person behaves according to his own nature, there is a danger that he might be seduced into perversity by his need for self-fulfillment. To counter this, Twain stressed the values of education for establishing criteria that would direct each person's passion for self-approbation into meaningful paths.

II   *Education and life*

But how can the school initiate the child into a world that is so frequently inconsistent with the saccharine precepts spoon-fed to the believing child by unworldly schoolmarms? Hjalmer H. Boyesen's idealistic aims for the lower schools include a strong brief for the realistic preparation of children. His article, "A Doll-Home" (*Cosmopolitan*, November, 1893), is still pertinent today, especially in the schools of suburbia, which are finding it difficult to rationalize the city's ghettos to their sheltered charges. Conversely, how can the ghetto teachers justify the suburban Edens to the ill-housed, asphalt-tied, and often famished child-cynics whom they are supposed to enlighten? Boyesen argues that: "every child, whether male or female, that comes into the world, has, abstractedly speaking, a full right to know the life into which it is born, to test its educational value, and by its rough and trying discipline to develop whatever powers there may be slumbering in it. You cannot artificially limit experience without impairing growth, diminishing the chances of survival, and stunting the stature of manhood or womanhood."[11]

III   *The Need for Practical Education*

In his *Talks to Teachers*, William James stresses that man is a practical being "whose mind is given him to aid in adapting him to this world's life."[12] Since only few children are educable, argues Albert Jay Nock, those not educable should be trained, a distinction that he elaborately demonstrates in his provocative *Memoirs of a Superfluous Man*.[13] Defending intellectual aristocracy in education, Abraham Flexner, like Nock, implies that the best education rewards excellence handsomely and provides for the vocational and civic needs of the vast majority of students who will not pursue the higher learning. A democracy that ignores excellence is in danger of losing its freedom, "for in very truth an aristocracy of excellence is the truest form of democracy."[14] Happily, Flexner applies seemingly classless tests to the sifting of the wheat from the chaff — the children of the wealthy are to be subjected to the same standards as the children of the poor — but one might argue with reason that the tutor-guided, prep-school graduate has an advantage over his slum-school counterpart. Peter Dooley was calm in his appraisal of educational equality; it really doesn't matter whether education is free or not since "men that wants it 'll have it be hook or crook, and them that don't ra-ly want it it never will get it,"[15] a common-sense philosophy that is only partially valid.

Literature provides many informal instances of education that are not readily transferable to the schools. Huck Finn's epic voyage down the Mississippi in the company of Jim, the runaway slave, is an admirable episodic educational itinerary; before Huck returns to "civilization," he is transformed into a worldly young man, aware of the foibles of the human race, portions of which had trooped across his magnificent stage, heightening his perception of human personality and endowing him with a compassionate regard for mankind's fallible ways. As a cub-pilot aboard a side-wheeler, young Twain was masterfully taught the mysteries of navigation and, perhaps even more important, the sacredness of human responsibility by one of the most brilliant unlettered teachers in all of literature, the inimitable Mr. Bixby. William Faulkner, too, has portrayed the remarkable education of a Southern boy in "The Bear." The mysterious forest is the young boy's school; his teachers are aristocratic white hunters, a half-breed Indian, and a black man. Each adult adds to the boy's lore; they do not sanction his solitary venture into the woods in pursuit of the mythic bear until he has demonstrated his readiness for the adventure. His teachers do not press him; there will be time for his meeting with the magnificent bear when he passes his preliminary tests.

But in the actual business of education there is little room for such romanticism. More or less, the public subscribes to the cynical educational generalizations of Ambrose Bierce: learning is "the kind of ignorance distinguishing the studious"; education is "that which discloses to the wise and disguises from the foolish their lack of understanding;"[16] and an academy is "a modern school where football is taught."[17] American education is divorced from life, and its methodologies are hopelessly outdated.[18] How can education that pays teachers to teach doctrines of heaven and hell to innocent children,[19] that petrifies the minds of teachers and students alike,[20] and that ignores the harmonization of emotion and intellect[21] claim to edify the nation? Furthermore, Lincoln Steffens's criticism of education, namely, that "educated people were the slowest to move toward any change," had been voiced earlier by Ralph Waldo Emerson and Wendell Phillips.[22] William James said in 1903: ". . . vice will never cease. Harvard men support Tammany. Harvard men defend the treatment of our Filipino allies 'as a masterpiece of policy and morals.' Harvard men will sell their pens to whoever buys them."[23]

IV   The College: Does it Educate?

Henry James, like his friend Henry Adams, was appalled by the "absolute and incredible lack of culture that strikes you in common travelling Americans,"[24] a theme epitomized in Mark Twain's *The Innocents Abroad*. Since the American worker and farmer could hardly afford to vacation in Europe, the American Babbitts must have been representatives of the nation's prosperous classes, including graduates of college and university. It seems that the higher learning in America had failed to create the type of educated gentleman envisioned by Henry James and his like-minded contemporaries. To inspire a love for culture the college should dispense with athletic patronage and encourage more democracy in the college's societies.[25] In his novels of college life, Sinclair Lewis mocks the limited cultural aspirations of America's provincial colleges. At Adelbert College, Hatch Hewitt belittles the school's educational worth to Gideon Planish: "I got what education I could reading at the branch library. I don't think so much of colleges, but maybe I can learn some economics here, and some vocabulary besides 'holocaust' and 'suspended sentence.' "[26] For a time Jack London believed that college would help him, but he was not impressed with the competition for high grades since "it is a matter of common knowledge that the one who captures the prizes for scholarship and the fellowships rarely does anything in his or her after-life."[27] Later, London said that he learned nothing about his future vocation during his year at the University of California. His professors were not interested in contemporary writing. Frank Norris said he had wasted nine years of university study on secondhand ideas in books of others.[28]

In Babbitt's praise of the B. A. to his son Ted, Sinclair Lewis reflects the shallow meaning of the degree to many of its possessors. Babbitt's eulogy is rhetorically vulgar, but sophisticated Babbitts have restated its theme in more cushioned jargon: "I've found out it's a mighty nice thing to be able to say you've a B. A. Some client that doesn't know what you are and thinks that you're just a plain business man he gets to shooting off his mouth about economics or literature or even foreign trade conditions, and you just ease in something like 'When I was in college — course I got my B. A. in sociology and all that junk.' Oh it puts an awful crimp in their style!"[29]

Babbitt's know-nothing philosophy is sad, but critics of American college life of this period are generally in agreement with Lewis' criticisms. Henry Seidel Canby found the American college wanting. College did not educate its students, lamented Canby, "for we were ready to organize a trust or go to war, but not to control the one for human uses and to stop the other before it began."[30] But the adult community was too narrow in its thinking. William James despaired of middle-aged apathy in the search for truth. The adult's desire for disinterested inquiry is torpid; in youth it is strong.[31] In Elmer Rice's play, *We the People* (1933), a student on the college board demands specific student rights in a tone that would be used by student militants of the 1960s:

All right. The way I look at it is this. A university should be something more than a place where you come to soak in a lot of facts. A college student should not only familiarize himself with the social system in which he is going to function, but he should learn to view it critically and with a certain amount of skepticism. Progress comes through change. We cannot hope for innovation and change from those who are past the prime of life. If we are against militarism, against war, against social and economic injustice and political corruption, we must make ourselves articulate, right here and now. I don't agree with Schwarz that protest is futile. My opinion is that if you have convictions, you shouldn't be afraid to express them.[32]

V   *The Social Goals of Scholars and Colleges*

The articulate student is often confused by the apparent dichotomy between the man thinking and the man acting. A man might rage awesomely in type against a social evil, but he will hesitate to join a small band of vulnerable dissenters. William James taught that "in theory as in practice, a man must take his part, believing something, fighting for what he believes, and incurring the risk of being wrong."[33] In more direct language, Wendell Phillips informed a Phi Beta Kappa audience at Harvard in 1881 that "it is the duty of the scholar to help those less favored in life,"[34] a belief shared by Jack London.[35]

George William Curtis passionately reminded scholars that they were the conscience of the state: "At every cost, the true scholar asserts, defends, liberty of thought and liberty of speech."[36] A conservative force for intellectual and moral freedom, the scholarly class has a sacred mission — "the elevation and correction of public sentiment."[37] But this ideal cannot be attained, wrote Lincoln Steffens, since universities in Berlin and California, for example, "were organized to teach the known — not for inquiry and research into the unknown."[38] How can the scholar appreciably improve society if he is conditioned to delve into the past, mull over the present, and afraid to leave the secure confines of tradition for the uncertainities of the future? Wendell Phillips was too blunt for the academicians of his day. Imagine the consternation of his Harvard associates who chanced upon this diatribe in lecture hall or in the press! "When I was asked the other day, how it happened there was so much learning at Cambridge, I answered: 'Because nobody carries any away.' "[39]

VI   *The Curriculum Under Fire*

For restless spirits like Jack London, a confining college curriculum was death. He countenanced a set curriculum for the "ordinary run of humanity," but recommended a more liberal curricular diet for the explorative student.[40] The library was a delightful substitute for classwork to creative students. Joseph Wood Krutch learned more from the college library and wise librarians than from some of his courses. Carl Becker attributes his interest in history and teaching to the tolerance of a stern librarian who permitted him to borrow a copy of *Anna Karenina*, a book strongly censured in nineteenth-century Iowa. Krutch recalls that his independent reading of Shaw at college sparked his passion for literature and teaching.[41]

Today, when independent study programs are common, Jack London might have found a course of study consonant with his needs. In *Martin Eden*, he ridicules a system of education that violates every sound principle of interest and motivation. Martin expounds a criticism of mass education that cannot be refuted by honest teachers: "The speed of a fleet, you know, is the speed of the slowest ship, and the speed of the teacher is affected the same way. They can't go any faster than the rush of their scholars, and I can set a faster pace for myself than they set for a whole schoolroom."[42]

VII   *Harvard's Intellectual Fare*

Harvard is damned and praised by its eminent alumni. George Santayana, a son of Harvard, said that the university taught a little of everything but nothing thoroughly.[43] In his novel, *The Last Puritan*, Santayana writes unflatteringly of the college's courses of study. Peter Alden thinks little of the curriculum; he devotes a fraction of his time to study and engages himself in theatricals, sports, and school journalism.[44] But Santayana's views on Harvard were not shared by William James, who wrote in 1882 that no German university was doing as much for its students as Harvard was. Harvard employed superior methodologies and offered broader and more cosmopolitan courses.[45] Pierrepont Noyes, the son of the founder of the Oneida Community, longed to transfer to Harvard where he believed history was taught well. At Colgate, he lamented, history courses were "made for Baptist preachers."[46]

VIII   *President Eliot and the Elective System*

Harvard has had two presidents, both chemists, who were controversial innovators. President Charles W. Eliot assumed his chair in 1869 and soon after shocked the sedate Harvard community with his plan for an elective system that would permit the undergraduate to pursue mainly those courses that interested him. Henry James lauded Eliot's revolutionary changes. There would be a proliferation of advanced courses, and to teach these courses competently, teachers would have to read more widely and broaden their intellectual horizons.[47] Lewis Gannett defends Eliot's elective system with reservation: "If one floundered about the classroom in Eliot's Harvard, I am not sure that the floundering was a bad experience. It taught one something of the size of the universe."[48] In Robert Herrick's fictional version of the history of the University of Chicago, Norman Beckwith, an inspired teacher, fears that the abolition of the elective system at Eureka University (Chicago's fictional name) would turn the college into a trade school.[49]

But the opponents of the elective system were powerful. Boyesen thought that the American student, unlike his supposedly more mature German counterpart, could not cope with an elective system;[50] Albert Jay Nock pronounced the elective system a failure after forty years;[51] and Abraham Flexner boasted that there was no froth in the Johns Hopkins University of his time. His college had "no special schools for the things that cannot be taught anyway, such as journalism, business, and education. . . ."[52] John Kendrick Bangs dismisses electives humorously in his satire "On Short College Courses." The Pedagog is incensed over Eliot's sponsorship of short courses at Harvard, but the Idiot, who generally shows more sense than his pompous professional friends, praises the short courses since they will allow a man to enter his field at twenty-one instead of thirty-one. To accelerate the learning process, Gramophone courses that could give the undergraduate a degree in forty-eight hours might be instituted, but the athletic departments would probably object, because students studying *in absentia* would not be available for the rowing and football seasons.[53]

IX   *On the Classics in the Curriculum*

The supporters of the classical curriculum saw the elective system as the death of their beloved Greek and Latin studies. Fred Lewis Pattee points out that during the flowering of literature in New

England no courses in English were offered in American colleges; Greek and Latin were prescribed for all. But the sons of the Transcendentalists who studied English and philology failed to make their marks in literature.[54] Albert Jay Nock attributed his literary skill and his awareness of social and political issues to his excellent classical education in a small college.[55] Barrett Wendell regretted the lack of intellectual tone in nonclassical schools;[56] John Jay Chapman viewed the classics as hallmarks of educated people;[57] Willa Cather, although disappointed with her pedestrian teacher of the classics at Nebraska, never forgot her introduction into classical studies;[58] and Ida Tarbell paid homage to George Haskin's, her classics teacher at Allegheny College whose lectures on Cicero, Tacitus, and Livy "could have taught her more than she knows today about the ways of men in their personal and their national relations, more of the causes of war, of the weaknesses of governments."[59] The inspired classics teacher truly believed that "Greek would be a universal window to all learning, . . . a clue to general knowledge of all human beings."[60] James Russell Lowell advocated translation as great training because the Greek tongue, in illustration, is precise and yet flexible enough to make translation both accurate and pleasant.[61]

But the classical tradition was dying. It was replaced by a trivial, easy-going, cribbed and sham education.[62] Van Wyck Brooks wrote a distressing eulogy for the passing of the classical curriculum:

Disregarding secondary writers, all of the first-rate writers of the later age, even those who knew the classics well, suffered as regards their style, from a vital indifference to the classics. Few of their books have the authentic ring that marks the best pages of Thoreau, Dana, Hawthorne, Motley, etc., etc., who were steeped in Greek, Latin, and the Bible. The "vices" of their style were almost as marked as their "beauties": the thin facility of Howells and the earlier Henry James, the obscurity of the later Henry James, . . . the perversity of Emily Dickinson, the awkward, metallic or inexpressive quality of much of Henry Adams's writing, especially the later chapters of the *Education.* . . .[63]

But the classics died a slow death; as late as 1917, professors united to preserve the classical curriculum.[64]

X *The Teaching of Philosophy and Science*

Teachers of philosophy were having major problems, too. William James cautioned his colleagues not to offer philosophy to immature students.[65] In an anonymous article to the *Nation* in 1876, James characterized the philosophy teacher as a college president, a minister of the Gospel lacking speculative penchants, a lifeless, uninspiring teacher in the classroom. His contemporary, G. Stanley Hall, in another article to the *Nation*, deplored the lack of philosophical studies in the best colleges.[66]

Historians like Henry Adams saw in the rise of new sciences a language that their old training had not prepared them to read. A humanist, Boyesen felt "that no man can ignore it [science] without a very great detriment to his intellectual life,"[67] a point of view that is becoming increasingly valid today. Science and technology are the pets of American education, since they are vital to our economic and military supremacy. Woodrow Wilson believed that technical schools "are proper parts of a university only when pure science is of the essence of their teaching, the spirit of pure science the spirit of all their studies," but he was unable to utilize science as effectively to maintain peace as he used it to wage war.[68] The lessons of World War I were apparent to Randolph Bourne in 1919; technology can be manipulated for good or evil. To insure that our technological tools do not become destructive Golems or Frankenstein monsters we must quicken our cultural studies, use our social and human institutions to eradicate evil, and wed the humanities with the technologies to ward off doomsday.[69]

XI *On the Teaching of English*

A native-born American studies English for eight years in elementary school, four years in high school, and, possibly, for two more years in college. Why, then, the almost universal outcry against the slovenly speech and the immature writing of the graduates from our schools at all levels? In 1892, when the Harvard freshmen were a select group, the Report of the Committee on Composition and Rhetoric to the Board of Overseers of Harvard College complained that as the Department of English at Harvard "is organized, under the existing standards of examination, the college seems compelled, during the freshman year, to do a vast amount of elementary work which should be done in the preparatory schools."[70] Barrett Wendell, after decades of teaching English at Harvard, painfully admitted that it is almost futile to teach English composition.[71] It would be interesting to ask five hundred English teachers to react to Wendell's final appraisal of the composition course: ". . . in the opinion of occasional observers, no teachers and no methods have as yet justified, by irrefutable results, the still general faith that if you try honestly to teach youths how to write English they will learn to write with idiomatic freedom."[72] Wendell's "occasional observers" included Professors Childs, Lounsbury, Cook, and Beers, all giants in their fields. William Lyon Phelps attested that Yale sophomores who had taken literature courses in their freshmen years wrote as well as the sophomores who had elected the preparatory composition course first.[73] And to the fledgling writer who seeks to advance into professional authorship, Willa Cather cautions "beware!" Schools and courses for writers are useless; they teach only what others have done and cannot inspire originality.[74]

Not until 1879 was American literature a popular course in American universities.[75] Inveterate classicists like Albert Jay Nock insisted that Greek and Latin studies precluded the need for courses in composition and literature. A reasonably educated college man should use the library to study literature.[76] A poor teacher of literature can ruin a student's taste for reading forever. Eugene O'Neill wrote of his literature course at Princeton: "I was studying Shakespeare in classes, and this made me afraid of him. I've only recently (1920) explored Shakespeare with profit and pleasure untold. . . . Why can't our education respond logically to our needs? If it did, we'd grab for these things and hold on to them."[77]

XII *Those Wasteful Education Courses*

O'Neill studied in a liberal arts college. His professors were not examples of the allegedly semiliterate professors of infamous schools of education. Yet, for all of their scholarship and specialization, they taught poorly. Apparently, men like Frank Dobie who abhor schools and professors of education, overlook the deadening lectures, eccentricities, and deficiencies of a goodly number of liberal arts professors. Dobie is bitter because of the time he wasted in education courses, none of which added "a whit to my fitness to teach anything or anybody."[78] Intelligent students at Southwestern University in Texas avoided education courses. How can education courses endow a student with "common sense, a sense of humor, imagination, tact, graciousness, and a mastery of the subject . . . the true requisites of a teacher?"[79] Dobie calls education professors victimized quacks who transmit their diluted learning to others. A race of cunning climbers, they are censors of curiosity and apostles of religion who are "more lethal enemies to society than all the communists dreamed up by Senator Joe McCarthy and set down in book by Hoover."[80]

Professors of the history of education escaped Dobie's wrath, for their course "is a legitimate subject."[81]

XIII   Some Unlikely Curriculla

Mr. Dooley will have his jests with the colleges. He suggested the following courses for the modern university:

1. Beauty
2. Puns. Pothry on the Changin' Hues iv the Settin' Sun
   Platonic Love Nonsence Rhymes
   How Green Grows the Grass
   Relation iv Ice to the Greek Idie iv God[82]

Dooley is quite up-to-date. One of the students takes hashish every morning and studies with Purfessor Maryanna. Dooley's creator, Finley Peter Dunne, strips men of their pomposities.

Ambrose Bierce indeed deserves his sobriquet "bitter Bierce" for his caustic satire. He proposes a state university that will include departments of mechanism, horse-shoeing, wagon-making, and rail-splitting. "This latter," he explains, "would also keep green the memory of one of the most carefully uneducated men of modern times, who nevertheless became President of these United States, as every graduate of the university will have a chance to do, despite a peculiarly similar obstacle."[83]

XIV   The Good Teacher in Fiction and Reality

President Coit Gilman's educational philosophy was "brains, not bricks and mortar"and Abraham Flexner saw the main problem of American education, as "how to prevent the bricks and mortar from obtaining greater importance than they deserve."[84] Whether American education would be more meaningful if administrators and trustees had invested more in academic brains than in elaborate campus architecture cannot be determined. Perhaps in the pretechnological period a Lavoisier, Priestley, and Franklin might engage in successful experimentation in physics and chemistry on a kitchen table, but today's sophisticated scientific instrumentation requires housing in vast experimental arenas.

The criteria for good teachers proposed by educational philosophers are impractical. To expect a land that celebrates the self-help ethic to pay for excellence in teaching when the marketplace is usually well stocked with hungry pedagogues is naive. Poor Richard's sermons on rugged individualism, an ample reservoir of frontier land, and an expanding industry enticed ambitious go-getters into more profitable vocations. Yet the profession has not been without its sacrificing teachers who love children, teaching, and mankind. But even our finest teachers contradict themselves when they talk shop. After his retirement from Harvard, William James wrote of two professorial functions: (1) to be learned and distribute bibliographical information; (2) to communicate truth. Although James felt that item 1 is essential, he cared only for item 2, but his weakness in learning gave him uneasiness throughout his teaching days.[85] Perhaps that is why he advised teachers to prepare themselves so well that their classroom lectures would be almost spontaneous. As a corollary to this injunction, James instructed teachers never to ask their pupils to do things that they themselves cannot accomplish.[86]

Good teachers are brave teachers, but outspoken teachers are not usually supported by their tenure-minded colleagues. In *Chimes*, Norman Beckwith is tolerated by the administration even after he asks an indifferent faculty, "What is a university for — athletes, fraternity houses, or scholarship?"[87] Another gadfly at Eureka University, old Professor Harden who hated faculty meetings, committees, and public dinners, spoke scornfully of the university's values at a cap and gown dinner sponsored by the trustees. He asked for libraries, seminars, and capable students. But he was passed off as an eccentric not to be taken seriously.[88]

Who are the teachers whom the students respect and admire? They exhibit combinations of these qualities according to the authors cited:

1. The ability to sustain spontaneous student interest.[89]
2. The offering of meaningful learning that is readily distinguishable by students from chaff and sawdust.[90]
3. A willingness to learn from students.[91]
4. A delight in awakened minds.[92]
5. A boldness that may succeed because of its stimulating indiscretion.[93]
6. A respect for the student's interest.[94]
7. Interest in both the weak and strong points of a student.[95]
8. An indifference to geniuses and dunces.[96]
9. An enthusiastic regard for the detection and encouragement of student talent.[97]
10. A concern for the "grinds" and a disregard for the socialites.[98]
11. The willingness to sacrifice lucrative business offers for the love of teaching.[99]
12. The ability to communicate educational values in time spans of "fruitful brevity."[100]

XV   A *Gallery of Honored Teachers*

The roll call of eulogized teachers in this period is impressive. Henry Seidel Canby recalls Henry Augustin Beers as a gentle inspirer of men who was defeated by a system which demanded exact practitioners in the humanities.[101] Santayana admired Professor Bowen — "a dear old thing and an excellent teacher" who made history live.[102] Gruff and irascible teachers are admired also. Joseph Wood Krutch writes fondly of Professor James Douglas Bruce who would announce before exams: "When I ask you a question I want you to tell me exactly what I have told you. I am not interested in your opinions because I do not think that they are of any value."[103] John Roderigo Dos Passos liked the old-fashioned ways of Dean Le Baron Russell Briggs of Harvard. An exposer of sham and a reverent apostle of neatness of language, Dean Briggs was accessible to all who sought him.[104] William Allen White respected James H. Canfield, his social science teacher at Kansas, for his humor, his inspiration, and especially his direction of classroom discussion, which did not encourage "ignorant opinion in the name of free discussion."[105]

Frank Norris dedicated his novel *McTeague* to Professor Lewis E. Gates, a gifted teacher of writing. Gates succeeded in developing the literary instincts of his students, a virtue that Norris found lacking in his literature professors at the University of California.[106] Edmund Wilson attributed his achievements in literary criticism to Christian Gauss of Princeton, a teacher who "taught much in insisting little."[107] Only later do some students appreciate this method of teaching. Bliss Perry, in a discussion with Professor Dodd of the faculty of Williams College, remarked: "Dr. Hopkins taught us nothing about the history of philosophy." Dodd replied, "No, he taught you nothing about philosophy, but he taught you to philosophize."[108] Ezra Pound was generous in his praise of Assistant Professor of Latin Walton Brooks McDaniel of the University of Pennsylvania and of Professors Joseph Darling Ibbotson and William Pierce Shephard of Hamilton College for encouraging him to write poetry.[109]

The consensus of biographers on the personality of William James as a teacher seems to support the testimonial accorded to James at his funeral by the Reverend George A. Gordon: "After all is said and done, it is the human aspect that lasts the longest. The scholar, thinker, teacher is merged at last in the human being. The man is the ultimate and the everlasting value."[110] At Harvard, Robert Frost found strength, enlightenment, and justification for his behavior in the works of William James,[111] and Gertrude Stein found in him a tolerance and understanding that is rare in humankind. As secretary of the Philosophical Club at Radcliffe, Miss Stein knew James as a friend as well as a teacher. Not inclined to take a test one day, she excused herself from class. James sent her a consoling card: "I feel like that myself somedays."[112]

Lincoln Steffens was grateful to Louis Loeb for teaching him "that it is worthwhile going to college if only to know what is not there."[113] But usually the tribute of a writer to his teacher is more concrete. For example, Barrett Wendell praised James Russell Lowell for teaching the spirit of literature, not the letter. Inspired by Lowell, Wendell read Dante better in a month than he had ever learned to read Greek, Latin, or German.[114] Lowell lived to hear of Wendell's praise; he was so touched and pleased with his student's gracious words that he was freed from wondering again "whether in his years of teaching he had not wasted rather fruitlessly time he should have given for literature."[115]

Max Eastman worshiped Henry Loomis Nelson, his teacher of English constitutional history. And why not? Is it every undergraduate who is told by his teacher that "he wrote better than Stuart Pratt Sherman?"[116] At Southwestern University in 1906, Frank Dobie adored Albert Shipp Pegues, his English teacher: "He drilled us on metrics and illuminated the language and thought of poets; above all he made us enjoy poetry. . . . No other teacher I came under . . . so enlarged and enriched life for me, so started up growths inside me.[117] Another English teacher, William Lyon Phelps of Yale, was remembered by many students in their writing. Phelps' inspiring lectures induced a passion in Randolph Bourne for literature.[118] Sinclair Lewis remembered Phelps as a great lover of human beings and literature, a guide to perplexed freshmen, and a humanizer of the fear-gripped campus.[119] But H. L. Mencken was disappointed in Phelps' *Advance of the English Novel,* a book hardly worthy of "a college professor shaken free of the class room, a pundit emancipated from superstition, the White Hope of the Seminaries."[120]

And the honor roll continues. Carl Van Doren's talks with Stuart Pratt Sherman on books, music, and art shaped his literary destiny.[121] Carl Sandburg was fortunate to have Professor Wright at Lombard College publish his early poetry in 1904. The professor recognized Sandburg's greatness and wrote a foreword to the book praising his young find.[122] Charles Townsend Copeland, a maker of writers, was affectionately called Copey by his students and close associates, including George L. Kittredge, Bliss Perry, and Barrett Wendell.[123] He was admired for many reasons: Walter Lippmann saw him as "a very distinct person in a unique relationship with each individual who interested him";[124] John Reed viewed him as a revealer of the beauty in books and world;[125] John Tunis cited him as an inciter of dissent because of his popularity with the undergraduates, his scorn for Ph. D.s, and his refusal to write scholarly books;[126] and finally, Walter Lippmann again praised Copeland — as a magical teacher "who has drawn out of a long succession of pupils whatever gifts they had for writing in the English language and of appreciating what has been written in English."[127]

But not all of Copeland's students deified him. T. S. Eliot disliked his teaching methods and derived little from the course; Conrad Aiken resented Copeland's vanity which was inflated by his clique of student adulators; and John Dos Passos described their relationship as "one of armed neutrality."[128]

XVI   In Praise of Philosophers and Scientists

It is to the credit of William James that he was man enough to overlook the eccentricities of Charles S. Peirce, "a hopeless crank and failure in many ways," and recommend him for a lectureship at Harvard.[129] Writing to President Eliot that "I should learn a lot from his course," James stressed that Peirce's "personal uncomfortableness" was a minimal deficiency in view of his intellectual strength.[130] John Dewey, too, was known for hiring teachers who compensated for some lack by their willingness to learn as they taught. When John Dewey appointed Max Eastman to teach the "Principles of Science," young Eastman was fearful of accepting the offer because of his ignorance of science. But Dewey assured him that there was no better road to learning than the coeducation of teacher and pupils.[131] Dewey, aware of his own rhetorical problems, one day remarked to Eastman: "You know how to write. I wish you'd show me how it's done."[132] Such humility prompted Eastman to write: "John Dewey's instinctive and active deference and unqualified giving-of-attention to whatever anybody, no matter how dumb and humble, may have to say, is one of the rarest gifts or accomplishments of genius."[133]

A science teacher at Oglethorpe, Professor James Woodrow, influenced Sidney Lanier to respect facts and to scan them carefully.[134]

William James wrote in homage to his comparative anatomy teacher, Jeffries Wyman, a scientist unknown away from Harvard because he did not publish.[135]

XVII   *To Teach or to Write*

Can a man write as well as he might and still teach a full college course load? Apparently not. Teachers are always seeking sabbaticals, grants, and leaves without pay to find the time and peace of mind necessary for scholarly or creative projects. How many English teachers would continue teaching if their income from writing were substantial? Do not many teachers secretly agree with Alves Preston in *The Web of Life*, who says of teaching, "I hate it. It takes a little of one's life every day, and leaves you a little more dead."[136] English professors advise their brilliant graduate students to go on for the doctorate. Carl Van Doren was urged by Stuart Pratt Sherman to take his Ph.D. in English because writing would not support him,[137] and Boyesen accepted a teaching position at Columbia in 1881 because he could not earn a living by his pen. Later, when his health grew poor and he had to make a choice between writing and teaching, he chose the pen.[138]

Ida Tarbell taught only as a stepping stone to another career.[139] Had she been a dedicated schoolteacher, it is probable that her major work on the Standard Oil Company would not have been written. Is it not fortunate for letters that Ezra Pound developed a distaste for teaching at Wabash College in Indiana?[140] Or might pedagogical success have contained his passionate social irritabilities and reduced his penchant for hatred?

In his letter of resignation from Harvard to President Abbott Lawrence Lowell, Santayana rationalized his farewell to the lecture hall: "But although fond of books and young men, I was never altogether fit to be a professor, and in the department of philosophy you will now have a chance to make a fresh start. . . ."[141] Actually, Santayana preferred writing to teaching; his modesty does not ring true.

William James felt his retirement unshackled him. A professor's life is awful — he is paid to "talk, talk, talk!"[142] He confided to his brother Henry that "to be at Cambridge with no lecturing and no students to nurse along with their thesis-work is an almost incredibly delightful prospect."[143] In another letter he spoke of his freedom to "live for truth pure and simple, instead of for truth accommodated to the most unheard-of requirements set by others. . . ."[144]

XVIII   *The Timid and Useless Scholar*

In his commemorative poem for Harvard's 250th anniversary, Oliver Wendell Holmes included a quatrain on the unappreciated scholar:

> I see gray teachers, — on their work intent,
> Their lavished lives in endless labor spent,
> Had closed at last in age and penury wrecked
> Martyrs, not burned, but frozen in neglect.[145]

Ambrose Bierce viewed all schools above grammar school as pernicious factories of untruth and called for their abolition, but he would spare one or two universities to turn out great scholars and to engage in original research.[146] If Henry Seidel Canby's typing of college teachers is accurate, Bierce's diatribe has validity. Why tenant the schools with surly escapists from industrial competition, mild sadists, inconclusive clerics, cunning or rich lovers of leisure, and seekers of cultural amenities?[147] Carl Van Doren is frank; like half the college professors in the United States he was a teacher by inertia.[148] Boyesen, who taught because he could not earn enough from his writing to support himself, wrote that his colleagues were usually failures who turn to education as a last resort.[149]

A serious critic of higher education accused teachers of studying everything but their students. This professorial indifference, charged Henry Seidel Canby, provoked the students in the academic citadel "to go over later to the enemy."[150] George H. Fitch wrote: "How a professor can . . . get so many degrees that his name looks like Halley's Comet with an alphabet tail, and then teach college students for forty years without even taking one apart to find out what he is made of, beats my time!"[151] In *Upstream*, Ludwig Lewisohn is harshly critical of the majority of professors; they "are dreary specialists with angular, strawy minds" who "often teach their subjects competently in the narrow, technical sense but without richness or savor or human and philosophical implications."[152]

The catalog of pompous, indolent, arrogant, and shallow college dons continues! Frank Dobie was startled to learn that the Ph.D. overlords in universities held back English instructors who had "a passion for literature and an ability to engender that passion in students;"[153] Willa Cather sought in vain at Nebraska for the inspired teaching she later represented in Gaston Cleric — as recalled by Jim Burden in *My Antonia;*[154] Robert Frost wrote bitterly of his freshman composition teacher, an arrogant and suspicious grader who gave him a B for the course — an outrage to Frost, who believed that he had earned an A;[155] and Mary Ellen Chase shared Frost's anger when her composition teacher countered her criticism of his C grade for her one expert paper with a nonchalant, "Why do you mind? These letters, they are nothing."[156]

Sinclair Lewis seems to delight in denigrating teachers in his novels, although in Max Gottlieb of *Arrowsmith* fame he fashions an exemplary pedagogical archetype — the passionate seeker of truth who transmits the sacred fire of learning to his adoring disciples. But in *Elmer Gantry,* Brother Karkis, a divinity student, despises the faculty of "book adulterated wobblers in the faith" whom he tolerates only because they will advance him to a degree and a profitable job.[157] Even spirited teachers like Professor Clavercin in Robert Herrick's *Chimes* cannot do much for his students, time-robbed as he is by nonacademic trivia.[158]

XIX   *The Charge of Timidity*

Upton Sinclair did not publish *The Goose-Step* until 1923, but in *Love's Pilgrimage* (1911) he wrote a fictionalized autobiography of his youth, education, and early writing efforts.[159] Thrysis, his fictional counterpart, lashes out against the higher learning in America with the same arguments that Sinclair later used in his muckraking classic: "Thrysis believed that the stagnation of the university [Columbia] was partly due to the connection it had with a great theological seminary. These future ministers, men of low ideals, represented a backward place in the national culture. Men of vital nature turned from the subsidized world, and to it came feebler minds, or those who wished to live at ease, and not inquire too deeply in the difference between truth and falsehood."[160]

George Fitch portrays the professor's social status poignantly in this little gem of irony: "I'll tell you it fills a chap with awe to see a man teaching along for twenty years at eighteen hundred dollars per, and buying books, and going off to Europe now and then on that princely sum — and coming through it all happy and content with life."[161] Happy? Not really. Professor Clavercin at Eureka University viewed his colleague Professor Memnor pityingly; poor, unkempt, greasy, ill-clad Memnor tutored after classes and taught evening classes as well to support his family. "Why," asked Clavercin, "should education be left to the unkempt, the sallow, the anemic? . . . You couldn't get the graces and abilities for $1,800 annually. Education was always an impoverished calling."[162] Later, Eureka lost its brilliant teachers. The old professors grumbled but stayed on. Where could they go?

Even fair Harvard overworked and underpaid its teachers, charged Santayana, and he did not endear himself to many of his former colleagues with this telling but perhaps too cutting metaphor: The faculty "was an anonymous concourse of coral insects, each secreting one cell, and leaving the fossil legacy to enlarge the earth."[163] Stephen Vincent Benét implied as much when he wrote of the "ludicrousness of the contrast between the salaries paid American teachers and the energy, personality, and wide knowledge expected of them."[164] Since the professional salaries were not forthcoming, many American professors were true Memnors — ill-paid, rarely promoted, moonlighting scarecrows, who like Markham's peasants become blind to "the swing of Pleiades" and deaf to "the long reaches of the peaks of song."[165] The talented teacher longs to sing in his specialty, but his honorariums (a degrading euphemism) are too skeletal to afford him the leisure he needs to convert his latent genius into tangible creativity. For ten years Robert Herrick taught English classes and hacked away at textbook writing to supplement his earnings. Finally after ten years, he found himself as a novelist, free to write as he pleased.[166]

Because of the miserly salaries paid to professors, their wives resign themselves to lives of impoverished provincialism. Unfortunately, administrators prefer to pay young teachers poor salaries.[167] Why not? Two assistant professors can be bought for the price of one experienced full professor. The cheap labor supply available for universities is endless; young assistants and fellows, moonlighting and daylighting part-timers, teachers, indigent pensioners, and bored housewives teach the same college courses that career teachers prepare themselves for. Boyesen was shamed by his $1,500 salary at Cornell in 1879. Many of his graduates were earning more than he.[168] John Erskine was offered $1,500 in 1903 for a teaching position in English at Amherst,[169] but scientists fared better at Eureka (Chicago), because business or commercial labs bid higher than the college for their services.[170] Things were not much better for teachers at the University of Missouri, according to Orrick Johns. An economy-minded legislature encouraged the trustees to hire inexpensive teachers — either too young or too old to bargain for decent wages — who turned out to be less competent than high school teachers. One in a thousand of the students developed into a scholar, and few of the undergraduates, save those in law and engineering, expected to find grace in life after their four years of study.[171]

Oliver Alden, Santayana's fictional Harvardian, speaks as disparagingly of his Harvard experiences as the actual Santayana does. Oliver's notes on his professors make one wonder how a school so ineptly staffed succeeds in contributing a handsome quota of creative and productive men to the nation. Are these the characteristics of a majority of Harvard teachers? (1) "Prof talks through his nose in a see-saw." (2) "Instructor very young and easy going. Sits on the desk and lets the class do all the talking." (3) "Lectures like a gramophone and quotes statistics." (4) "Too old. Coughs and spits into a bandanna handkerchief and reads extracts out of his own works."[172]

Santayana is not any kinder to Harvard professors in his autobiography, *Persons and Places.* The lecturers are no better than dull ministers; their sermonlike pronouncements tire the student mind.[173]

Another Harvard man, John Tunis, resented his professors' aloofness, boring note-reading, and clock-watching.[174] William James wrote candidly to Professor Alexander Forbes on the academic's sorry penchant for lecturing. Forbes had written of lecturing to James in 1909, and James wrote back sympathetically: "I think you're entirely right, but your learned professor would rebel. He much prefers sitting and hearing his own beautiful voice to guiding the stumbling minds of the students. I know it myself. If you know something and have a little practice there is nothing easier than to hear yourself talk, while to direct the stumbling minds of the students soon becomes unbearable."[175]

Charles M. Flandreau's fictional account of Marcus Thorn's attempt to ingratiate himself with his students shows the pitfalls of this practice. Hating to dine with his peers whom he regarded as bores, Thorn elects to dine with the boys in his undergraduate club.[176] But he detects a polite indifference to him in their relationships; they call him Mr. Thorn and go with him only when they have nothing else to do. Thorn later commits an unpardonable academic sin. Seeking the approval of Prescott, a popular athlete, he generously passes the incompetent student on the first examination. Exalted by his achievement, Prescott takes Thorn's measure by cutting classes and failing to submit written exercises. Finally, fearing to examine Prescott's final paper, Thorn throws the blue booklet into the fire and gives the delinquent student a C for the course. After a brief talk with Prescott, Thorn sickens inwardly, intuitively sensing that the boy whom he had adulated was a fraud, that he had handed in a blank examination book.

XX   *Faculty Meetings*

If college teachers are timid, apathetic, servile, and dishonest timeservers, their meetings should reflect their collective weaknesses. Henry Adams saw his colleagues as futile practitioners of what should be a noble art. College society was a "faculty meeting without business,"[177] but even faculty meetings with business were boring to Santayana, who hated the poor speeches and the general apathy.[178] Royce felt similarly: "I have no difficulty with Hegel's Absolute; that is simple. What I cannot follow are the discussions at faculty meetings."[179]

Randolph Bourne was never hesitant to expose shallowness, deceit, and self-seeking in education, but he concluded that despite all the criticism of American college teachers "it is becoming more and more common now when you touch a professor you touch a man and not an intellectual specialty."[180] Unfortunately, American writers have frequently exposed teachers who are not men in the sense that Bourne implies.

XXI   *The College Student: His Intellect*

The recent trend to open enrollment in many large universities has shocked educational conservatives — and some liberals also. Thomas Jefferson's basis for selectivity in education is predicated on a theory of natural aristocracy that has a democratic ring to it. Neither birth nor inheritance shall advance the scholar; only intellectual excellence, be it resident in the mind of poor or rich, is requisite for advancing its possessor up the ladder of learning. What, however, of the tenement child, ill-fed, ill-housed, and often unloved? How will his seed of intellect flower in the slum that envelops him? One can sympathize with Abraham Flexner's problem at Johns Hopkins, where the scholarly diet was too rich for many of the boys.[181] A Babbitt-like character in *At Good Old Siwash* reduces the mind of the undergraduate to absurdity in this sad oration by a garrulous alumnus: "Mind you . . . I'm not saying that a little eddication isn't a good thing in a college course. I learned a lot of real knowledge in school myself that I wouldn't have missed for anything, though I have forgotten it now."[182] Fitch exaggerates, but serious educational commentators tend to corroborate many of his witty insights. Theodore Roosevelt was upset by the small number of Harvard undergraduates who came there to learn,[183] a feeling that caused no end of grief to President Eliot, who wrote: "The striking things about the American boy from well-to-do families are his undeveloped taste and faculty for intellectual labor, the triviality of his habitual subjects of thought, the brevity of his vocabulary, and his lack of judgment and sense of proportion in historical, literary and scientific subjects."[184]

At Columbia, Randolph Bourne had similar reservations about the undergraduate mind. The college was a glorified prep school for hedonistic revelry. Professors despaired of their students' apathy, their inability to cope with abstractions, and their rejection of the humanities. Nurtured in well-to-do homes by "nice" people, they develop a taste for sentimental music, repeat the shibboleths of an amiable religiosity, and acquire a "vague, moral optimism" that "is alien to the stern realism of secular college teaching."[185] Reared in this congenial middle-class society, the young collegian prized conformity, rarely concerned himself with disinterested scholarship, and devoted his four-year sanctuary from life to vocational aims.[186] Perhaps learning is repulsive to youth because it is measured out to him mechanically, said James Russell Lowell.[187] But academic inventiveness cannot always cope with student ingenuity. Henry Adams tried many motivating techniques to bestir his apathetic students, but after evaluating his teaching effectiveness he concluded that "no man can instruct more than half-a-dozen students at once," seeing the "whole problem of education" as "one of its cost in money."[188] But Robert Herrick argues in *Chimes* that small classes do not necessarily encourage real teaching since "young minds are . . . rather cloudy and lethargic, unless prodded by competitive excitement."[189]

William James complained to his wife of the immobility of his students' minds, which consumed a half-hour to transfer from one idea to the next. Intellectual change was not characteristic of students.[190] Ezra Pound attributed the mediocrity of American universities to their adamant stand against awarding fellowships for creative ability.[191] The grade-conscious American student is not usually creative, a view propounded in 1887 by Emerson who opposed grading in colleges as "an ungracious work to be put on a professor."[192]

But some writers have kinder recollections of the undergraduate.

Abraham Flexner's college years at Johns Hopkins were not diluted with the attenuating pleasures of secret societies, fraternities, organized athletics, and undergraduate publications. What the college lacked in pretentiousness it compensated for in genuineness. A college should admit only students who match their aspiration with their productivity. Less dedicated students "should procure in some other kind of institution such technical or other instruction and discipline as they may require or desire."[193] The serious student, called a freak by his scoffers, is careless of his dress, grooming, and tastes. He might be a son of the wealthy or of Europe-trained artistic bohemians. A potential homosexual or bizarre in behavior, he despises athletics, fraternities, and student clubs.[194]

Such a "freak" is Santayana's Oliver Alden, a Harvard undergraduate of whom the novelist writes:

He was set down as belonging to that odious category of outsiders who hung loosely on the fringes of college life: odd persons going about alone or in little knots, looking intellectual, or looking dissipated. They were likely to be Jews or radicals or to take drugs; to be musical, theatrical, or religious; sallow or bloated; or imperfectly washed; either too shabby or too well dressed. The tribe of these undesirables was always numerous at Harvard. Nothing was ever to be got out of them for the public good — not even money.[195]

XXII *On the Social Life of the College Man*

Alumni convocations on alma mater's beloved campus rarely attract the "freak" or "grind" who passed four harrowing years at the college. In *Tea and Sympathy*, Jim returns to the school that had expelled him to recapture a sense of the beautiful that a gracious faculty wife had engendered in him when he was undergoing a severe emotional crisis. As he walks alone on the grounds he passes raucous, back-slapping, classmates who are as adolescent as ever in their values and perspectives. They have been well-initiated into the anti-intellectual sporting philosophy — "a win or lose syndrome" that wanes after the event has been resolved. The faculty and the alumni encourage this philosophy, naively missing the point that things are not won or lost in education.[196] Randolph Bourne, a giant mind in a pitifully deformed body, might be accused of hating competition because of his physical grotesqueness; John Erskine supposedly said of Bourne, after Bourne had written disparagingly of Erskine's teaching, that "a deformed body must also have a deformed mind."[197]

The sporting philosophy tends to polarize the student body. Those who come to college to sing, cheer, drink, and compete for recognition and romance generally win the extracurricular prizes;[198] those who come to overcome the handicaps of birth and poverty generally amass the scholarly awards.[199] William Allen White semiseriously typed himself as "a poor student; a good mixer; a bit of a smart aleck; hail fellow, not afraid of being caught and taking blame; come easy - go easy; half student, half roisterer, who knew the students by name and catalogued them by their weaknesses; . . . college politician; figure-head for the fraternity; brother-in-law to the sororities."[200] Woodrow Wilson believed undergraduate life was too "frilly." To divert the young college man from his social preoccupations, Wilson recommended that older men associate with students.[201] But sports helped some students overcome their inverted tendencies; George Apley was accepted by his peers after he proved himself in boxing and rowing;[202] only sports and the theater helped John Tunis to survive his academic ordeal at Harvard, but he charged that organized sports in schools and colleges rarely have a good effect upon players and spectators.[203]

Humorists have endless material for satire in college sporting life. The congenial Idiot of John Kendrick Bangs proposes courses in the theory and practice of gridirony, baseballistics, and lacrossetics and recalls that when he was in college there was a special degree for the "footballers who didn't pass finals," the A.B. Sp. Gr. (by special favor of the faculty).[204] At Siwash the coach found bone-crushing Skjarsen in a lumber camp "and had to explain what a college was before he would quit his job. He thought it was something good to eat at first. . . ."[205] The student body was delighted with this find: "Everybody helped him register third prep, with business college extras."[206]

The biographical and fictional indictment of the nonacademic mores of student life is impressive. Ludwig Lewisohn and Randolph Bourne assail the philistinism of the college man — his adolescent worship of sports and snobbish adherence to puerile fraternity ritualism.[207] H. M. Pulham, one of Marquand's stereotyped Harvardians, witnesses a scene of collegiate fealty to the athletic overlords. Bo-jo Brown, a football star, is injured and will not play in the sacred game with Yale. His peers are all in tears as they stand vigil at his bedside. Later, Bill King is disgusted. He announces openly that Brown is not going to die and that a loss to Yale does not mean much. Heresy! Immediately, Joe Bingham wants to fight him and speaks vehemently against the traitor: "He's a radical bastard. Should have had the hell beaten out of him in some good school."[208]

Marquand will have his fun with Harvard. George Apley's father at first objects to his son's friendship with Henry Alger, but this antipathy for a son of supposedly lower class parents changes to warm acceptance after Apley senior learns that the Algers are the proprietors of the West Springfield Yarn Company.[209] In Marquand's previously cited novel, Bill King becomes increasingly lonely among Harvard's elitist sporting men. When Pulham accompanies him to lunch one day, King unleashes his bitterness toward Harvard's snobs: "You're the first person I've seen here who isn't a nickel-plated son of a bitch."[210]

Occasionally even the scions of the ultrarich were ostracized socially, sometimes because of envy, sometimes because of the raucous flamboyancy of the gilded one. In illustration, William Randolph Hearst, Jr. offended Harvard's sensibilities by smoking long cigars and exhibiting modes of behavior unbecoming a Harvard man.[211] At Princeton, too, according to F. Scott Fitzgerald, social distinction highlighted undergraduate relationships with one another. Snobbish prep schoolers kep apart from the lowlier high school population.[212]

XXIII   Campus Frivolities

American college students have always had their moments of prankishness and destructiveness, but they have never approached the intensity of political violence associated with their counterparts in Europe. Even the campus takeovers by dissident American students in the sixties were mere ripples of rebellion when contrasted to the waves of violence that erupted intermittently in Europe between town and gown. In America, student protest has generally been motivated by poor campus conditions, dislike of a college president, occasional dismissal of popular teachers, or spontaneous reaction to alleged mistreatment of a student. Henry Seidel Canby attributes student irresponsibility to a desire to escape from small-town conformity, dissatisfaction with dull bourgeois life, and a compulsion to challenge the discipline of boarding school life.[213] College histories, novels, and biographies cite numerous such incidents, many of which are fondly recalled by alumni at their reunions. At Old Siwash, students tipped over street cars, placed bronze statues on street car tracks, and called for an ambulance to service the alleged victim.[214] In *The Trail of the Hawk* by Sinclair Lewis, student gangs at Plato College painted memorials, stole signs, and created mysterious noises at night;[215] in Boyesen's novel, *The Mammon of Unrighteousness*, students celebrated Founder's Day by hauling a cow up the chapel-bell tower, secreting live mice in professors' desks, painting an unpopular college bust blue, and introducing one another to credulous farmers as celebrities;[216] at Madison College, now Colgate, Pierrepont Noyes witnessed his fraternity hauling up a heavy lumber wagon, piece by piece, through the skylight of East College to its roof, where they assembled the vehicle.[217]

XXIV   *More Serious Escapades*

Today's moralists who would condemn a student who occasionally partakes of an illegal drug to lifelong imprisonment or death might be shocked to learn that one of our most respectable secretaries of state, fashioner of much of today's American foreign policy, indulged in hashish-eating at Brown. A classmate of Hay recorded his friend's daring: "On one occasion, at least, his enthusiasm for literature was carried to excess. *The Hasheesh-Eater* had recently appeared (1857) and Johnny must needs experiment with hasheesh a little, and see if it was such a remarkable stimulant to the imagination as Fitzhugh Ludlow had affirmed."[218] In Frank Norris's *Vandover and the Brute*, young Vandover is a dude at Harvard; clad in corduroy vest and gray felt hat, he is a model of collegiate fashion. He puffs at his pipe, plays billiards, and attends important football matches. He drinks whenever he can.[219]

Upton Sinclair's puritanical idealist, Thrysis in *Love's Pilgrimage*, is appalled by the "blasphemous abandonment, orgy of obscenity, and disgusting wantonness" of the licentious tenants of a fraternity house of a fashionable university.[220] Abortion, too, is a campus problem. In one of his lost college plays, "Abortion," Eugene O'Neill describes the tragedy of Jack Townsend, a popular athlete who seduces Nelly, a village girl. Nellie dies from the effects of a crude abortion she undergoes, and Townsend, accused of the heinous crime by an undergraduate, commits suicide. His accuser goes to the police for help as the rah rah of the rooting crowd is heard from the stadium.[221] "Running" for membership in a college secret society may have tragic consequences. Peter Alden is commanded by his peers to steal the college Bible from the chapel. Unfortunately, he comes upon the watchman and strikes him on the head with the Bible. The coroner ruled that the watchman's death was accidental;

the associates of Peter pledged themselves to secrecy. To appease their genteel consciences, they established a fund for the widow.[222]

XXV   A Touch of Anti-Semitism

The influx of tens of thousands of eastern European Jews posed a problem to the middle and upper classes of America after large numbers of Jewish garment workers moved into the middle class. Fearful of this "alien" intrusion, the non-Jewish middle- and upper-classes introduced both explicit and subtle restrictions to exclude Jews from the mainstream of American social, educational, and financial life.[223] In *Up Stream*, Ludwig Lewisohn feelingly narrates how opposed the Anglo-Saxon heads of English departments were to hiring him even though Lewisohn's master's thesis was published while he was still a graduate student. Upton Sinclair read *Up Stream* and raged in *The Goose-Step* against the alleged anti-Jewish cabal in the colleges, asserting that "few indeed are the Anglo-Saxon professors who can demonstrate equal attainments."[224] Before leaving this ugly topic, Sinclair named Columbia, New York University, Barnard, Harvard, Pennsylvania, Denison University, and the University of Oklahoma as institutions that had quota systems for Jews or that barred admissions of more than token Jews by administering "so-called" psychological tests that were designed to eliminate Jewish applicants for admission.[225]

Santayana records in *Persons and Places* the social ostracism of his friend Loeser, the son of a "dry-goods" merchant. To Harvard undergraduates, Loeser was not a proper gentleman, so they "cut him off, in democratic America, from the ruling society."[226] So strong was class prejudice at Harvard that even an avowed radical like John Reed could not accept a Jewish friend. A lonely freshman himself — he thought that all of the 700 freshmen had friends but him — "he befriended a brilliant Jewish boy but parted from him because he couldn't enter the rich splendor of college life with him around."[227] George Oppenheimer found similar bias at Williams in 1916; Jews were barred from fraternities and other college social activities.[228] In Fitzgerald's *This Side of Paradise*, Amory and his friends delight in filling a Jewish student's bed with lemon pie, putting out his lights every night by blowing into the gas jets, and piling up his books and pictures in the bathroom.[229]

XXVI   Graduate and Professional Schools

Spurred on by their earnest scholars who had ascended to doctorhood in the hallowed universities of Europe, proud and self-conscious American universities encouraged their native sons to acquire their advanced degrees at home. Robert Herrick ridicules the mania of American college presidents, especially heads of newly established colleges, for enticing Ph.D.s to their provincial campuses. In illustration, President Harris of Eureka University (fictional for President William Rainey Harper of The University of Chicago) jovially salutes his new English professor, fresh from Harvard,

"Glad to see you, Dr. Clavercin —"
"Mr. Clavercin."
"Ah, not yet taken your doctorate? We'll make that right soon."[230]

Clavercin might have been tempted to paraphrase George Lyman Kittredge's famed rejoinder to those who questioned his refusal to toil for the doctorate: "Who at Eureka can examine me?" But, a novice at the trade, he was more circumspect. There was no one at Eureka who could match him in his field. In time, his earnest teaching and publications would more than compensate for his dodging of the most coveted academic degree. The undecorated but talented teacher had a strong champion in William James. To James the Ph.D. degree was a passport to academic Elysium given to technicians whose adeptness in passing examinations had little relevancy to good teaching.[231] Bliss Perry, who shared James' abhorrence of the "dessicating and pedantifying" processing of the American Ph.D.,[232] preferred to study ideas, not sterile courses. He was himself a professor without a doctorate, and he wrote: "None of us dreamed, of course, that within the next thirty years American colleges would insist upon a Ph.D. degree as a requisite for promotion, that its commercial value would consequently be reckoned with the precision of an actuarial table, and that all academic "go-getters" would take it in their stride."[233]

Stephen Vincent Benét wrote that the Ph.D., "like the poor, is almost sure to be with us no matter what world upheaval impends."[234] But talented men like Sinclair Lewis, John Erskine, and Ezra Pound agreed that the Ph.D. is not necessarily a good teacher. Lewis wrote that "humanity outweighs the humanities";[235] Erskine said of the Ph.D. that, although he is a reservoir of knowledge, he may not necessarily be a good teacher;[236] and Ezra Pound wrote to a classmate of his that anything more than an M.A. and a fellowship smacks of professionalism and for that reason he would not seek the Ph.D. degree.[237] In *Chimes*, Clavercin pities the teachers in graduate schools who starve their minds and bodies in their pursuit of the lofty degree. Most of their dissertations would be valueless; only one of a hundred would be worth reading.[238] Yet many of these sincere but mediocre graduate students would be offered college teaching jobs. Later, when tenured and the author of several articles, some of these passported professors in the liberal arts schools would turn on their lowlier brethren in the education schools and denounce them. Mary Ellen Chase tries to correct the unfounded notion that liberal arts teachers are pedagogically competent because of their superior degrees: "I have found from long experience that the teacher of freshmen who has had past experience in secondary schools is far more likely to succeed in college teaching, with or without the doctorate, than one who has gone directly from the bachelor's degree to further study."[239]

Professional schools come under frequent attack in memoirs of their graduates. The playright Elmer Rice recalls his law school days with pain. The courses were boring, easy, and valueless. Students were drilled to pass examinations; professors consumed two hours in rehashing one half-hour of reading. Rice did not complain, however, since his ability to fake attention in class enabled him to read hundreds of books. Of this boon, he wrote: "I shall always be grateful to New York Law School for the knowledge of literature I acquired there."[240]

Disappointed in his law studies at Columbia, Theodore Roosevelt regretted that he had not studied at Harvard Law School, where he might have realized that "the lawyer can do a great work for justice and against legalism."[241] Upton Sinclair, whose troublesome muckraking book, *The Jungle,* irritated the flamboyant Rough Rider, was more critical than Roosevelt. He charged in *Love's Pilgrimage* that "the law students were not going out to battle for truth and justice. They were interested in cunning, in sharpening their wits to make them useful tools for the opening of treasure chests."[242] But Archibald MacLeish relished his stay at Harvard Law School, since "learning the law there provided a sense of the tradition of human conduct, action, knowledge, values, morality, and so forth. The glacier slowly moves, and you felt yourself part of the glacier. For the first time you were drawn into something."[243]

English graduate students are frequently exposed as frauds by writers, many of whom were themselves English majors. Bliss Perry pitied the students who were destined to be taught by the ill-read Harvard graduate students. Ignorant of foreign writers, many professed no knowledge of Petrarch, Rabelais, Diderot, Goethe,

Voltaire, Franklin, and Jefferson.[244] Great names on the faculty avoided undergraduates; only Santayana and Copeland felt a kinship with the undergraduate.[245] Thrysis, Upton Sinclair's starving writer in *Love's Pilgrimage,* was amused to find men at a college town near New York "who were counting up the feminine endings in Shakespeare's verse, and writing elaborate theses on the sources of Spenserian legends. To these entrapped students nonentities in literature and philosophy appeared as geniuses. Thrysis writes reprovingly: "And this was the education that was dispensed at America's most aristocratic university — for this many millions of dollars had been contributed, and scores of magnificent buildings erected!"[246]

Mary Ellen Chase criticized the teaching of English in the West. The "subject-damaged" teachers of teachers at the University of Minnesota in 1917 were passionless, and, sad to relate, the most learned teachers were also the most benumbing. And sadder yet, it seemed as if "anyone possessing a bachelor's degree from any miserable institution in the country can storm the walls of most graduate schools if he has but the desire and sufficient money."[247]

Ambrose Bierce surveyed the American campus and laughed cynically. The professional schools annually poured thousands of men into the job market. The less fit of these are forced into meaner professions which tend to corrupt them. Consequently, "the learned professions are little more than organized conspiracies to plunder."[248]

XXVII   *Presidents and Deans*

Until the last quarter of the nineteenth century, the college president was the master of the faculty and the student body. An unapproachable campus deity, he was subject only to the whims of the trustees. In Noah Porter, D. D., President of Yale College, William James portrayed a type of college administrator unknown today. Porter was "a very peculiar type of character, partly man of business, partly diplomatist, partly clergyman, and partly professor of metaphysics, armed with great authority and influence" in an important college.[249] Today's sophisticated chief campus executive never teaches, meets his students only at convocations and athletic matches, manages the school plant like a corporation head, tours the nation to raise funds, lectures to adulating women at clubs, assists at Rotary clubs, adorns himself peacocklike at commencements, and absents himself from the campus intermittently.[250]

The old-time college president demanded unqualified respect from students. Pranksters paid severely for their jests. President James McCosh of Princeton suspended an entire freshman class for rioting before his house, but he fancied students who demonstrated interest in psychology, philosophy, and metaphysics, disciplines ardently loved by him.[251] Bliss Perry remembers President Francis Landey Patton of Princeton fondly; when he was made aware of the lawns ruined by short-cutting students, Patton replied: "Are not pleasant relations between students and faculty more important than a little grass?"[252] In Edmund Wilson's ironic praise of another famed Princetonian, President John Grier Hibben, he succinctly degrades the office: "But he was, I think, by no means the worst of our mediocre American college presidents, who seem sometimes not to have any competence at all in any of the departments over which they preside."[253]

According to Henry James, the freedoms granted to Harvard's undergraduates by President Charles W. Eliot did not endear him to them. Forgetting the annoying regulations that he had abolished, they disliked him for the regulations that he introduced.[254] Barrett Wendell, though, had a kinder regard for the president who hired him to teach English even though he was inexperienced;[255] Wendell disputed the allegation that Eliot was a dictator, praising him as a rational, just, and impartial administrator, unlike McCosh of Princeton who pounded the table at meetings until his opposition was silenced.[256] But Santayana sorrowed over Harvard's decline in Eliot's waning years. Eliot defended the Harvard Fellows, a lot of businessmen charged with investing Foundation funds. Harvard's end, concluded Santayana, "was service in the world of business."[257] But President Eliot's successor, President Abbott Lawrence Lowell, was a villain to John Reed who protested Lowell's modification of the elective system, herding of freshmen into one dormitory, and general abridgment of freedom.[258]

Eight years before Upton Sinclair caricatured Nicholas Murray Butler in *The Goose-Step*, Randolph Bourne satirized Columbia's newsworthy president in the *New Republic* (September 4, 1915), thinly disguising Butler's name as Dr. Alexander Makintosh Butcher, President of Pluribus University. Butcher was a political opportunist rising from ward captain to district leader. As a scholar and educator he upheld the shibboleths of the Republican party, especially the war cry "we should never change any form of government." A great fund raiser because of his communion with corporate trustees, he lived as a prince in the $125,000 mansion built for the president's use by the college.[259]

Flexner praises President Daniel Coit Gilman of Johns Hopkins unstintingly. Gilman was never fettered by the trustees, and in turn he never fettered the faculty. His concern was for a sound faculty, a meaningful curriculum, and a diligent student body; buildings and trimmings would come later.[260] Although he was generally critical of higher education, Lincoln Steffens saw merit in President Van Hise's attempt to "distract the living interest of our students from sport to the intellectual field" at Wisconsin.[261]

XXVIII   *Some Fictional Presidents*

Rare is the college president who is presented fictionally as a man worthy of the respect of his faculty and students. It may be argued in defense of the college president that fictional writers are generally unhappy with their college experiences. The writer is an individualist; consequently, he rebels against what he believes to be the president's arbitrary imposition of regimentation and conformity on the campus. But not all writers represent the college head as an unmitigated scoundrel. Charles Monroe Sheldon, a pastor whose now little read novel *In His Steps* sold more than twenty million copies, illustrates the conflict of interests that troubles every sensitive executive. President Donald Marsh knows that he has been a faithful teacher of ethics and philosophy, but he knows also that he is not following Jesus faithfully. Secure in his academic sanctuary he has never protested the rule of corrupt leaders. Would Jesus have done this?[262] Even Sinclair Lewis' President Wood of Plato College is not completely demolished in this uncomplimentary characterization: "O harassed, honorable, studious, ignorant, humorless, joke-popping, genuinely conscientious thumb of a man."[263]

To the laity and educators not particularly concerned with educational history the accomplishments of President Harper in founding and nurturing the University of Chicago — with John D. Rockefeller's munificence — was a notable achievement. But G. Stanley Hall regarded Harper as an academic pirate who came to Clark University and stole away — with their consent — many of the university's best teachers. Robert Herrick who taught English during Harper's reign was always hostile toward "the energetic westerner, with his salesmanlike approach to higher education. . . ."[264] Weary of the rigors of academic life, Herrick wrote to his colleague Robert

Morss Lovett: "Harper a little rottener than usual; the shop stinks a little more from the unwashed; the future righteousness a little further away."[265] In *Chimes*, Herrick's vendetta with Harper continues. President Harris wears soft, unshined shoes, short trousers, and a black frock coat besprinkled with dust and dandruff.[266] But more distasteful to Clavercin than Harris' personal appearance was his emphasis upon numbers, an emphasis alien to Clavecin's Harvardian preference for quality.[267] Yet Herrick does not totally obscure some of Harris' altruistic traits. When Professor Dexter's wife is arrested for shoplifting, Harris reminds the vindictive trustees who seek Dexter's resignation that it is not easy for a professional man with a wife and three children to live comfortably on $2,400 annually. Harris vows to raise Dexter's salary to $4,000 per annum; in addition, he arranges for Mrs. Dexter to enter an asylum for treatment of her alcoholism, and, although she dies there six months later, Harris keeps his promise to Dexter and raises his salary to $4,000.[268]

XXIX   More Administrative Sins:
Hiring, Doings of Deans, and Honorary Degrees

Angered because he had been rejected at many universities by men who professed to be "pillars of the democracy, proclaimers of its mission to set the bond free and equalize life's opportunities for mankind," Ludwig Lewisohn never hesitated to expose what he believed to be academic fraud.[269] He noted that at one commencement 70 percent of the graduates were frauds. Illiterate in thought and culture, they were replicas of those "conferring the degrees or orating."[270] Obviously, college administrators would seek passive professors. In *Love's Pilgrimage*, Upton Sinclair wrote: "And when it came to the selecting of the college professors, of the men who were to guide and instruct the forthcoming generations — what precautions would be taken then! What consultations and investigations, what testimonials and interviews and examinations!"[271]

When Bliss Perry attended Williams College, the academic post of dean had not yet been invented.[272] Today's legions of deans probably dislike Perry for writing: "It is, I am told, an honor to become a dean; but it is dearly purchased if it means the temporary or permanent end of a scholar's productivity. The whole tendency of American institutions is to breed ten administrators to one real teacher."[273] Edmund Wilson wrote disparagingly of Dean Andrew West at Princeton, a man who sat at the deathbeds of affluent men to get bequests for the college.[274] But John Kendrick Bangs draws a pleasanter picture in his gentle twitting of Dean Van Amringe of Columbia. Bangs suspected that Van Amringe had given him his B.A. against the wishes of the faculty. Twenty-five years after his graduation he thanked Van Amringe in these amusing lines:

> Who flunked me even with a face
> So genial I ne'er felt disgrace,
> But rather that I owned the place?
> Van Am!

> Who when a bootless facultee
> Declined to give me my A.B.
> Went out and got the same for me?
> Van Am![275]

Unlettered men who ordinarily despise the trappings of academic ritualism do not disdain the honorary degree. Sherwood Anderson rose to fame after working as a laborer, farmhand, and factory worker. In the winter of 1899, he completed a semester at Wittenberg College, Springfield, Ohio. Later, he was called back for a doctor's degree, an event that gratified his ironic sensibility.[276] In his deliberate pose of naiveté, Mark Twain reduces the honorary degree to absurdity. He knows nothing about art and Yale makes him a Master of Arts; he is not fit to doctor anybody's literature but his own and Yale makes him a Doctor of Literature; and he knows nothing about laws but how to evade them and the University of Missouri makes him a Doctor of Laws. But this was bravado. Twain envied the lettered men at Cambridge, and when he was awarded an honorary degree by Oxford he boasted that he was one of the ten Americans so honored by Oxford and was not a degree from Oxford worth twenty-five degrees of any other college?[277]

XXX   *The Unhappy Trustees*

Representing the established order in the control of higher education are the trustees, usually successful men in the business world and in the professions. Thorstein Veblen wrote that science and scholarship represent virtue, business, vice. Governing boards, he wrote, "are an aimless survival from the days of clerical rule, when they were presumably of some effect in enforcing conformity to orthodox opinions and observances, among the academic staff,"[278] but today businessmen "meddle in academic matters which they do not understand."[279] Usually, those boards that are granted power to choose academic heads choose men who will be subservient. Upton Sinclair repeated Veblen's views with a more obvious socialistic bias: "The master-class . . . had founded the colleges and named the trustees, who in turn named the presidents and professors. . . ."[280] Robert Herrick deplored the founding of schools of business, education, and journalism at the University of Chicago. The emphasis of the board of trustees upon business ideals and business methods would subvert the humanistic ideals of the university.[281] In *Chimes*, Professor Sanderson delights the trustees with his idea of a business college.[282] Ambrose Bierce, enraged by the arbitrary dismissal of professors, called the California Board of Regents "a precious set of muttonheads." He censured them for deeming themselves "worthy of founding, guiding, and developing a state university" without ever having seen a college building.[283]

Willa Cather exposes academic nepotism in *The Professor's House*. Disgusted with the teaching of Horace Langtry, a nephew of a trustee, Professor St. Peter notified the Board of Regents of Langtry's incompetence. The vindictive board responded by threatening to dismiss St. Peter; only the support of St. Peter's former students saves the good professor's position.[284] Sometimes a board acts to defend a "good" professor from student harassment. William A. White reports that at Kansas State in 1888 he once had a seat "in front of the chancellor's office when the Regents were in session, roaring clamoring, and hooting because they were trying to suspend or exile the editor of the college paper for criticizing a professor.[285] Although most fictional trustees are depicted as Philistines or Babbitts, Robert Herrick presents Samuel Gorridge, president of the board of trustees of Eureka University, as a cultivated man sympathetic to the problems of teachers and a champion of higher education even though he was not a college man himself.[286]

XXXI *Donors*

Tycoons, moguls, and lesser millionaires have donated hundreds of millions of dollars to their favorite universities, most with stipulations for special use of their endowments. A humorous doggerel encourages philanthropists to

> Learn to give
> money to colleges while you live.
> Don't be silly and think you'll try

> To bother the colleges, when you die,
> With codicil this and codicil that,
> That Knowledge may starve while Law grows fat;
> For there never was pitcher that wouldn't spill,
> And there's always a flaw in the donkey's will.[287]

Fictional writers have a low esteem of college donors. Edna Ferber is not wholly enthusiastic over a coal-oil tycoon's contributions to Mid West University, which he founded in 1893 with a $30,000,000 grant.[288] Upton Sinclair's naive intellectual hero in *Samuel the Seeker* engages in an economic dialogue with a professor of sociology, who argues that in the struggle for existence those who amass the greatest power and fortunes are in essence the wisest men in the land. Samuel agrees, for do not the great captains of industry endow the colleges and choose the professors? This logic is irrefutable to Professor Stewart. Samuel's unsophisticated reasoning makes him wince.[289] Professor Clavercin learns on his first day at Eureka what the academic priorities of donors and their followers, the administrators, tend to be. A young man points out the university gymnasium and temporary library to him. Clavercin, fresh from Harvard, mutters disdainfully, "temporary!"[290] When Elmer Gantry receives a D.D. degree at Abernathy College, three other worthies are honored with him — the governor of the state, a divorce lawyer who facilitated the public service corporation's theft of the state's water power; B. D. Swenson, the auto manufacturer who donated a football stadium to the college; and Eva Murphy, the noted author, painter, lecturer, and musician who wrote the new college song.[291]

Hjalmar Hjorth Boyesen, who opposed Ezra Cornell's open enrollment policy at Cornell in 1874, fearing an influx of cranks and misfits, satirized Cornell in his novel of academic life, *The Mammon of Unrighteousness*.[292] The Honorable Obed Larkin, a rich lumberman, had founded the university at Torryville, New York, to educate poor men's sons in a coeducational institution that would sanction "no high living, no frills and flummery, no Oxford gowns."[293] Larkin was a frugal man who never smoked or drank. A martinet, he demanded complete loyalty of his professors, for had not he founded the college and paid their extravagant wages? Today, Larkin would be idolized by those who champion open enrollment at college. He stormed at professors who failed applicants on entrance examinations; any serious boy could, he said, succeed at college.[294] His goal was to have one thousand boys and girls at the college, and to his nephew Aleck's question — "What could the nation do with such a mob of scholars?'' — he replied that no man is embarrassed with learning.[295] In his will he left $1,000,000 to Larkin University, $50,000 to Hampton College for the education of blacks, and $20,000 to the Carlisle School for Indians.[296] His ideals and benefactions compensate somewhat for his authoritarian meddling with the university's affairs. As limned by Boyesen, Larkin is not totally devoid of virtue and high aspirations. His cards, at least, were truly on the table; one knew at once where he stood with the founder.

XXXII   Academic Freedom: Its Multifaced Enemies

Historical generalizations are as valid as the cumulative strength of their particulars, but it would be hard to refute C. Wright Mills' characterization of the period from 1866 to 1914 as an age that witnessed a transfer of initiative from government to corporation in which senators and judges were unduly influenced by an economic elite.[297] George William Curtis assailed the retreat of the educated classes from responsibility; in an address given at Brown University in 1882, Curtis castigated the church for having supported slavery, and the learned professions for tolerating drinking and for raising the cry of communism in disputes between capital and labor without studying the issues objectively.[298]

If the business ethic is accepted by the campus majority, trustees and administrators can exclude dissenting professors from participation in the school government,[299] and dismiss those who oppose the interference of politicians in university affairs.[300] Albert Jay Nock saw the state university as even more oppressive than private institutions because the administrators of state universities feel they must stress patriotism, nationalism, flag worship, hero worship and synthetic duty to one's native land.[301] Obviously, state legislatures express the will of the more affluent classes, and it is naive to assume that state governments will tolerate teachers who boldly speak out against corruption and favoritism in government. But whether in private or in public college, candid professors were outlawed. In illustration H. L. Mencken made much copy of Scott Nearing's dismissal from the Wharton School of Finance of the University of Pennsylvania in 1915 because of his liberal social views, especially his outspoken attack upon child labor. Nearing's case gave Mencken ammunition for his tirades against the timid scholars and banker trustees of colleges. "If you want to know what happens to a professor who departs from it [the college program] in the field of social theory, examine the crimes, trial, condemnation, and execution of the late Scott Nearing, B.S. B.O. Ph.D."[302] John Jay Chapman despised college presidents who were the lackeys of millionaires. Thorstein Veblen alleged that "fear of the academic blacklist has kept many professors from speaking in support of a fellow teacher who has fallen under executive displeasure,"[303] a charge supported in a dramatic simile by John Jay Chapman: "The average professor in an American college will look on at an injustice done to a brother professor by the college president with the same unconcern as the rabbit who is not attacked, watches the ferret pursue his brother up and down through the warren to predestinate and horrible death."[304]

Canby observed that almost all scholars were conditioned to be safe in their public and private lives;[305] Robert Herrick sorrowed that scholars who were supposedly bold seekers of the truth sacrificed ideals for security;[306] and even President Eliot of Harvard, the innovator of the elective system, was in Santayana's view subservient to the Fellows, six Boston businessmen who were the legal owners of Harvard. Harvard's end, said Eliot, "was in the service of business,"[307] a statement consistent with the later enormous expansion of Harvard's School of Business Administration.

Short shrift was often made of student editors who boldly but unwisely attacked administrative policy. Orrick Johns, who lampooned the faculty and allegedly wrote disrespectfully of the Virginian founders of the University of Missouri, was suspended for his editorial rashness.[308] Joseph Wood Krutch had the audacity to attack prohibition in a literary magazine at the University of Tennessee; for this heinous offense he was threatened with expulsion.[309] Upton Sinclair blamed the Philistinism "embodied in the banker trustees" of Columbia University for MacDowell's dismissal,[310] but Lionel Trilling, a literary critic who wrote a history of Columbia University, sees the unhappy event in a different light. Professor George Edward Woodberry, a distinguished poet and critic, and composer Edward MacDowell "represented laudable efforts of the University to bring creative artists to Columbia College. But they were not fitted for the academic life as it then existed, and it would be less than fair, in either instance, to put the whole blame for their separation upon the University alone. Their resignations left wounds that were long in healing, yet their having taught in the University, Woodberry for twelve years, MacDowell for eight, cannot but be counted for good."[311] Randolph Bourne had no love for President Butler who dismissed many eminent teachers at Columbia. Nevertheless, Bourne said that Columbia breathes the finest spirit of freedom in the city of New York.[312]

Perhaps it is to literature's benefit that Ezra Pound was dismissed from Wabash College in 1907. There are various versions of Pound's abrupt departure from teaching, but Pound's own narration of his derring-do at the college reads amusingly:

Two stewdents found me sharing my meagre repast with the lady-gent impersonator in my privut apartments. keep it dark and find me a soft immoral place to light in when the she-faculty-wives get hold of that jewcy morsel. Don't write home to me folks. I can prove an alibi from 8 to 12 p. m. and am present lookin for rooms with a minister or some well-established member of the facultate. For to this house come all the travelling show folk and I must hie me to a nunnery ere I disrupt the college. Alrady one delegation of about-to-flunks have awaited on the president to complain erbout me orful langwidge and the number of cigarillas I consume.[313]

XXXIII *Fictional Instances of Assaults upon Academic Freedom*

Writers tend to accentuate the evils they see in the nation's schools. The American novelist Winston Churchill accused Harvard Law School of teaching the law as "an infallible shield to spare the Constitution profanation."[314] Stover, the hero of Owen Johnson's *Stover at Yale*, agrees wtih Veblen's argument that business controls education.[315] In *Samuel the Seeker* by Upton Sinclair, Samuel doggedly follows Professor Stewart's delineation of social Darwinism. A convert to Stewart's creed, Samuel refuses Stewart's hospitality since charity is inimical to the laws of the survival of the fittest. Before he leaves Samuel notices that "Professor Stewart turned back to his work-table, upon which lay the bulky manuscript of his monumental work which was entitled 'Methods of Relief; A Theory and a Programme.' Some pages lay before him; the top one was headed: Chapter LXIII-'Unemployment and Social Responsibility.' And Professor Stewart sat before this title, and stared, and stared."[316]

Professor Stewart's dilemma — how to profess his belief and yet retain his chair — is faced by many sensitive teachers who are torn between dedication to truth and compromising for bread. Sinclair Lewis' self-righteous Babbitt expounds on the subversive teacher at a meeting of the Zenith Real Estate Board: Teachers who are critical of the American way of life — "long-haired gentry who call themselves 'liberals' and 'radicals' and 'non-partisan' and 'intelligentsia' — . . . constitute the worst of this whole gang. . . ." Babbitt grows more excited as he excoriates the un-American professors on the faculty of the state university, likening them to "snakes to be scotched."[317] Patriotic teachers should "whoop it up for national prosperity" and civic-minded businessmen should fire "blabbermouth, fault-finding, pessimistic, cynical University teachers."[318] In Herrick's *Chimes,* Will Ampthill is warned by his superiors to take "impersonal and scientific views on public utilities,"[319] an attitude easily detected by wide-awake students. In *We, the People* by Elmer Rice, a young man and a young lady discuss her college experience:

ALLEN: Are you sorry you left college?
MAY: No, of course not. I could not stay there, Allen. It is only a place for hiding the truth from people, for making students satisfied with the present condition.[320]

The novelist may reveal what the professor may fear to express about the presence of antidemocratic practices on the campus. Sinclair Lewis' exposure of academic deceit, cowardice, and anti-intellectualism in the university is painful reading. In *The Trail of the Hawk,* Lewis describes provincial college life in the United States. At Plato it is ill-advised for a professor to discourse on Bernard Shaw, H. G. Wells, and socialism. Professor Frazer's lecture was a tame presentation for our times, but in 1905 he had to contend against classroom spies who conveyed his ideas to Civil War veterans and to the town's worthies who preached the gospel of law and order.[321] *The Plato Weekly Times* attacked seditious professors who brazenly praised anarchist Bernard Shaw; in another lecture, the editor of the newspaper and a conservative professor of Greek heard Frazer appeal to this students to give labor a sympathetic hearing. But he invited administrative enmity by charging a trustee with ownership of land rented to two saloon keepers. His naive charge earned him the reputation as a crank, "so much does muck resent the muck-raker."[322] Interestingly, one of Frazer's supporters is Carl, a popular athlete. Meanwhile, the professor of Greek succeeds in bringing Frazer to trial. Eleven assistant and full professors constitute the jury.

In a dramatic scene, Frazer is condemned by his peers. President Wood knows he has the faculty and student body in hand. He asks student supporters of Frazer to stand. To the amazement of all, Carl rises. Only Gene, a fifteen-year-old "grind" and Plain Smith, a thirty-one-year-old high school teacher join Carl in opposing the cabal of teachers, students, and administrators against Frazer. Plain Smith resigns from Plato secure in his belief that honesty must be supported. Carl is censured by the dean who bids him apologize to President Wood and the faculty. Carl refuses to trim his sails. The machine is too strong for him. Later, *The Plato Weekly Times* lauds President Wood for crushing a student rebellion in the chapel. Wiser and sadder Carl leaves Plato for good. He had received an unexpected education at Plato.

XXXIV   *Evidence of Academic Freedom*

William James acknowledged in later life that he had not always fought vigorously against bigotry in the university, but in his lectures he often denounced misrule and malpractice. In *Talks to Teachers*, he sets forth his belief that man thinking without acting accomplishes little:

The more ideals a man has, the more contemptible, on the whole, do you continue to deem him, if the matter ends there for him, and if none of the laboring man's virtues are called into action on his part, — no courage shown, no privations undergone, no dirt or scars contracted in the attempt to get them realized. It is quite obvious that something more than the mere possession of ideals is required to make a life significant in any sense that claims the spectator's admiration.[323]

In an address that he delivered at Harvard in 1902, James paid a tribute to intellectual courage that should be read to every teaching candidate: "Those who anticipate the verdict of history, the abolitionists, *les intellectuels,* as the university professors were called who stood out for Dreyfus, the present anti-imperialists etc. — excite an almost corporeal antipathy. . . . Often their only audience is posterity. Their names are first honored when the breath has left their bodies, and like the holders of insurance policies, they must die to win their wages."[324]

How courageous it would be even today for a professor to repeat James's memorable words that must have disturbed many of his audience at the Harvard commencement in 1903: "Our undisciplinables are our proudest product. Let us agree together that the output of them will never cease."[325] It is an undisciplinable, Dr. Zechlin at Mizpah College, who tries to create a skeptical attitude in

Elmer Gantry's thinking. The theological heretic tells Elmer that "doubting is a very healthy sign, especially in the young," and then confronts him with this gadfly question: "Don't you see that otherwise you'd simply be swallowing instruction whole, and no fallible human instructor can always be right, do you think?"[326]

Undoubtedly John Jay Chapman was sincere when he encouraged radicals to "do what you will, but speak out always. Be shunned, be hated, be ridiculed, be scared, be in doubt," he urged, "but don't be gagged!"[327] Yet brave as these words are they ask others to take risks to do what the writer can do with reasonable impunity. A renowned scholar and writer like Charles A. Beard can resign from Columbia University in protest against administrative mistreatment of supposedly competent teachers, but to ask the same heroics of a young, untenured teacher who might face an academic blacklist for life is to expect sainthood. How many men can say as peasant-born Professor Friedrich Paulsen of the University of Berlin said of himself in 1907, "I will not crook my knee to the military gentlemen of the Court?"[328] In 1918 Paul Elmer More asked his colleagues to participate in the urgent affairs of the state — that professors should be like Moses, not like Princeton dons.[329] Paul Goodman found James McKeen Cattell's proposed university beautiful in concept; in 1906 Cattell suggested that the university corporation be composed of professors, officers, alumni, and all dues-paying members of the community. The professors alone would elect the president; the corporation would elect trustees to care for the college property.[330]

Even Upton Sinclair begrudgingly acknowledged that Harvard was more dedicated to academic freedom than any other college — a concession that he makes in *The Goose-Step* after flaying the administrators and trustees at Cambridge severely. William James spoke unequivocally of the need to teach philosophy with complete freedom,[331] a stand endorsed by President Eliot with one major stipulation — that the teacher "cannot authoritatively impose his personal opinions upon the students."[332] Harvard did not oppose the formation of a Socialist Club on the campus, and to rebels like John Reed the club was an intellectual boon. Its program carried him to events of significance outside the collere walls[333] and undoubtedly led him from Cambridge to Moscow. At the school itself, the Socialist Club invited noted radical speakers; in addition, the club advanced interest in music, art, and the theater, and, inevitably, promoted a more progressive outlook in the college newspapers. Walter Lippmann and Lincoln Steffens instituted an experimental program subscribed to by twenty-one teachers and interested seniors. Nonacademic speakers were asked to lecture; these included journalists, Wall Street men, and sociologists.[334] Free expression was not hushed at Harvard. And for this respect for freedom of expression, Harvard was suspect in the eyes of ultraconservatives. And still is.

XXXV   The Value of College to The Writer

Hundreds of noted writers had little or no university training. It is impossible to determine the relative worth of a degree to an accomplished writer. The writers speak for themselves, but their comments are sometimes unreasonably critical. For example, Henry Adams condemned Harvard's system; fallacious from beginning to end, a Harvard education "was more mischievous to the teachers than to the students."[335] Adams protested too much. Harvard gave him more than he remembered her for. Perhaps his self-education propelled him much faster through the tunnel of learning than his courses did. Perhaps geniuses should not be goose-stepped at uniform pace from class to class for four years.

Scores of writers have seconded Adams' complaint. Pearl Buck wrote off her college experience as "an incidental interlude out of the mainstream of life" that taught her very little.[336] Robert Sherwood felt that his two and a half years at Harvard were a waste of time,[337] a sentiment shared by fellow Harvardian John Tunis, who belittles himself too much in this confession: "I failed to obtain an education in college, and as a consequence, like so many Americans, I have been scrambling after one ever since."[338] Harvard is roundly scored by her eminent sons: Adams pitied his students whose "minds burst open like a flower at the sunlight of a suggestion," although for the most part they were "ignorant of all that men had ever thought or hoped."[339] What irked him most about his students was their materialism. What could a professor say to an undergraduate who boasts that "the degree of Harvard College is worth money to me in Chicago?"[340]

Theodore Roosevelt objected to the narrow scientific training he had received at Harvard. A natural scientist must be more than a tissue-sectioner or a microscope gazer. As an adult he said that Harvard had been of little specific value to him, especially the required course in political economy that never acquainted him with the collective responsibilities that the fortunate have to the unfortunate.[341] Lincoln Steffens agreed; the colleges had failed to inspire him with an ethical sense since all they were concerned with "was the long story of what man had thought about right or wrong."[342]

Sinclair Lewis fretted his youth away at Yale, irked by the courses which he felt were useless to him. Edmund Wilson blamed Princeton's worship of money and prestige for Scott Fitzgerald's unhappiness and inability to realize his full genius in writing.[343] Robert Frost learned at Dartmouth College that self-education is the best education.[344] Bliss Perry labored through large freshman classes at Williams College doing stultifying exercises, some dating back to 1848.[345] William A. White got little out of the College of Emporia in Kansas whose six rooms on the third floor of a brick building tended to the needs of seventy-five boys and girls.[346] Joseph Wood Krutch learned little at the University of Tennessee in 1911 because of the inability of antiquated teachers and the indifference of the genuine scholars;[347] and Ezra Pound found the college library at Wabash "utterly useless."[348]

XXXVI   *General Criticisms of College Education*

Henry James' longing for European culture is evident in his educational criticism as well as in his literary essays. Alas, America had "no great universities nor public schools — no Oxford, nor Eton, nor Harrow."[349] Although he was not so explicit in his admiration of European culture as James was, Henry Seidel Canby missed in American college life the intellectual power of a church and the elements of a culture.[350] Instead, the ideals of American college life lend themselves to the indoctrination of students with a zest for the harsh competition of capitalism.[351] Unfortunately, the business mind at the helms of most large colleges exploits the resources available in massive, often frilly and ostentatious, building projects.[352] Consequently, large schools with limited curricula and overcrowded classrooms were poor centers for the intellectual development of both teachers and students.[353] The older university was able to function adequately because its clients were prepared soundly for their intellectual jousting in the college, but in the modern intellectual factory the undergraduate enters the humanities class passionlessly and apprehensively.[354]

Joseph Wood Krutch, upon reading the platitude "The Love of Learning Rules the World" on a brass plaque in the entrance hall of the University of Arizona, remarked: "On this occasion it struck me, that of all the lies which have been cast in eternal bronze, this is probably the most barefaced."[355] Such lies are distressing to serious students. Jack London believed that students supposedly learning the truth at college were asleep, while poverty brutalized the masses. He longed to incite them to think — "even at the risk of being called a long-haired anarchist."[356]

XXXVII   College Versus Life

At the University of California, Frank Norris found the scholarship of his instructors unrelated to the reality of life. Norris was attuned to the present, not to the past. He left Berkeley for Harvard and under the guidance of Professor Lewis Gates, Norris was able to work on his naturalistic novels, *McTeague* and *Vandover and the Brute*.[357] Lincoln Steffens was equally unhappy at Berkeley where "knowledge was absolute, not relative, and it was stored in compartments, categorical and independent. The relation of knowledge to life, even student life, was ignored. . . ."[358] Stephen Crane preferred to study humanity, since the college curriculum was unreal. How much more could be learned studying passing trains, people, and faces![359] Theodore Dreiser found the life in town more educative than his courses at Indiana University; students were overly solemn and given to much pomposity and show.[360] At Columbia Frank Dobie found more vital living in the city than at the conformist university.[361]

Wendell Phillips wrote that to the shame of the university, "almost all the great truths relating to society were not the result of scholarly meditation, but have been first heard in the solemn protests of martyred patriotism and the loud cries of crushed and slaving labor."[362] Professors at Yale failed to inspire their students with a love of culture. Unlike the dons who initiated the Oxford movement in England. American professors were content to have their charges swim aimlessly in the shallow and sterile streams of their specialties.[363]

XXXVIII   Fictional Values of College

Plato College is described by Sinclair Lewis in an effective simile. The college "is as earnest and undistinguished, as provincially dull and pathetically human, as a spinster missionary."[364] Lewis is fond of attributing sound, unschooled wisdom to eccentrics and backwoodsmen. In *The Trail of the Hawk*, Bone Stillman, the town eccentric, advised Carl that Plato College is "a shortbit freshwater sewing-circle . . . where an imitation scholar teaches you imitation translations of useless classics, and amble-footed girls teach you imitation party manners that'd make you just as plumb ridic'lous in a real salon as they would in a lumber-yard."[365] Elmer Gantry attends Terwillinger College in 1902, one of ten denominational colleges of the East-Middle Kansas Conference, "all of them with buildings and presidents and chapel service and yells and colors and a standard of scholarship equal to the best high schools." Gantry hated Terwillinger. He would have been happier in the prize ring, the fish market, or the stock exchange than "poking through the cobwebbed corridors of Terwillinger."[366]

In *The Last Puritan* Santayana reproved Harvard's leadership — 1905 vintage — for its surrender to mean tastes and values. Caleb Wetherbie, a crippled convert to Catholicism, speaks movingly to Oliver Alden of Harvard's decline and of his hopes for the school's regeneration:

Boston and Harvard have need nowadays of new blood, of fresh spiritual courage. They are becoming too much like the rest of the country, choked with big business, forced fads, and merely useful knowledge. Our fearless souls of other days have left no heirs. We need to break away again . . . from intellectual professionalism, from the slough of standardised opinion, from the dulcet mendacity of the pulpits, from the sheepish, ignorant, monotonous, epidemic mind of our political rulers, well meaning and decent as a whole, but oh, how helpless.[367]

Humorists find ample comic material in college life. George Ade occasionally lampooned the credulous commoner who sacrificed the best years of his life to see junior through college. In illustration, a farmer brought his son to a college that would prepare him for a school superintendency at $990 per annum. Alas, the son returns in full collegiate regalia, a fop who disgusts his disappointed father.[368] This paragon of fashion is questioned by his stunned parent:

"What do they teach you up at your school — besides murder? I thought you wanted to be County Superintendent of Schools."
"I've outgrown all these two-by-four ambitions. I'm going to be on the Eleven next Fall. What more could you ask?"[369]

The delightful Idiot in John Kendrick Bangs' *Coffee and Repartee* is a realist. Unlike the farmer, he believes that "in the chase for the gilded shekel the education of experience is better than the coddling of *alma mater*"; besides, the explosion in the college population has necessarily lowered the quality of the plant's products.[370] This proliferation of schools is unhealthy, Ambrose Bierce cautioned. "Still we go on with a maniacal hope, adding school to school, college to college, university to university and — unconscious provision for their product — almshouses, asylums, and prisons in prodigal abundance."[371]

XXXIX Advantages of College

Even in their censures, diatribes, and lamentations, men of letters betray a concern for the school that affected them for better or worse. John P. Marquand is gentle in his exposure of Harvard's shams and occasional pomposity. In *The Late George Apley*, Harvard of the eighties mirrors the nation's materialism; its new buildings, laboratories, and gymnasiums fortunately do not overshadow its role as repository of the best of New England culture.[372] Harvard's merit is not in its preparation of young men for the specialties, Oliver Wendell Holmes said in 1884, but in that all-pervading aroma of high feeling that lingers in its halls, a higher purpose is sensed by all who have ethical and cultural affinities.[373]

Ludwig Lewisohn initially praised Columbia for its elective system. In his autobiographical novel, *Haunch, Paunch, and Jowl*, Samuel B. Ornitz praises the intellectual standards of the College of the City of New York. Besieged by thousands of learning-mad sons of immigrants, the free-tuition college was an academic mecca. Many of the matriculants dropped out; no mercy was shown by the faculty to those who could not keep up with their brisk pace.[374] Mary Ellen Chase had kind words for the superb assemblage of graduate teachers at the University of Minnesota;[375] Edmund Wilson cited Yale for respecting academic achievement;[376] and Stuart Pratt Sherman defended the State University of Illinois in 1913 as a great university that shows the world that "the search for light is not a sacred possession of old New England colleges."[377]

Albert Jay Nock never regretted his education at a college that restricted its student body to one hundred youths. Most of the students were rural-bred, resourceful young men who ate their plain food contentedly and devised their own recreations. The teachers were learned but aloof gentleman.[378] Perhaps something has been lost as colleges have grown. Critics of the soulless multiuniversity long for the peaceful simplicity of Nock's halcyon college days, but in education as in life, "the moving finger having writ. . . ." And those who never had an alma mater feel "like an orphan child." Poor John Burroughs gazed sadly upon the faces of the 3,500 students, well-dressed and well-behaved, who attended a football match between Princeton and Yale and sighed, "Alas! that I have no college associations. It is a great loss."[379]

Henry Seidel Canby was realistically critical in his exposition of the deficiencies in college education, but he paid homage to the lasting values that Yale inculcated in her more successful sons. "This college seldom educated us," he wrote, "but it did temper the excesses and sweeten the content of our real, our preferred education, in college life, and it sowed in our inattentive minds seeds of ideas which often sprouted later."[380] George William Curtis stoutly defended scholarship; although "the educated class is denounced as impracticable and visionary," it must be remembered that "the Constitution of the United States is the work of American scholars."[381]

XL　*The Alumni*

The alumni, like veterans of foreign wars, cling to their memories of their youthful associations. Those writers who refuse to be drawn into this pantheon of sham deities are perhaps overly critical of their Rotarian fellows who perpetuate a puerile loyalty to tinsel rituals. Sensitive critics of American college graduates have much to complain of in the antics of alumni who go to silly plays, read silly books, and uphold "every poisonous fallacy in politics, religion and conduct."[382] Canby accuses the colleges of failing to educate the alumni to temper competitive aims with the reasonableness of analysis.[383] Babbitt at sixty — paunchy, bald, and wrinkled — adopts an air of false joviality at the dinner of the class of 1896. Cries of "You haven't changed a particle," college cheers and songs fill the air. Men attired in dress-clothes and men in ordinary suits signal the class separation among the once-supposedly classless undergraduates.[384] Nostalgically, the beaming pillars of industry recall how they beat up the hick "constabule" and hung a stolen pants-pressing sign on Professor Morrison's door.[385]

The alumnus is an educational conservative. He stresses practical courses, but speaks fondly of the old culture, including Greek, which he flunked, and literature, which he tolerated as a useless requisite for his degree.[386]

XLI　*Conclusions*

The pre - World War I college graduate has been charged by Henry Seidel Canby for part of the violent inconsistency of

American policy in the postwar period. The miseducation of college men who led the nation in 1917 and thereafter contributed to these contradictions in twentieth century American history:

1. An extraordinary organization for the war in 1917 - 1918; and a complete disorganization in the handling of the peace.
2. An incomparably efficient organization of industry in the boom decade; and an almost complete anarchy of business and financial control of that boom, ending in an unparalleled smash.
3. A magnificent extension of philanthropy and science applied to humanitarian ends, extending beyond our boundaries around the world; and a failure, almost complete, to organize a radical reform of our own social ills, although every corrupt municipal government has been flying flags of distress.
4. The most elaborate school system in the world; and the highest percentage of crime.
5. Wealth so great that it had to be given away; and inexplicable poverty, less desperate but even more destructive than the poverty of Europe.[387]

Professor Canby's strong indictment of the educated classes reinforces Wendell Phillips' abrasive indictment of timid scholars in his Phi Beta Kappa speech at Harvard in June 1881. "Corruption does not so much rot the masses," he warned. "It poisons Congress. Credit Mobilier and money rings are not housed under thatched roofs; they flaunt at the Capitol."[388] Warming to his subject he gazed directly at his aghast audience and continued: "It is not the masses who have most disgraced our political annals. I have seen many mobs between the seaboard and the Mississippi. I never saw or heard of any but well-dressed mobs, assembled and countenanced, if not always led in person, by respectability and what called itself education."[389]

To follow Phillips is to strip oneself of all personal, egoistic, and hedonistic goals. If one must "give hostage to fortune," he cannot follow in Phillips' train. Phillips demands what Jesus demands: unconditional adherence to truth. But in a society that worships competition as the eleventh commandment — "thou shalt compete with thy fellow man" — there is an overt conflict with the medieval injunction, namely, "thou shalt not rock the boat." And in education it behooves a rising schoolmaster to vie furiously with his peers for elevation to a deanship, a presidency, or a superintendency since, like Samuel the Seeker, he has been taught that only inferior pedagogues remain in the classroom.

In fiction, Sinclair Lewis's Bible Belt Plato College, Robert Herrick's Eureka University, Boyesen's Larkin University, Fitch's Old Siwash, Fitzgerald's Princeton, Santayana's Harvard, Edna Ferber's Mid-West U., Upton Sinclair's College of the City of New York, and Sheldon's Lincoln College tend to expose the unpleasant and destructive traits of American college life. Outmoded curricula, tired, incompetent, and apathetic teachers, pompous and self-seeking administrators, conservative and unbending trustees, ill-mannered and indolent students, cunning and greedy athletic coaches, and money-grubbing professionalism stigmatize the colleges as hypocritical agents of an acquisitive society. Men like Albert Jay Nock and Abraham Flexner celebrate the small college of the past that honored learning, shunned athleticism, and inculcated a sense of the scholar's mission in the minds of its students. Severe academic critics like Canby and William James suggest that a great university, weak as it may be, nevertheless imbues its more sensitive youth with a feeling of purpose and independence that transcends the value of the formal learning.

Canby attributed part of the post - World War I chaos to the failure of the schools to educate men for the exigencies that will confront them after commencement. But this criticism leads to a circular argument. If the schools reflect the aims and ideals of the society that funds them, can they be expected to turn against their patrons? "Dare the schools change the social order?" asked Professor Counts, but few indeed in the schools dared to test his query. Despite all the professors attesting to the freedom of expression in the schools, there always exists in the minds of men competing for tenure a fear that, if they protest too much against injustices, they will compromise their standing in the promotional combats.

The novelist or educator turned author writes freely because of his independence from academic overlordship. It would be instructive to have the anonymous reactions of thousands of teachers to novels and plays critical of college life. Their opinions would be a plausible indication of the validity of much of the fictional criticism of education.

CHAPTER 4

The United States after 1918

World History is more likely to be shaped by American history for the next half-century [from 1948] than by any other element in its making; but how it is to be shaped depends on how Americanism is shaped, and that is still a question to which no answer has been given.[1]

I The Pessimism of Henry Adams

IN his famed autobiography, *The Education of Henry Adams*, a book which should be required reading for all politicians, Adams lamented that the evolutionary theory was negated by the election of a man like Ulysses S. Grant to the presidency two thousand years after Alexander the Great and Julius Caesar had exercised their "brief authority" in their respective empires. A master of hyperbole, Adams wrote that "that the progress of evolution from President Washington to President Grant, was alone evidence enough to upset Darwin."[2]

Grant's incompetence and possible corruption disillusioned Adams, who had investigated Jay Gould's attempt to corner the gold market in 1869. Convinced that Gould would not have undertaken his grandiose scheme without assurances of noninterference from the White House or the Treasury, Adams undertook to unravel the intricate meshes of the Gold Conspiracy. As the tragedy unfolded Adams sorrowed that Grant should have fallen "within six months into such a morass," leading the nation into scandals which "smirched executive, judiciary, banks, corporate systems, and people, all the great active forces of society, in one dirty cesspool of vulgar corruption."[3]

The Gold Conspiracy, Teapot Dome, and Watergate; what price education? What has man learned from his foibles? Happy Henry Adams! His return to earth in 1938 would not have assured him that "for the first time since man began his education among the carnivores, they [John Jay, Clarence King, and himself] would find a world that sensitive and timid natures could regard without a shudder."[4] Happy Henry Adams! Had he chosen to return in the 1970s how much gloomier his visit would have been. Man has not melted his swords into ploughshares; hunger and pollution portend catastrophic events for the most of the world; and racial hatred creates walls between peoples that can only intensify isolation and consequent violence. And in the schools millions of students pass through pedagogical treadmills, discovering more or less as Henry Adams had that schooling teaches little.

II   *An Academic Takes the Nation into War*

How was a high school freshman to know in 1914 what Woodrow Wilson intimated when he warned that a German victory would compel the United States "to give up its present ideals and devote all of its energies to defense, which would mean the end of its present system of government?"[5] Of what value to them was Wilson's advanced eulogy for the class of 1917 which he uttered to his secretary, Joseph P. Tumulty, after returning to the Capitol from the White House, his ears still tingling from the raucous applause of Congress and the spectators who had heard his war speech? "My message today was a message of death to our young men. How strange it seems to applaud that."[6]

What happened in the United States after Congress declared war upon the Central Powers vindicated Wilson's warning that total armament meant the end of democracy in its present form. To rationalize his war policies, Wilson recruited legions of scholars and scientists to give intellectual support to the war.[7] Opponents of the war were arrested or silenced. Eugene Debs was sentenced to ten years of imprisonment for condemning the war effort and denouncing the prosecution of alleged seditionists. Randolph Bourne found publishers indifferent to his pacifist books; Columbia University dismissed antiwar professors, and at the University of Nebraska twelve professors were tried for disloyalty.[8] German-Americans were baited, and German culture was demeaned. Senator La Follette, formerly popular, was burned in effigy and censured by the faculty of the University of Wisconsin. The statue of General Von Steuben was removed in many cities, and the small-mindedness of many "patriotic" Americans narrowed to the extent that they forbade the study of German in the schools, the preachment of sermons in German, and the sale of pretzels in Cincinnati.[9] A friend of Wilson,

George Creel, organized 150,000 lecturers, writers, artists, actors, and scholars to mobilize American support of the war. As the war progressed, so did hysteria. Dissidents were whipped, tarred and feathered, and lynched. Of 2,168 prosecutions under the Espionage and Sedition Acts, 1,055 were convicted, but only ten for sabotage. Historians Arthur S. Link and William B. Colton write that "the war hysteria seems the most fearful price the American people paid for participation in World War I."[10]

III   *The Hectic Twenties*

Wilson's League of Nations, even if subscribed to by all of the major powers, was merely a papier-mâché organization according to Thorstein Veblen, since the league introduced no new measures "to avoid the status quo out of which the great war arose."[11] The election of 1920 was a sad sequel to the death of Wilson's dreams. H. L. Mencken summarized the choices offered to the American people: "I am an old friend of political shows, and witnessed both the nomination of Harding at Chicago and that of Cox at San Francisco. It would be difficult to imagine more obscene spectacles. Who, being privy to their disgusting trimming, their mean courting of mean men, their absolute lack of any sense of dignity, could vote for either?"[12]

But the people voted for Warren G. Harding, as they later voted for Calvin Coolidge and Herbert Hoover, both apostles of the high tariff and of low income taxes for the rich.[13] In his *Mind in the Making*, James Harvey Robinson anticipated in part the thesis of C. Wright Mills' *The Power Elite*, charging that "businessmen, whether conspicuous in manufacture, trade, or finance, are the leading figures of our age. They exercise a dominant influence in domestic and foreign policy; they subsidize our education and exert an unmistakable control over it."[14]

The raucous twenties were years of masked aspirations and tinsel integrity. In the train of the war to make the world safe for democracy came fascism in Italy, communism in Russia, and nazism in Germany. And as the great political dramas evolved in the Far East innocent peoples were caught and torn by the talons of massive conglomerates of robot-men called armies. In the United States, Eden was promised by industry's publicists. Henry Ford urged the world to produce and consume! Buy what you do not need and replace it before it is worn out. And, scoffed Kenneth Duva Burke, "if our normal wastage fails, war can take up the slack."[15] Even divorce adds to our economy; separated couples need two apartments, two sets of furniture, two automobiles, two of everything.[16]

In 1928 Haldeman-Julius, the publisher of the ubiquitous *Little Blue Books*, reported a sale of twenty million of these self-educators. Although hundreds of titles ran the gamut of intellectual and cultural literature, the best-selling books were on sex, love, and self-improvement in that order.[17] For those too impecunious to matriculate at the Harvard School of Business, the *Little Blue Books* were a godsend. The road to managment was outlined in their succinct pages. For a dollar one might absorb the "go-getting" wisdom of twenty pundits of business and finance. Haldeman-Julius was the twentieth-century reincarnation of Franklin's Poor Richard.

The world of the novelists of the twenties was gloomy — perhaps "the most gloomy in the whole of literary history,"[18] possibly because the writers themselves were among the most tormented and the most pessimistic of all Americans. Perhaps the twenties were carefree years to the perennial partygoers one meets in Fitzgerald's novels, but even they seemed to be affflicted with the gloom of purposeless ennui. The struggles between capital and labor, the plight of the veteran, the immoralities spawned by prohibition, the racial tensions threatening to explode momentarily into full-fledged war, the dramatic Scopes trial, the traumatic Sacco and Vanzetti case, and the disruption of family life by technological change provided novelists with an amplitude of motifs for their literature of woe and despair.

The apathy of the government in enforcing prohibition has been the theme of scores of novels and moving pictures. The consequent disrespect for the law affected all classes.[19] That corruption had infiltrated into the precints of the White House was made clear when Secretary of the Interior Albert B. Fall was convicted for conspiracy to obstruct justice in the Teapot Dome scandal.[20] But Fundamentalists were more concerned with the literal truth of the Scriptures than with the morality inscribed therein. In Dayton, Tennessee, where religion replaced golf, bridge, music, art, literature, dancing, tennis, and clubs, the foes of hellish Darwin, led by their prophet William Jennings Bryan, proclaimed to the world that not one word of the Bible is suspect and that evolution is the Devil's preachment.[21]

In 1927, Sacco and Vanzetti went to the electric chair for a murder which they denied knowledge of. Their case rocked the world. Protest meetings were worldwide; many of the greatest intellectuals in numerous lands pleaded with the governor of Massachusetts to stay the execution. Conservatives and liberals argue the merits of the case to this day. Upton Sinclair based his long novel *Boston* on the struggle of the doomed men for acquittal. Scores of poems have been written in honor of these immigrant laborers. But the jury had spoken, the men were executed, and within the framework of American jurisprudence justice had been done.

IV   The Plight of the Immigrant

The immigrant's lot should be studied in the lower schools. Young Americans should learn why their classmates are sometimes called kike, mick, dago, chink, kraut, hunk, jap, spick, shine, nigger. Ironically, the black man, first of America's non-Anglo-Saxon immigrants, is still called by the distasteful epithet "nigger," openly in some localities, covertly in others. The history of American immigration is a history of expediency and conscience. When the plains had to be wrested from the Indians, when the railroads and canals had to be built, when the giant factories had to be manned, the call went out from the land to foreign strands — send us your people to make our nation strong. Sometimes, when the nation heard the cries of tormented poeple, it opened its doors to tens of thousands of them, as the nation did for the Jews of Czarist Russia who fled the merciless land of czar and cossack. But in the second decade of the twentieth century American compassion for the persecuted or impoverished foreigner became more selective. Quotas were placed upon immigration of non-Anglo-Saxon peoples. Although Presidents Taft, Cleveland, and Wilson vetoed literacy tests for immigrants, Congress succeeded in passing legislation in 1917 that made the ability to read English a requisite for anyone seeking entrance to America.[22]

The Immigration Law of 1917 was praised by Professor Robert D. C. Ward, a geologist at Harvard. Ward argued that the country would benefit from its refusal to accept inferior people who included radicals and criminal types.[23] From 1924 - 1947 only 2,718,006 immigrants arrived in the United States, and from 1929 - 1947, the yearly average of entry was inconsequential, if the number of departing aliens is deducted from the number of entries.[24] The McCarran-Walter Act of 1952 restricted the number of immigrants on a racial and national basis; but in World War II, alien labor was contracted from Mexico, Jamaica, and the Bahamas to keep war production booming.[25]

Herbert Hoover, champion of free trade, free enterprise, open markets, and open opportunities, shunned economic planning as the instrument of dictators. But when the dreams of the "great engineer" were transformed into an endless nightmare by the sudden paralysis of free enterprise, the stage was set for Franklin Delano Roosevelt's exploitation of the domestic tragedy. Inheriting a depressing legacy of 12 - 15 million unemployed Americans subsisting on charity, and a drop in national income from 81 billion dollars to 40 billion,[26] Roosevelt saved the nation from disaster and "is bound to be," in the words of Richard Hofstadter, "the dominant figure in the mythology of any resurgent American liberalism."[27]

V   *The Depression Years*

Among the millions of insecure Americans in the thirties were thirty million new Americans of foreign stock. These sons of immigrants could not readily insinuate themselves into the mainstream of American life. They spoke with foreign accents, they were given inferior jobs, and in school ignorant teachers and students made sport of their foreign-sounding names.[28] Unaccepted by their fellow Americans and lacking cultural ties with their old countries, these unhappy new Americans sailed precariously between the Scylla of the old and the Charybdis of the new. Some sought escape by running away from their homes or by Anglicizing their names. Still othes, to demonstrate their Americanism, exaggerated their patriotism, indulging in flag-waving and chauvinistic fancies.

But life was hard for all lower-class Americans, native or foreign born. The nation disagreed with the Republican argument that "things could have been worse" in the three years of business stagnation that witnessed bank failures, farm foreclosures, and massive unemployment.[29] Although the press was almost unanimously opposed to him in the campaigns of 1936, 1940, and 1944,[30] Roosevelt's charm and charisma, materially abetted by his famed fireside chats, gave the lie to the popular myth that the newspapers control the minds of the people. Emulating Wilson's reliance upon scholars in World War I, Roosevelt gathered together a so-called "brain trust" of university men, authors, and librarians to shape his policies; thousands of young intellectuals entered government service in the crusade to destroy the depression. But many of the president's staunchest liberal supporters had misgivings about their leader when he decreed a state of neutrality during the Spanish Civil War. Perhaps President Roosevelt felt that the time was not yet ripe to challenge Hitler on the Continent, but resistance to nazism waned sharply after Franco's victory. Probably much of the apathy of the French to Hitler's invasion of their territory stemmed from the cynicism of the French people after Hitler's victories at Munich and Madrid.

VI   *Post - World War II Values*

Calling in 1940 for a change in values in Western civilization, Lewis Mumford warned that the West must eschew the old trinity of the establishment, namely, profits, power, and special privileges, if it is to preserve democratic values and liberties.[31] But the war ended and the old ideals prevailed. An astute columnist, James Reston, said of President John F. Kennedy what applied to his predecessors and followers alike: he "aimed to avoid alienating any major groups that might wreck the major objectives of trade and economic expansion."[32] Reston was not kind to President Kennedy and probably displeased many ardent Kennedy lovers with this deflating announcement: "He came into society just a year ago on the narrowest of election margins sounding like a liberal crusader. He is ending it like a calculating machine."[33]

For a large majority of Americans life was never prosperous, even in the best of times. In 1929, 42 percent of the population earned less than $1,500 annually.[34] In 1959 the average family had an income of $6,250, but the median salary of teachers was considerably lower than this.[35] The nation spent $1,000,000,000,000 on the military in twenty-five years.[36] These military costs obviously limit the money available for humanitarian projects, a truism stated feelingly by Henry Wadsworth Longfellow in 1841 as he stared sorrowfully at the "burnished arms" in the arsenal at Springfield:

> Were half the power, that fills the world
>   with terror,
> Were half the wealth, bestowed on camps
>   and courts,
> Given to redeem the human mind from error,
> There were no need for arsenals nor forts.[37]

VII   *The Continuing Battle of Blacks for Equality*

If a significant portion of that $1,000,000,000, 000 had been given as retroactive awards to blacks for the ill-use of their ancestors who had helped build this land with blood, sweat, and tears, it is possible that the demeaning confrontations between blacks and whites since 1945 might have been avoided. But the ugly ghettos swell, the barriers between black cities and white suburbs become more defined, and the tasks of reconciling the races grows almost hopeless. The violence of Reconstruction days had a resurgence after World War I. The lynching of a black in Omaha touched off an orgy of shooting and pillaging. Thousands of "respectable citizens stood by as mobsters killed, burned, or looted."[38] In 1917 there were thirty-four lynchings; in 1918 the number rose to sixty; and in 1919, seventy blacks including ten servicemen were murdered by white mobs. In 1919 race riots in Chicago, Washington, D.C., and Longview, Texas, were among the twenty-five riots throughout the nation that left hundreds dead and thousands homeless.[39] In the twenties there were five million in the dues-paying army of the Ku Klux Klan,[40] a legion of hate-filled patriots who added Jews and Catholics to their list of enemies.

To keep the blacks from ascending in the social order, the South deliberately, and the North, with less openness, provided inferior education for blacks.[41] Although some Southern states tried to furnish good education for blacks, most Southerners agreed with Booker T. Washington that vocational education was best for the unskilled black child.[42] As late as 1945, an anecdote in *Time* magazine illustrated pointedly the feelings of the white population toward the education of blacks. After a successful run in Manhattan, Arthur Laurent's play "Home of the Brave," dealing with anti-Semitism at an outpost in the Pacific, opened in Dallas and Texas. In Dallas, after overhearing playgoers' comments on the play, a black elevator operator summed up their observations: "Well, I'll tell you, 99 percent of the people say its educational; the other one percent say it's good."[43] Apparently, the Dallas playgoers did not find virtue in a play exposing racial bigotry. If "educational" dramas are not to be equated with good ones, especially if the specific "good" is education for racial harmony, a syllogistic conclusion follows — education that attempts to develop racial equality is no good.

Americans, North and South, were not yet ready to accept blacks as first-class citizens. Ten years after the momentous 1954 desegregation decision of the Supreme Court, 75 percent of the Southern district schools were still segregated.[44] William Faulkner, although opposed to compulsory racial inequality, spoke for millions of Southerners in his "Letter to the North." The South, he warned, would never accept integration forced from without; Southerners themselves had the responsibility to cure the South's unique racial problems.[45] Blacks should temper their militancy with restraint, since their hasty attempts to alter Southern mores might boomerang.[46] To this plea, James Baldwin said no. The Southerner would never change his spots voluntarily.[47] For the black man the time is now, a view grudgingly accepted by Martin Luther King.[48]

There was some governmental action in behalf of the nation's blacks after World War II. The Committee on Civil Rights reported in 1946 that "the United States is not so strong, the final triumph of the democratic ideal is not so inevitable that we can ignore what the world thinks of us or our record." But an America grown so strong and so self-righteous cared little for "the decent respect for the opinion of mankind" that the Founders believed in so strongly.[49] Had we not destroyed tyranny in two major wars? Had we not contained communism in Korea and Vietnam? And where in the world was there so much abundance as in the United States?

To millions of blacks in the ghettos or on sharecropper farms this rhetoric was meaningless. Governmental laxity in enforcing civil rights laws offended them. Violent riots erupted in the sixties culminating in the tragic burning of Watts. Chicago and Newark experienced major riots, and peace between the races seemed impossible to attain.[50] In the seventies, black consciousness manifested itself in every phase of American life. Liberalism's creed could not appease black disdain for half-measures, and black leaders now realized that "an oppressed people can depend on no one but themselves to move that long distance, past all distance, to genuine dignity."[51] White liberals rationalized that they were not wanted and increasingly separated themselves from black novements, especially when integration came closer to their schools.

VIII   *Educational Problems of Our Times*

It is unfortunate that ultimately education becomes a matter of money. It is almost obscene to think that parents will vehemently oppose excellence in education because of the tax rate. If only people would be one-tenth as extravagant in educating their progeny as they are in building war machines, how advanced might our educational systems become!

The rise of the high school population from five hundred thousand in 1914 to four million in 1926 imposed great hardships on the taxpayer,[52] but people grumbled and continued to support the public schools. The greatest savings in educational costs were made at the expense of grade school teachers, an unhappy lot of quasi-professionals who avoided unionization. For their dedication to a genteel educational tradition — impoverishment — teachers' salaries in 1927 were never "equal to the minimum standard of living as proclaimed by trade unions and social reformers."[53] As high taxes and poor business conditions became more pronounced, especially in the Midwest, a movement arose to dispense with vocational training, sports, and recreational programs and to return to the three R's.[54] When the depression was at full tide school expenditures dropped 18 percent nationally and as much as 41 and 52 percent in Michigan and Mississippi, respectively. College enrollment decreased by 8.5 percent, and state university budgets were cut severely.[55] Teachers' salaries were appreciably cut, but senior teachers on tenure lived comfortably on salaries that had barely provided them with necessities in prosperous times. Legions of college graduates competed for post-office jobs in 1937. Unfortunately, the college men who had no interest in postal careers acquired most of the postal positions, and to the old-timers who sorted or carried the mail the new class of mailman was a strange breed. The unlettered career men frequently scorned the newcomers and scoffed at their useless degrees.

In the twenty-year period from 1940 to 1960, the nation's public elementary and high school population rose from 25,434,000 to 36,305,000. In the same period the number of pupils enrolled in private schools rose from 2,611,000 to 6,100,000. Since 350,000 teachers had left the profession for better paying jobs before the end of World War II, the schools were faced with a lack of trained teachers.[56] College enrollment doubled in the same period as tens of thousands of veterans took advantage of Public Law 346.[57]

During the same time, an ideological battle was fought between educational progressives and traditionalists. At the end of World War II educational thought was "saturated with progressivism."[58] Traditionalists like President Robert Maynard Hutchins of the University of Chicago found progressivism wanting because it lacked a system of philosophical values, but progressives rejoined that traditionalism encourages authoritarian and undemocratic tendencies in children.[59] Harold Laski, a British scholar who had taught for many years in American universities, discovered nothing subversive to the American tradition in progressive schools.[60] In the progressive school, the child asserts his individuality — he creates, explores his talents, sits informally in class with his peers, and with them, participates in activities demanding his cooperation, initiative, and adjustment to novel situations. The teacher, however, really leads the class.[61]

As early as 1940, Walter Lippmann wrote that, in the schools, "there is no common faith, no common body of principle, no common body of knowledge, no common moral and intellectual discipline."[62] These criticisms plagued the schools for decades. Progressivists were assailed on two fronts: traditionalists, superpatriots, and witch hunters were troublesome assailants, but the most serious onslaughts came from intellectuals, academicians, and the informed laity, many of whom were apostates from progressivism.[63] Laymen, for the most part, found the mystique of progressivism baffling. Perhaps the most grievous fault of the progressive philosophers was their inability to communicate effectively with the public.[64] By the fifties, progressive education was under massive frontal assault by all of the media. The elementary schools allegedly failed to communicate the elemental wisdom of the human race to the young, the high schools coddled their adolescents, and the colleges were mediocre, failing in their mandate to train leaders. Furthermore, God was being kept out of the schools and parental privileges were being usurped by teachers. Leading in the attack upon progressivism was Mortimer Smith; in *And Madly Teach* he urged parents to rise up against teachers who deny the role of education as a "moral and intellectual teacher."[65] Arthur E. Bestor, an accomplished and respected scholar, charged in *Educational Wastelands* that the function of a school is to teach students how to think. But a program of education that does not firmly ground the student in history, science, English, mathematics, and foreign languages deprives him of knowledge requisite for sound thinking. Teachers' colleges were wasteful; their curricula were designed primarily to train administrators. Especially distasteful to Bestor were the educational courses required for certification.[66]

According to Lawrence A. Cremin, progressivism collapsed because it became schismatic, failed to assert itself positively against its opponents, exacted too many virtues and talents for the average teacher, ignored the laity, and failed to keep pace with American society.[67] Although the progressive movement succumbed, the new education incorporated the essential ideas of progressivism.[68] In addition, progressive education had the role of a gadfly. "In this sense," wrote Adolphe E. Meyer, "Its work, though oftentimes at odds with the common beliefs of the time and often enough leading to wild claims and fancies, is nonetheless desirable, nay, it is indispensable."[69]

In education as in all other tributaries of America's business mainstream, its explorers must not stray too far from its source. Since most trustees are businessmen, they demand financial success. The president must elicit sizable endowments from foundations, wealthy men, and corporations. But to do so he must be deferential, humble, and even obsequious before the lords of philanthropy. The college president, generally a conservative, seems to defend liberalism in commencement day speeches, but more often than not he is also prepared to denounce those who supposedly deviate from the accepted bounds of liberalism.[70] At Amherst, in 1935, President James B. Conant of Harvard University declared that "we must have our share of thoughtful rebels on our faculties, and our students must be exposed to the 'clash of opinion.' Only from continued debate can new vistas be opened."[71] But Henry Steele Commager recalls how during the McCarthy era regents and trustees shamefully punished teachers for conduct that civil authorities did not regard as unlawful.[72] And later, during the student uprisings of the sixties, was the record of presidents and deans in dealing with dissident students worthy of their office? Professor Commager thought not:

"Why should president or deans indulge in the vanity of supposing that they can somehow commit great universities? Yet here they stand numbed by timidity, palsied by indecision, taking refuge from the obligation to confound great moral questions by escaping into the easy activity of applying petty disciplinarian measures to students who embarrass them.[73]

The success of the Russian Revolution engendered intense fear of radical subversion in the United States. The Lusk Committee set up in New York investigated the state school systems, introduced loyalty legislation, and generally played havoc with freedom of speech in the schools. At the same time, the New York State Legislature barred five elected Socialists from taking office on the ground that Socialists were a potential menace to the nation.[74] The period from 1940 to 1960 was a difficult one for teachers. Progressive and nonconformist teachers were linked with communism, nativism deprived teachers in Oklahoma of their civil rights, and loyalty oaths were administered at the University of California. Liberal teachers were silenced; some even embraced orthodoxy to avoid controversy.[75] Later, governmental agencies like the CIA and USIA appeared on campuses; Professor Commager denounced their presence because they "repudiate or paralyze the principles of freedom."[76] Even reputable scholarly journals have found themselves duped by CIA "free lancers," clandestine operations that expose "the entire publishing and scholarly enterprise to suspicion."[77] Commager is strong in his condemnation of educators who were silent during the great political debates of the sixties, reserving his praise for the students who marched and protested the Vietnam war, the racial injustices of the period, and the exploitation of the university by government. Many will question his courageous stand, but he is in good company — that of Emerson, Whitman, and Wendell Phillips — in his denunciation of intellectual apathy:

If presidents, deans, trustees, and regents are unwilling to protect and exalt the dignity of the university, they should be grateful to students who have remembered it and exalted it. If universities have refused to face the major moral issues of our day, they should rejoice that they have, somehow, helped to produce students who are neither paralyzed nor timid, who are sensitive to moral issues and prepared to respond to them, however convulsively.[78]

When Johnny-College came marching home again in 1918, he was no longer the idealistic enlistee of 1917. The war had disillusioned him. Unemployed, dislocated and perplexed, he saw that the adult world had no concept of history, that all was flux, that the war had perhaps been fought in vain.[79] The college graduates of the twenties were standardized products; there were few rebels.[80] The high school was steeped in athleticism. Team stars were deified; fraternities and sororities selected their society and closed their doors upon the rest.[81] The great American paradox — a national belief in education and an indifference to intellectual distinction — troubled only a small segment of the population.[82]

What was the value of a college diploma? In the thirties John Tunis reported on the status of his Harvard classmates in an article, "Was College Worth While?" His conclusions do not exalt the Harvard degree for, while "studying that group of men, a picture developed of a group of middle-aged Americans with keen ambitions to break eighty, to stay off the breadlines, and to vote the straight Republican ticket."[83]

When one contemplates the years of study, both undergraduate and professional, amassed by the culpable, the indiscreet, and the neutralists directly or indirectly involved in the infamous Watergate scandal of the 1970s, he is appalled by the failure of their valued education to influence them morally. Many respected attorneys on the White House staff advised clients to omit, to forget, or to doctor testimony, and these were all college educated men sworn to uphold the law. How is democracy to flourish when sophisticated young men learn soon after leaving college that party loyalty, corporate loyalty, and Mammon loyalty are surer roads to affluence than loyalty to truth, to conscience, and to mankind?

An American born in 1916 and living today has witnessed wars, revolutions, massacres, famines, and racial turmoil of unprecedented magnitude. He has seen technology produce frightful engines of war. He has lived through depressions and might yet witness another one. He has seen the nation torn apart on racial issues, on conservative versus liberal ideology, on the shibboleth of law and order. Education has apparently effected little change in man's moral tone and aspirations.

CHAPTER 5

American Writers on Philosophical and Administrative Problems in Education, 1918 - 1970

To the extent that I am genuinely educated, I am suspicious of all things that the average citizen believes and the average pedagogue teaches. Progress consists precisely in attacking and disposing of all these ordinary beliefs. It is thus opposed to education, as the thing is generally understood, and so there should be no surprise in the fact that the generality of politicians are bitter enemies to all new ideas. [H. L. Mencken][1]

I   Some Problems in Education

IN *The League of Frightened Philistines,* James T. Farrell writes that "the story of Studs Lonigan was conceived as the story of the education of a normal American boy" whose saga begins during the zenith of Woodrow Wilson's power.[2] Contributing to Stud's education were home, family, church, school, and playground, but these institutions collectively failed to elevate Studs from his street-gang culture in Chicago's slums.[3] Although Studs and his cohorts seemingly enjoyed freedom from parental mores, the pool rooms, basement clubs, street society, and vocations they encountered were essentially adult-spawned and nurtured, for, as John Dewey wrote, "adults consciously control education of the immature by controlling the environment in which they act, think, and feel."[4] Unfortunately, Dewey assumes in this statement that parents are necessarily more mature than their progeny, but history nullifies any such notion. How diligently and altruistically have adults striven to eliminate the gross social injustices around them? The slums that Studs Lonigan grew up in are still with us, although they have new lodgers, mainly blacks and Puerto Ricans. Corrupt politics, wars, and intolerable economic injustices continue to plague the citizens of the seventies. To conservatives like T. S. Eliot, modern secular education is wanting in moral force. Eliot argues that "since educational theory is derived from our philosophy of life, we must regard education as a

religious problem."[5] But would Eliot be happy with Southern education, dubbed the "Baptist Seminary standard" by H. L. Mencken?
Thomas Wolfe called them "priest-ridden schools" in which
educated men denied evolution and used the Bible as an arbiter in
all disciplinarian disputes.[6] Recent theological trends in the United
States do not offer significant hope for the emergence of a
monolithic Anglo-Catholicism to gratify Eliot's disciples.

To educators or laymen who misinterpret John Dewey's advocacy
of permissiveness, the following passage should help clarify his
ideas:

> To talk about an educational aim when approximately each act of a pupil
> is dictated by the teacher, when the only order in the sequence of his acts is
> that which comes from the assignment of lessons and the giving of directions
> by another, is to talk nonsense. It is equally fatal an aim to permit capricious
> or discontinous action in the name of spontaneous self-expression. An aim
> implies an orderly and ordered activity, one in which the order consists in
> the progressive completion of a project.[7]

Perhaps Dewey's ideas on transforming the school into a center for
social change are vulnerable to criticism. If the function of a school is
to provide a simplified environment to accord individuals opportunities to escape social limitations of birth,[8] what happens to the
child when he returns to the ugliness of the slum? What indoctrination can the school give him to spare him the contradictions that
envelop him on his street, on his rambles through affluent
neighborhoods, and in his Mitty-like fantasies via film and television
fixation?

"Elementary education," writes Mark Van Doren, "can do
nothing better for a child than store his memory with things deserving to be there."[9] But the "things deserving to be there," have been
the subject of argument between educators and laymen at school
board meetings throughout the land. Robert Hutchins cautions
educators "that the purpose of education is not to fill the minds of
students with facts; it is not to reform them or amuse them, or make
expert technicians in any field. It is to teach them how to think, if
that is possible, and to think always for themselves. It is of the
highest importance that there should be some place where they can
learn how to do it."[10] If each child is taught to think objectively, can
our society exist in its present form? If each child grows into an in-
quiring Ralph Nader, he will question each act of his government,
each advertisement, each act of bigotry. He will deluge his represen-

tatives with objections should they betray the electorate who chose them. All these civic responsibilities should be taught in the schools, but even John Dewey wrote "that we are doubtless far from realizing . . . that it [education] represents not only a development of children and youth but also of the future society of which they would be the constituents."[11]

Speaking at the University of Virginia in 1958, William Faulkner emotionally instructed his hearers that, had the South heeded Virginia a century ago, perhaps the bitterness between the sections might have been avoided. In an eloquent finale, he promised:

But this time we will hear you. Let this be the voice of that wilderness, speaking not just to Mother Virginia but to the best of her children - sons found and chosen worthy to be trained to the old pattern in the University established by Mr. Jefferson to be not just a dead monument to, but the endearing fountain of, his principles of order within the human condition and the relationship of men with man - the messenger, the mouthpiece of us all. Show us the way and lead us in it. I believe we will follow you.[12]

Less sanguine about education's supposed meliorative societal potential, Theodore Dreiser presents a naturalistic philosophy in this passage from *Dawn*:

I have no quarrel with education as a serviceable means of passing the time, or giving one a method of making a living, or some little sense of the present or recent past, or of making the shifting scene more physically endurable. None. But as for counting all this more than just that, or believing that it leads to some divine far-off event, or that it is directed for the benefit of man and to end of his eventual dominance, not me. The thought of it is as petty as it is preposterous, as asinine as it is vainglorious. It is really fantastic and points more clearly to the unintelligibility of matter and of man in his relation to the whole universe than almost anything else. . . . The thing that I object to is the dull assumption that in this or that way lies the so-called "true" spiritual development or improvement or ultimate perfection of man. Bunk. A temporary means to a temporary end, a temporary experience leading to what important end? Lord![13]

Albert J. Nock, humanist, classicist, and debunker of what he alleges is pap in modern education, nears Dreiser in his fulminations against what we call progress. Although modern man has vindicated Goethe's predictions, much of this advance has been achieved without a corresponding elevation in intelligence. Cynically, Nock sees modern science as a Golem or a Frankenstein monster; lacking wisdom, we create to destroy.[14]

Paul Goodman reminds us that the word "school" is the Greek work for serious leisure. The Greeks were content to have their children play games, sing, and enact Homer in school.[15] But such progressive Greek notions are not much admired by contemporary lovers of classical humanism. Perhaps the Greek philosophers believed as T. S. Eliot did that "it is a part of education to learn to interest ourselves in subjects for which we have no aptitude,"[16] but apparently many of them studied on the elective principle. Reviewing our present systems of education, Paul Goodman finds them so wanting in aim and effectiveness that he doubts that "going to school is the best use for the time of life for the majority of youth."[17] In *The Empire City*, educator Mynheer sets forth Goodman's educational views dramatically. Mynheer's school is the city. Groups of boys aged nine or ten are chaperoned through the city to learn about life. The curriculum is revolutionary; the children are taught skills and sabotage which will enable them to penetrate corporate bureaucracy. Sabotage becomes honest service, since the establishment will not grant privileges to the people voluntarily.[18] The aim of education is to adapt the child to life in the Empire City — to temper his experience to his growing powers and to teach him to cultivate the art of nonattachment, since no one really wants to feel at home in the city. Students would study strikes, interview pickets, and examine the attitudes of stockholders, panhandlers, and job seekers.

American education is eclectic according to Walter Lippmann. Since it has no dogmatic base it lacks a system, but men proceed by "unending inquiry and debate, having agreed as best they can, because there is no other way they can combine freedom with order."[19] But accompanying the American belief in education is an anti-intellectualism that scorns the academician as an effete egghead.[20] Critics of American education, themselves products of American schools, spare no facet of the educational program.

Interestingly, when Upton Sinclair muckraked American higher education in *The Goose-Step* (1923) and lower education in *The Goslings* (1924), he was praised by some of his ideological foes and disparaged by many of his socialist friends. In brief, both of his books purported to be documented studies of the control of education by American capitalists. In higher education, trustees on college boards, indistinguishable from trustees heading the major corporations, select college presidents who are loyal to corporate interests. In turn, these captains of erudition, so named by Thorstein Veblen, hire administrative subordinates who will be safe, conservative, and loyal to the corporate ideal. In the humanities and social sciences, textbooks critical of the existing society are avoided. To divert students from careful scrutiny of their government and culture, alumni encourage large-scale athleticism. State universities face greater problems, because state legislatures are easily corrupted by local industrialists and financiers who will brook no economic heresy. Private boarding schools and academies are similarly oriented in favor of big business. And public schools, subject to the control of boards of education, which are controlled by the American Chamber of Commerce and its adjuncts, teach a narrow doctrine of Americanism to their lockstepping clients.[21]

The Goose-Step by Upton Sinclair is hardly known today; even professors of educational philosophy rarely accord it a footnote in their works.[22] But in 1923, it upset many prominent teachers, administrators, and businessmen. Not always careful in his documentation, Sinclair was warned by his socialist associates that ideological bias in the book would weaken its message. But Sinclair received support from a Tory critic who hated the ways of American education bitterly. Before reviewing *The Goose-Step*, H. L. Mencken sent this note to Sinclair: "It [*The Goose-Step*] is not only a fine piece of writing; it is also a sound piece of research. I shall let out some whoops for it at the first chance. Once the news of it gets among the colleges it should be read very widely. On all sides a revolt is rising."[23]

Another writer, John Jay Chapman, praised the thesis of *The Goose-Step*, although he did not accept Sinclair's socialism. In a letter to Sinclair, Chapman wrote: "The masses of illustrative material which you brought together speaks for you, and will remain as a valuable deposit, a sort of lurid mass of hot smouldering coals, at which historians may warm their hands."[24]

If today's educational critics do not accept Sinclair's thesis of direct or surreptitious control of their administration by big business, they nevertheless support many of Sinclair's educational criticisms. Max Lerner deplores the crowd culture of the school, the spread-eagle "rhetoric of national pride" that is substituted for democratic ideals, and the uncritical acceptance of success, power, and prestige as life goals.[25] Paul Goodman sees the schoolchildren in a lockstep atmosphere centered around extramural demands. Education becomes a rat race for high grades leading to high-salaried jobs. In the frenzied tempo of aptitude testing, achievement testing, advanced placement, and National Merit competition, the child requiring individual help drops out unnoticed.[26]

John Dewey hoped to reconcile man's political action with his economic determination. Education should be the great reconciler of "the dispositions of all members of society."[27] But Paul Goodman dismisses this as sheer naïveté, since no society will encourage reforms that might undermine its power.[28] Real or imagined threats to its security intensify the government's control over education. The atomic age, the Sino-Soviet bloc, and Russia's pioneering sputnik catalyzed governmental and corporate subsidization of American education, especially science and technology. Technicians and engineers were turned out by the thousands in the fifties, many of whom, alas, were unemployable in the seventies. A few professors protested this massive technological emphasis, but the program rolled on unchecked.[29] Two great eastern universities were almost completely funded by the government; corporations subsidized special courses and deducted the expense from their income taxes. Meanwhile, class size increased, lectures became standardized, and tutors were underpaid.[30] Lerner was dismayed; large segments of universities were converted into Armed Forces satellites.[31] And throughout all this hectic financing, the humanist languished in the background, envying his more affluent brethren in technology. Albert Jay Nock, in a sentence of masterful irony, illustrates the contempt that practical rulers have for "eggheads" and humanistic reformers: "The State has little use for men of wisdom and learning. England in 1914 would have drafted a Jesus, a Confucius - what other uses would the State have for them?"[32]

Robert Maynard Hutchins, warning that "education will at intervals be at the mercy of politicians, large taxpayers, and cranks," called upon educators to make it clear that their calling "has standards, ideals, and traditions to enforce" which can give teaching independence from pressure groups.[33] Unfortunately, the American teacher is a sycophant who follows his master's educational fiats implicity.[34] Perhaps Mencken exaggerates when he characterizes the teacher as a dupe of his masters who command him to manufacture proper Americans ready to accept unquestioningly what they are taught, what they read, and what they are told is official gospel.[35]

Less caustic than Mencken but also critical, Jacques Barzun exposed what he feared were major faults of American education, namely, too many courses, repetitious teaching, overweighted survey courses, wasteful conferences, excessive emphasis upon publication, dishonest leaves, poor writing, and vainglorious status-seeking.[36] T. S. Eliot had surveyed this scene many years before and asked: "Who shall be educated, how and why?"[37] Eliot advised nations with little money to provide a superior elementary system for their young, the greatest number of whom will never go beyond the lower school. He believed the college population should be reduced to one third of its present number,[38] a view consonant with Tory ideals. H. L. Mencken agreed. But Albert J. Nock believed that a distinction must be made between education and training. Since "most students are ineducable beyond the thirteenth year" of school it is idle to encourage them to seek the higher learning.[39] Had not the Jesuits demonstrated three hundred years ago in their *Ratio Studorium* that not everyone is educable? Education cannot raise the nation's level of intelligence. Actually, popular education has made men more gullible. But this view is hard to accept in view of the centuries of superstitious servility of peasants. William Faulkner, like Nock and Mencken, objected to an education that neglects the gifted student.[40] He saw the schools as state-supported baby-sitters staffed by indifferent and underpaid teachers. He called for a two-school system, the second one for the student who "can't or won't do the work of the first one." Color should not be a reason for assigning a student to a superior or inferior school.[41] But Martin Luther King did not trust such pronouncements of intellectual integrity. He wanted immediate equality of education for his people, despairing of the promises of well-intentioned whites to integrate the schools. In his famed letter from Birmingham Jail, he challenged the right of white people to legislate education for blacks: "For years now I have heard the word 'wait!' It rings in the ear of every Negro with a piercing familiarity. This wait has always meant 'never!' "[42]

II *The Trustee and Board Member*

Henry Mulcahy, the "radical" professor in *The Groves of Academe*, feared that he was being fired to appease reactionary trustees and fund raisers.[43] The trustees in Stringfellow Barr's *Purely Academic* are solid businessmen, loyal Republicans, and very conservative. Joe Stanforth, a trustee, is blackmailed to support Dr. Nast's bid for the college presidency. In return for Stanforth's cooperation, Dr. Nast will not publish his book exposing the trustee's shady financial dealings.[44] In *The Man Who Stole A University*, General Fenton threatens to draft the students at Wellington College who are supporting a faculty protest movement. Earlier, General Fenton had fired Ward Perry, a brilliant physicist, who was uninterested in publication. Incensed by the firing, Ward's department head tells the startled trustee: "You mouth platitudes like a ventriloquist's dummy, and you've got just that much brains. There isn't one man on faculty row who hasn't squirmed under that idiotic, dogmatic nonsense, and it's time to get rid of it."[45]

The businessman trustee is also likely to be an ardent sports enthusiast. Trustee Sayre in Howard Nemerov's *The Homecoming Game* demands the resignation of Professor Solomon for failing star athlete Blent on the eve of a crucial game.[46] Trustee Edward R. Keller in *The Male Animal* is a football fan who supports young athletes as spiritedly as he denounces young radical professors.[47]

To a handful of novelists and playwrights, trustees are like "boy scouts on duty." They are respectful, well-mannered, and exhibit a unique form of decency not readily found in other enterprises. But in most college novels trustees are more rascally. For example, in *The Worlds of Color* by Du Bois, Miss Jean du Bignon was tried and acquitted for supposedly indoctrinating her classes with the tenets of communism. To no avail. The board of trustees fires her because she is suspected of treason.[48] President Purdy, in Elmer Rice's play *We the People*, accuses Professor Hirschbein of presiding over a student protest meeting that is objected to by the dean. The business-minded board of trustees asks Hirschbein to resign or be fired,[49] a typical administrative ruse to avoid the unpleasant publicity associated with academic dismissals.

White trustees of black colleges are not portrayed favorably by black writers. Ralph Ellison's "invisible man" recalls his unfortunate role of chauffeur to Trustee Norton in his junior year at college — a one-day role that changed his life forever. The young driver saw Norton as "a face pink like St. Nicholas's, topped with a shock of silk white hair. An easy, informal manner, even with me. A Bostonian, smoker of cigars, teller of polite Negro stories, shrewd banker, skilled scientist, director, philanthropist, forty years a bearer of the white man's burden, and for sixty a symbol of the Great Traditions."[50] Norton is a romantic and speaks dreamily of man's fate to his uneasy companion: "You are bound to a great dream and to a beautiful monument. If you become a good farmer, a chef, a preacher, doctor, singer, mechanic — whatever you become, and even if you fail, you are my fate. And you must write me and tell me the outcome."[51] Alas, when the narrator meets Norton in New York City several years later, Norton does not even recognize him, nor does he associate with their earlier meeting the young man's reminder that the two were linked by destiny. In Du Bois's *Worlds of Color*, Harry Hunt, president of a black college in North Carolina, tells his peers of his feelings toward the trustees: "I've got a Board of complete sons-of-bitches, but they're cheap and inexperienced whites. If I let one steal a hundred dollars, he'll vote through five thousand dollars of needed repairs. It's their habit of direct insult in dealing with us that rankles me."[52]

III *Financial Support of Schools and Colleges*

In The Thread That Runs So True, Jesse Hilton Stuart directs a Christ-like diatribe against the politicians who starve education to death: "O hypocritical, short-sighted, ignorant politicians, living in the middle of the twentieth century, allowing schools to remain closed for lack of financial appropriations, perpetuators of continued ignorance and future crime, I at least shall go on record to rebuke you! Tax us. Tax us to death to pay our teachers. Let them work upon immortal minds to brighten them to all eternity. We educate our people or we perish. . . ."[53] But the people will not be taxed to provide better schools and better pay for teachers. In prosperous times teachers leave teaching for business careers; in hard times they are content with security. Boards of education rarely feel that teachers are hard to procure.

A nation that spends eight billion dollars annually for liquor, nineteen billion dollars for automobiles, and only five billion dollars for education is not achieving its potential.[54] Local control of education tends to dilute opposing educational viewpoints. The exodus of males from the teaching profession weakens the collective will of teachers to resist political pressures. Since an ill-paid man is not a free man, teachers have poor standing with pupils and the community.[55]

If the motivations of politicians are sometimes suspect, what motivates private donors to grant millions to their favorite schools? The classical view of radicals and liberals regarding donors is succinctly expressed by John Jay Chapman in a letter to Upton Sinclair: "The historians will be apt to say that our millionaire barons of today did no worse than other rich men have done in former ages; they attempted to enslave society by bullying and bribing the Education of Society to favor their own interests and prejudices."[56] Percy Marks opposes this criticism of donors. He writes that men donate large sums of money to schools because there is an intangible virtue in a college "that uninspired administration officers, stupid professors, and alumni with false ideas cannot kill."[57]

But many donors, like their counterparts who subsidize political campaigns, occasionally demand something from those whom they endow. Upton Sinclair, consistently a critic of college donors, has Nicola Sacco expound on the aims of donors in *Boston:* "So sometimes you see the Rockefellers, Morgans, they give fifty — I mean they give five hundred thousand dollars to Harvard College, they give a million dollars for another school. Every day say 'Well, D. Rockefeller is a great man, the best man in the country!' I want to ask him who is going to Harvard College? What benefit the working class they will get by those million dollars they give by Rockefeller?"[58]

Sinclair's trustees are two-dimensional — they are usually villains of the robber baron variety. More culpable than Harvard's donors are the millionaires who contribute to the plant of Southern Pacific University, a school that had grown enormous "upon the money of an oil king who had bribed half a dozen governments in Mexico and the United States." The founder of Ross Consolidated· Industries planned to donate a building for teaching oil chemistry to the university, that is, if his son prospered academically at the school.[59] Ernest Aloysius Saybrook, D.D., another of Sinclair's college presidents, was able to wrest large grants from rich donors by shedding tears opportunely,[60] an act that probably would repel today's sophisticated donors.

Donors occasionally stipulate that a a new course of study be added to the curriculum. In *Purely Academic*, Stringfellow Barr wryly notes that "the alphabetized list of courses an undergraduate might elect began to look like a Sears, Roebuck catalogue."[61]

In *The Invisible Man*, Ellison describes the appearance of donors at a convocation in the chapel of a black college: "Here upon the stage the black rite of Horatio Alger was performed to God's own acting script, with millionaires coming down to portray themselves, not merely acting out the myth of their goodness, and wealth and success and power and benevolence and authority in cardboard masks, but themselves, the virtues concretely."[62]

Alas for the college that offends donors. Individual offenses on campus such as pregnant girls, thefts from the library, plagiarism, alleged race discrimination, alcoholism, homosexuality, food strikes, and religious proselytism can induce a donor to eliminate the college from his list of beneficiaries.[63]

In *Native Son*, socialite Mrs. Dalton brags that her husband had given five million dollars to found and maintain "Colored Schools,"[64] and in *The Man Who Stole a University*, millionaire Harry Hertz is moved to aid Wellington College by Emory Monck, the president of the college. Donor Hertz admits that he had "never thought about higher education except vaguely as a home for underpaid professors,"[65] a naive but honest estimation of a professor's worth by a successful businessman.

IV   *Foundations*

Are foundations dedicated to the advancement of scholarship or are they adjuncts of big business, cunningly masked to give the public the impression that they are engaged in scholarly projects? Stringfellow Barr has Director Denby of the Winthrop Foundation respond affirmatively to Professor Schneider's frank question: "But is a foundation as much of a racket as a university?" Denby says the only difference between the two institutions is in detail. His job is easy but dull. Most money is given for some ill-disguised purpose thought up by a professor who will lead his team to tackle a problem which they will never solve.[66] However, Abraham Flexner, writing in the thirties, felt that foundations promoted neither conformity nor radicalism,[67] and that they were not interested in perpetuating the status quo.[68] Sinclair Lewis' Gideon Planish, as public relations man of an educational foundation, viewed the foundation as a mill that hired impecunious professors to grind out facts and write acceptable articles for the director to sign.[69]

A large portion of *To Make a World* by Theodore Morrison concerns itself with the award of a foundation grant in world affairs to Rawley College. Since the foundation desired to have Hans Richter, a nonacademic scholar, made the school's director, the faculty rejected the foundation grant.[70] Disillusioned, Richter commits suicide, a victim of foundation stubborness and faculty independence.

How true can a foundation director be to his principles? Ezra Pound scored Nicholas Murray Butler, director of the Carnegie Peace Endowment and president of Columbia University, for abandoning the cause of peace while he directed the foundation.[71] But so had others, including socialists like Upton Sinclair, who was soundly chastised by H. L. Mencken for preaching peace and acting war in 1917. In recent years, leading foundations, including the Ford and Rockefeller Foundations, have been attacked for sponsoring alleged liberal and radical projects, but these conservative protests have not appreciably altered the type of projects supported by the foundations. Adolphe E. Meyer writes:

Taking one with another, the foundations have done a good job. Granted some of their subsidies to learning have added little to our fund of knowledge, and some might just as well have been lavished on another cause. Yet one magnificent blast like the survey of Dr. Flexner [*Medical Education in the United States and Canada,* (New York: Carnegie Foundation for the Advancement of Teaching, 1910)] more than makes up for all of the dreary zeroes. Nowadays, moreover, with the cost of research reaching to newer and giddier heights . . . the foundation money is clearly a boon — indeed without it, tracking down the rarer and more exotic truths would be impossible.[72]

V *Administration of Lower Schools*

Paul Goodman does not care for modern school administration, which "isolates the individual, the groups, and the studies, and, by standardizing and coordinating them, reconstructs a social machine." Unfortunately, the machine is wasteful educationally. New York State has more educational executives than can be counted in all of Western Europe.[73] A major study of administrative practices might be helpful in reshaping American educational philosophy.

The problems confronting American educators are bluntly listed by Mr. Cleary, director of guidance of the Pequot schools, in John Hersey's novel *The Child Buyer.* Mr. Cleary complains that "I am supposed to solve and cure insubordination, goldbricking, dullness of mind, smoking, drinking, sexual promiscuity, law-fracture, money madness, suicidal selfishness, aggression, contempt for property, want of moral anchorage, fear of failure and of fear."[74] A formidable list of student problems to which he might have added racial tensions.

Fictional writers do not dwell solely on failures in our schools. Writers like Jesse Hilton Stuart try to uplift American education by stressing the sacrifices of educators. George Gallion, the idealistic principal of Kensington High School in Greenwood, Kentucky, is

Jesse Stuart's fictional counterpart. Warned by his doctor not to return to administrative work because of his weakened heart, Gallion bravely assumes the principalship of the high school which cannot attract good teachers because of its poor salary schedule. Gallion asks: "What in the hell has happened to one hundred ninety million Americans? Don't we give a damn for our youth? Can't somebody work for something that doesn't have the almighty dollar sign?"[75]

Gradually Gallion persuades gifted teachers to work with him, but the school's staff is still incomplete. Undaunted, he prevails upon the faculty to allow gifted senior students to teach — heresy from a union standpoint — and this expedient works well for the semester. Later, Gallion is plagued with another problem — stealing by boys because of hunger — but he eliminates this by offering the boys free lunches in return for work he will assign them in the school.

A dedicated urban school principal is honored by Joshua Craig in *Tales out of School*. Jim King, who heads the Millville elementary school, is told by his superintendent not to expect any help. "No complaints and you're a good administrator," is his parting advice to King.[76]

King advises frustrated teachers to handle their discipline cases individually. But when a teacher is assaulted by an aggrieved parent, King supports the teacher, places charges against the parent, and wins the respect of the neighborhood for his school.[77] Indirectly, King suffers because of his forthright action. Disgruntled students break the windows of his home and slash his automobile tires. Later, vandals break into the school, tear up textbooks, and scatter important records. But Jim King perseveres. When the new elementary school opens, he can say with pride that he has "led twelve hundred children and teachers of different races, colors, and creeds to a new promised land." He has taught them to love each other, understand each other, respect each other, and work together as one.[78]

In Edward Chodorov's play, *Decision*, Superintendent Riggs tries to match wits with a powerful political machine. Riggs heads the Citizen's Committee against reactionary Senator Dufresne and publisher Masters of the *Free Press*. When Riggs refuses to call off his campaign, Masters advises him to shun politics and attend to educational matters. Angered when he rejects the ultimatum, the reactionaries frame Riggs on a charge of sexual intimacy with a student. Offered a whitewash in return for abandoning the political scene, Riggs refuses to "play ball." He is arrested and jailed, and later is found dead in his cell, an apparent suicide. His son Tom, a veteran, vows to fight the machine to vindicate his father's name.[79]

It is common knowledge in the academic community that physical education directors and coaches are the "fair-haired boys" of administrators. There is little danger of radicalism or dissent among the athletic personnel of schools; besides, newspaper reporters and photographers give the schools ample sports coverage, a species of publicity that successfully balances the unpleasant references in the newspapers to student protests, strikes, and drug addiction. But in Principal Ek of Ithaca High School, William Saroyan depicts a fair-minded administrator defending a classroom teacher who has offended the track coach.[80]

VI *Fictional Headmasters*

The headmaster of a boy's private boarding school has unusual powers. Francis Prescott, D.D., fictional headmaster of Justin Martyn, an Episcopalian boarding school thirty miles west of Boston, reigned securely over teachers and students even in his eightieth year. Few of Martyn's graduates had neutral feelings about him; they remembered him either with hate or with love.[81] A foe of hazing and an apostle of truth, he refused to compromise his dedication to learning. In one instance he turned down a proposed $50,000 endowment by a rich father who insisted that his delinquent son be admitted to the school. Another fictional headmaster, Dr. Holt of Durham Academy, dismissed much of modern pedagogy as nonsense and proved his point by having all of Durham's students pass college entrance examinations.[82]

Dr. Holt, an adamant disciplinarian, has a serious problem with Benson Smith III. An individualist, Smith III will not go to chapel because he is an atheist.[83] Holt will not accept Smith III's protestations. He refuses to read Bishop Gore on *Christian Apologetics*. Holt roars, "Get out," gives the boy a month's detention, and compels him to attend chapel. Smith III has more brushes with Dr. Holt. Enamored of a young lady, twice divorced and the mother of a four-year-old child, Smith III finds her arbor more to his liking than Durham's precincts. But Holt tracks him down, confronts the enraptured lad and his amused paramour, and instructs Lorna to cease enticing the young man. Smith III is gallant; he unwisely but heroically tells his superior, "You talk to me, you rotten bully!"[84] Years later, a successful writer, Benson Smith III is invited to speak at an endowment-fund dinner at Durham. Recalling how Dr. Holt had humiliated him before Lorna, Smith is tempted to ridicule the old man but he cannot. Impulsively, he gives the school a greater pledge than he can afford, probably in homage to the revered headmaster who had really influenced him constructively.

But not all headmasters are praised by novelists. Holden Caulfield saw Headmaster Thurmer of Pencey as a pompous autocrat served by a sycophant faculty. Reviewing his feelings about Pencey's faculty to his sister Phoebe, Holden writes:

"Even the couple of *nice* teachers on the faculty, they were phonies, too," I said. "There was this one old guy, Mr. Spencer. His wife was always giving you hot chocolate and all that stuff, and they were pretty nice. But you should've seen him when the headmaster, old Thurmer, came in the history room and sat down in the back of the room. He was always coming in and sitting down in the back of the room for about a half an hour. He was supposed to be incognito or something. After a while, he'd be sitting back there and then he'd start interrupting what old Spencer was saying to crack a lot of corny jokes. Old Spencer's practically killing himself chuckling and smiling and all, like as if Thurmer was a goddam prince or something."[85]

VII *College Administrators in Non-fictional Views*

David Riesman categorizes three types of college presidents, namely, the president of a top college who is protected by tradition and faculty democracy; the college president of a middle college who protects himself by expert fund-raising; and the president of a lower college who exerts autocratic control over the school.[86] In 1927, Abraham Flexner gave cogent reasons for the exaltation of the American college president: "The executive is valued because the American loves administration and organization and esteems highly those charged with responsibility for it, whereas he gives less recognition to superior intellectual achievement."[87]

"How," asks John Ciardi, "can education be left to men who lack the time to read a book?"[88] Too often deans dictate policy that is properly in the teacher's domain; for example, deans frequently interfere in a selection of a new chairman. And when called upon to publicize the achievements of the college, deans often laud visual additions to the college — buildings, numbers, equipment, and alumni gifts — more than curricular innovations. With his usual flamboyancy, H. L. Mencken writes that the college president is a "so-called learned man who spends his time making speeches before chautauquas, chambers of commerce and Rotary Clubs, and flattering trustees who run both university and street railways, and cadging money from such men as Rockefeller and Carnegie."[89]

Ezra Pound wrote that some college presidents are chosen "for their sycophantic talents."[90] In 1931 Langston Hughes criticized the elderly white trustees of Hampton Institute for forbidding a student protest meeting called to memorialize the deaths of two blacks, one of them a college coach who was beaten to death by a mob. All the trustees could say was "we educate, not protest."[91]

In *The Goose-Step,* Upton Sinclair devotes several chapters to the amazing derring-do of Nicholas Murray Butler, president of Columbia University for almost four decades. Jacques Barzun attributes Columbia's greatness to "the handiwork of a brilliant empire builder," President Butler, who directed the scene "like a virtuoso conductor without crisis or rebellion."[92] Neither Upton Sinclair nor James Wechsler, author of *Revolt on the Campus,* would agree with this praise.[93] Mencken could not resist casting a minor barb at Butler "who is an absolute masterpiece of correct thought." Butler has never "cherished a single fancy that might not have been voiced by a Fifth Avenue rector. . . ."[94]

When the minimum wage law of Massachusetts decreed that the salaries of scrubwomen must be raised from thirty-five cents per hour to thirty-seven cents, Abbott Lawrence Lowell, another university empire builder, replaced the women with men. Heywood Broun wrote in protest that the education of Abbott Lawrence Lowell had not been altogether successful, since "he has failed to learn that there are things which men and colleges may not do with honor."[95] Unsatisfied with Lowell's promise to find work for the dismissed women, Broun wrote further that "a university is a living organism, and, when the heart has ceased to beat, death and corruption of flesh set in."[96]

How does one reconcile contradictory analyses in the works and thoughts of a writer? In his autobiography, *Upstream,* Ludwig Lewisohn writes that President Thompson of Ohio State had been a poor man "and he was understanding and helpful to his colleagues."[97] But in *The Goose-Step* by Sinclair, Lewisohn depicts President Thompson as an unfeeling man who summarily dismissed an excellent scholar "who did not indulge in riotous living, but found that with the increase of prices during the war his family could hardly keep alive." Lewisohn alleged that President Thompson fired this hapless professor after receiving a copy of an unpaid bill from an aggrieved department store for a pair of shoes that the professor had bought for one of his children.[98]

VIII *Fictional Adminstrators*

Novelists tend to emphasize the uncomplimentary traits of adminstrators. As education began to ape big business, the trustees sought executive types to fill presidential posts. President Engstrom of Jefferson Junior College is young, smooth-shaven, efficient, and limited,[99] remarkably akin to Shirley Jackson's clean-shaven golfer and women's club speaker who heads a college in her novel *Hangsaman*.[100] In Sinclair Lewis' *Gideon Planish*, Dr. T. Bull, President of Kinnikinick College, rose to the top rung of the academic ladder by virtue of his deceptive elegance, conversion to Episcopalianism, and business ideals. Against sloth, debt, the teaching of Greek, and the seduction of coeds, he seems woefully inadequate to guide the lives of the innocents who believe in him.[101]

Conservatism is the creed of many fictional college presidents. When the Boston police went out on strike in the twenties, Abbott Lawrence Lowell offered the city the services of one thousand students to patrol the city.[102] Howard Fast has further criticisms of Lowell; in the *Passion of Sacco and Vanzetti* Lowell is reputed to have referred to a professor of law as "that Jew," because he chose to defend "two Italian communists." Lowell proposed a quota system for Jews and other minorities at Harvard, but he found it harder to keep Jews out.[103] To Lowell's credit, however, he did defend Professors Laski and Frankfurter when hostile trustees who regarded them as radicals demanded their resignations.

The catalog of fictional college presidents is large. Edward Albee in *Who's Afraid of Virginia Woolf?* describes Martha's father as a Philistine president of a New England college who runs the college as a business, demands complete loyalty from the staff, and avoids controversies that might offend donor, trustee, and politician. His son-in-law George, a self-confessed abmaphid (A.B. . .M.A. . .Ph.D), has resigned from honest intellectual effort to please Martha's father. He will never publish and he no longer enjoys teaching.[104] The making of a college president, new style, is described in Randall Jarrell's *Pictures from an Institution*. President Robbins of Benton College taught sociology for one year, was elevated to dean of men in the latter part of the year, promoted to dean of the college of liberal arts two years later, and finally, at the age of thirty-four, proudly ascended to presidential rank.[105] Thereafter, he spent his time on fund raising tours, article writing, speechmaking, and petitioning Congress for sundry benefits.[106]

The eccentricities of fictional administrators are legion. Vridar, the hero of *We Are Betrayed* by Vardis Fisher, is astonished by the unseemly deportment of President Peter Matwick at a faculty meeting. After Matwick had admonished him not to be proud — there are great men at Watsach College — Vridar comments on the president's performance: "So this was a college president: this strutting Mormon, this humorless prig! This was the man who summoned the members of his faculty before him, and stood, short and hostile, with a clenched hand thumping his desk."[107]

Gerald Warner Brace's President Pomton of Wyndham College is reminiscent of Jarrell's President Benton. Pomton is a climber; aware that his school of education background will not help him advance, he left teaching for administration. He rarely published, but made himself known as an expert on the academic credit system. A popular speaker, he charmed Rotarians who were unaware that his speeches were ghosted by his aide, Miss Thelma Stilton, a literary genius.[108] To maintain his position, he learned to deal with trustees of dubious morality, powerful and uneducated alumni, and fatuous guests at cocktail parties.[109] When he is asked to speak at State A and M, Pomton is overjoyed. If he speaks well he might be asked to head State. He knows the formula that will please trustees: praise free enterprise and give Russia hell.[110]

Can an honest college president maintain his integrity? In *The Spire*, David Gaunt asks this question of Bill Pinney at an English department meeting, and Pinney answers him cynically: "My dear boy, no college president can retain his integrity. Haven't you found that out? He promises, he pacifies, he flatters and bribes, he plays both ends against the middle, he acts as God's personal representative — and as sure as sin he turns into a stuffed shirt."[111]

But there's another side to the coin: college executives "recognize that teachers and scholars are vain, touchy, and fanatically self-important."[112] When President Gidney's "publish or perish" mandate is challenged by members of Wyndham College's English department, he counters their objections wittily, "But often when a man can do nothing well, he assumes that he at least can teach."[113] Gidney, however, respects the real scholar who honestly believes that a dean is a sort of YMCA leader and headwaiter.[114] Deans can also be intense haters. In *No Villain Need Be* by Vardis Fisher, the deans of education and science are at war with each other. Dean William Tergaud of the sciences constantly attacks what he believes to be humbug pedagogy. Science alone is worth studying and his stinging, hot-tempered attacks upon the dean of education enliven the campus proceedings.[115]

Not all college presidents are described as villains by writers. Vridar in *No Villain Need Be* praises President Johnson for refraining from expelling Mike Rowe, the author of a supposedly obscene essay: "President Johnson is a pretty good president. He has a tough job here. . . . Imagine yourself with religious bigots trooping into your office every day and raising hell. Imagine yourself with all the fraternal orders of the city telling you what to do. Imagine yourself with a stupid and reactionary legislature. . . ."[116] Similarly, President Andrew Aiken of Rowley College will not be pressured into firing Maurice Holsberg, a rumored Communist.[117]

Rarely is a fictional college admistrator praised as highly as Emory Monck, chancellor of Wellington College, in *The Man Who Stole a University*. His dean of women, Esther Hollister, insists that he discipline a group of girls who resorted to stripping in their dormitories as a protest against the college's unduly restrictive rules. Chancellor Monck, who had been chosen by the trustees to head the college because of his financial wizardry, angers Dean Hollister by supporting the activism of the girls. A college "must provide a transition from childhood dependence into responsible adulthood," he tells her, but Dean Hollister is adamant in her denial of Monck's liberalism.[118] When Cecil Eliot, president of the student council, complains that there is no point in students making resolutions if the faculty overrules them Monck replies: "Try me. I'm the new chancellor. It's your function to set up reforms, work with the administration."[119] But Monck's liberalism and defense of academic freedom disturbs the conservative members of the board, especially General Fenton, a reactionary who believes that military discipline should be introduced into the colleges to suppress the excesses of radical students. To remove Monck from office is General Fenton's obsession. When Martha Yates, a Wellington student, steals into Monck's hotel room by posing as his wife, General Fenton is informed by ex-dean Hollister that Monck had planned the assignation. Gleefully, General Fenton, accompanied by several trustees, demands entrance into Monck's hotel suite. Happily for Monck, Denise Dempsey, whom Monck had appointed as Esther Hollister's replacement, arrives opportunely to save the day. Martha Yates and Cecil Eliot, she explains, have every right to be in Monck's suite since they were in town on educational business.[120]

In Maynard Hoar, president of Jocelyn College, Mary McCarthy creates a complex character. Henry Mulcahy, an outspoken teacher, had been turned down by many colleges because of his supposed radicalism. His friends suggested that he try Jocelyn where the liberal Hoar was attempting to discipline unruly students and hostile trustees.[121] Hoar himself had been under attack by a state legislator for harboring atheistic and communistic beliefs. What else might decent citizens expect of a man who had authored "The Witch Hunt in Our Universities"? Besides, Hoar had contributed to Vice-President Wallace's campaign fund, a truly un-American act.[122] Although Maynard had hired Mulcahy on a contingency basis, Mulcahy protested Maynard's decision to discontinue his position. The president is not pleased with Mulcahy's teaching performance,[123] and to a committee's plea to retain Mulcahy, he answers: "Can you have creative teaching side by side with the preoccupation with security, with the principle of regular promotion and recognition of seniority? God knows, in the big universities, this system has fostered a great many academic barnacles."[124] But Mulcahy has played his cards well; soliciting the support of liberal members of the faculty, he eventually succeeds in having Hoar renew his contract. Finally, believing that the college would never be rid of Mulcahy and his machinations, Hoar resigns for the good of the school, feeling that a new president might regard Mulcahy unemotionally and dismiss him without compunction.[125]

Few black teachers were hired in white colleges before 1950, and even today tokenism exists in many schools. Yet some college administrators today have gone beyond tokenism and have sometimes relaxed formal academic requirements for black teaching candidates. But in 1922, few colleges even had one black teacher. A light-skinned black might hide his racial ancestry and be appointed as in Alvin Johnson's story, "Black Sheep" (1922), a highly contrived story that successfully exposes bigotry on the campus. President Clark, sorry for Professor Harris, employs him as an instructor in elementary mathematics. But Harris disappoints Clark by failing one-third of his class.[126] The president admonishes Harris not to fail more than 10 percent of the class — "keep standards relative to the level of students," he warns — but Harris will not obey Clark's fiat. Clark is angry, and to test Harris further he orders him to give a conditional grade to the son of a banker friend. Harris refuses, but Clark is adamant. Finally, Harris accuses Clark of using his teachers as vilely as his father had used "niggers" in the South. Clark is disturbed by the word "nigger." Harris, it seems, knows the South too well. Besides, he perfumes his hair as blacks usually do. Could it be that Harris is black? Now a zealous sleuth, he traces Harris to Cleveland via postmarks on his mail. At the cottage from which the letters originated Clark is greeted by a mulatto woman. Harris is caught red-handed. The exultant president accepts Harris's letter of resignation and returns proudly and happily to his now lily-white college.[127]

William E. B. Du Bois fought all of his life to advance the education of blacks; in his realistic novels he combines history and fiction to illustrate the problems of black educators. Du Bois is not a black chauvinist. In *Mansart Builds a School,* he bitterly exposes the jealousies of black presidents who sought Mansart's job,[128] but in Mansart he portrays an unselfish, dedicated educator who believes in equal education and refuses to accept the "Uncle Tom" compromises acceded to by vocationalists like Booker T. Washington. Mansart, titular head of a new black college in Macon, Georgia, will not dishonor himself by accepting building contracts from Mr. Sykes, a board member who is also a contractor.[129] Jean Du Bignon, Mansart's light-skinned aide, further offends Mr. Sykes by insisting that he call Dr. Mansart by his name,[130] but the white Southerner is not yet ready to accept a cultured black educator as his equal.

A reprehensible but understandable black college president is created by Ralph Ellison in *The Invisible Man.* Servile to his white overlords, stern to his black faculty and black students, Dr. Bledsoe has learned that a black man can rise to eminence in the South by playing the role of sycophant. Although he rationalizes that by exacting tribute from the whites he is advancing the education of thousands of black youths, he really relishes his power as president.

At trustee meetings, convocations, and commencements, he would appear in striped trousers and swallow-tail coat, a servile harlequin happy to rub shoulders with the trustee elite.[131] Bledsoe, a statesman for the blacks, would carry their problems even to the White House. He maintained a large endowment fund for scholarships and engaged in extensive publicity campaigns to reach compassionate donors everywhere. To the novel's narrator "he was our cool-black daddy of whom we all were afraid."[132]

The young hero of the book is chastised by Dr. Bledsoe for having guided Trustee Norton through an immoral slum area. Bledsoe tells the guide he should have lied to keep Norton away from the black ghettos. The boy is shocked. Lie to a white trustee? Bledsoe becomes enraged and shouts: "The dumbest black bastard in the cotton patch knows that the only way to please a white man is to tell him a lie! What kind of education are you getting around here?"[133] The incredulous lad is shocked. Dr. Bledsoe, a black man calling his own people "black bastards." What kind of man was he? He soon finds out. Dr. Bledsoe threatens to dismiss him, even after he proposes to tell Mr. Norton of the whole affair. Bledsoe sneers. He would deny everything. No one would believe the wild story of a student. "Men like me who run the schools make it possible for the country to exist," boasts the confident president.[134] But he will not pardon the student. He allows the boy two days to pack and leave for New York City, where he will have an opportunity to earn tuition money for the next semester.[135] Bledsoe gives the boy letters of introduction to businessmen in the city, but after being refused employment by six of his supposed benefactors, the son of the seventh reads Bledsoe's letter to the startled lad.[136] Bledsoe had betrayed him. He will never admit him again to the college.

CHAPTER 6

The Teacher, the Curriculum, and the Student, 1918 - 1970

No printed word nor spoken plea
Can teach young hearts what men should be,
Not all the books on all the shelves,
But what the teachers are themselves.
For education is making men;
So is it now, so was it when
Mark Hopkins sat at one end of a log
And James Garfield sat on the other. — Arthur Guiterman[1]

I *The Teacher in the Lower Schools*

PERHAPS no other professional comes under such sharp critical scrutiny as the teacher. He must please his superiors, his board of education, his students, and their parents. In addition, his behavior is watched over by religious, patriotic, and service groups. The nation expects him to mold a race of matchless citizens. But since teachers are not magicians, they fail to convert the lads and lassies they coax, browbeat, or inspire into paragons of virtue. Ideally, as Jesse Stuart has written, "the teacher held the destiny of a great nation in his hand as no member of any other profession could hold it. All other professions stemmed from the products of his profession."[2] But how the self-made man in America would have laughed at this assertion! Commodore Vanderbilt, who boasted that he had not read a book until he was seventy, and his friends, the robber barons, had little use for teachers. Franklin, Edison, Ford, Rockefeller, and scores of other inventive and shrewd Americans had little schooling. In a land waiting for industrial and commercial exploitation, a degree in business administration served its owner little.

But if we are to have eclectic schools, let the teachers be intellectually honest, demands Ezra Pound, for "the humblest

teacher in a grammar school can contribute to the national education
if he or she refuses to let printed inaccuracy pass unreproached." In
addition, a teacher must feel a call for his profession; the classroom is
not a sanctuary for escapists. In *The Rector of Justin,* Headmaster
Prescott is interviewing David Griscom who wants to teach at Justin.

"Are you sure you want to teach, Davey?"
"If I could teach here, sir."
"No, that won't do. You'd have to want to teach anywhere to be able to
teach here — You must see more of the world first, Davey, if you're to teach
boys to deal with it."[3]

Prescott does not mention courses in pedagogy to Griscom. The
world is an ideal school of pedagogy, but the teacher must be "a man
who knows a subject thoroughly, a man so soaked in it that he eats it,
sleeps it, and dreams it —"[4] But Mencken gets out of hand at times
in his zest to shock readers. When he recommends "hanging all the
professors of pedagogy, arming the ma'am with a rattan, and turning
her loose,"[5] his humor fails. Mencken's friend Theodore Dreiser
could have told him what it is like to be educated by a ma'am let
loose with a rattan.

II   *The Good Teacher of Lower Schools*

Jesse Hilton Stuart, teacher, principal, and novelist, taught his
first class at the Lonesome Valley School in Kentucky. A high school
junior armed with a second-class teaching certificate, young Jesse
faced thirty-five students ranging in age from five to twenty.[6] To win
the student's respect, Jesse first had to thrash the class bully;
thereafter discipline was no problem.[7] But at Justin Martyn, a
private academy, discipline cannot be administered so forcefully.
Threaten the lads with poor marks, advises old headmaster Prescott.
And if this does not quiet the mischief makers, take away their
privileges. It's not a question of guilt or innocence. Impudence must
be met squarely.[8]

In Michener's *Fires of Spring,* Miss Chaloner is able to teach high
school mathematics without using discipline. Somehow, she is able
to inspire literary and graphic artistry in her geometry class, and she
stays willingly after class to teach seniors advanced mathematics.[9]

How do teachers motivate apathetic students? Jesse Hilton Stuart
cites the techniques of two successful English teachers. Mrs. Hilton
of the Plum Grove School invited her theme-frightened students to

write her letters explaining why they could not write compositions. Often, these letters turned out to be well-written themes that led the now excited students to write voluntarily.[10] The second teacher, Miss Kirsten of New York City, described her writing plans to Mr. Stuart: "I let them write their own thoughts any way they see fit. I give them all the freedom they want to express on any subject they choose to write. After they have written their themes we read them in class . . . We don't always correct all the mistakes. . . . We don't correct a mistake when it gives color and originality to a theme."[11]

Parents might be startled to see a teacher chasing a student with a harpoon during a lesson on *Moby Dick*, and they might question the sanity of an English teacher who talks about the Globe production of *Hamlet* to a bust of Shakespeare. And they would call for dismissal most probably of an old woman who hops on the desk, window pole in hand, immersed in enacting the lion-hunting scene in *Tartarin de Tarascon*. Yet, these are the types of teachers that students remember fondly. Socrates Makrites, in *Tales out of School*, delights his slumtown students with his oddities. A health faddist, he eats carrots constantly. He unceremoniously takes siestas on the school floor. He comes to school on a motorcycle, fittingly attired in a black leather jacket. A popular teacher, he visited sick children in hospitals, jailed students in prison.[12]

James Baldwin paid homage to substitute teacher Orilla Miller, who helped him in later life when he met white people who were not so nice. Teachers at De Witt Clinton High School (1939 - 1942) encouraged him to write, but he said that he hated Mrs. Whalen, the *Magpie* adviser, who boasted that she had discovered him.[13] Baldwin praised Wilmer Stone, also of De Witt Clinton, for his great teaching.

The great teacher is not always popular. When Van Artevelde, in James Gould Cozzens' "The Guns of the Enemy," refused to doff his hat at the passing of the colors of the student battalion, the students branded him as a traitor.[14] The antiwar teacher absented himself from a speech given by Major Loiseaux of the French army and further antagonized the self-righteous class by pointing out propaganda favorable to the French in the French textbooks — propaganda that only imbeciles would believe. Artevelde understands the patriotic fervor of the students; even when Potts, an irate student, knocks him down, he asks Dr. Holt not to expel the boy. Finally, Dr. Holt appeals to Artevelde to stay to guide the Sixth Form through the difficult days ahead.

III   *The Dismal Profession of Teaching in the Lower Schools*

H. L. Mencken believed that only fools teach, a belief that he shared with George Bernard Shaw. Teachers must have snarled when they read Mencken on teaching, especially this passage from *Prejudices, Third Series:* "Next to the clerk in holy orders, the fellow with the worst job in the world is the schoolmaster. Both are underpaid, both fall steadily in authority and dignity, and both wear out their hearts trying to perform the impossible."[15] Mencken goes even further in demeaning the teacher who, he writes, "must be essentially and next door to an idiot, for how can one imagine an intelligent man engaging in so puerile a vocation?"[16] We meet such teachers in fiction; for example, Headmaster Prescott's wife is bored with the pomposity of Mr. Ruggles, a history teacher at Justin, and she asks, "Why does teaching always seem to attract the intellectually flabby?"[17] A good question! According to Edna Furness in *The Image of the High School Teacher in American Literature* (1960) American high school teachers lead monotonous lives, are passive about the great issues of the day, and are generally regarded as social misfits.[18] John Updike highlights this public attitude in his short story "Sense of Shelter." When Mary Landes calls the cheerleading teacher Potbottom Porter, William Young, the girl's unsuccessful suitor, deplores her insensitivity and asks rhetorically: "Couldn't she see around teachers, into their fatigue, their poverty, their fear?"[19]

Fatigue, poverty, and fear. Young Mr. Armytage in Upton Sinclair's *Didymus* is tired, poor, and frightened. He teaches four crowded classes in high school, and he has hundreds of papers to correct weekly. But to advance in education he must complete his doctoral dissertation, "Sources of the New Testament Apocrypha." He lacks time and money to teach well and to maintain good standing in graduate school.[20] In *Mr. Gallion's School* by Jesse Hilton Stuart, good teachers are asked to teach six classes of mathematics without intervening rest periods.[21] Stuart is an idealist and approves of teachers' unions provided that they forfeit their right to strike; yet he exacts extraordinary labor from his teachers because the community is poor and cannot support good education. What he ultimately asks is that teachers become selfless, but teachers, like most other human beings, believe in a just wage for just labor.

It might be wise for teachers to tape their lessons. Might not an eighth-grade teacher blush to hear herself prefacing a lesson on "Evangeline" with this bit of nonsense? "We're coming to a long poem now, boys and girls. Now don't be babies and start counting the pages."[22]

Weak teachers are the easy prey for predatory students. George Caldwell in John Updike's *Centaur* is soft-spoken and gentle. He cannot cope with either the students or the faculty. He is ridiculed by the class, dismissed as a misfit by his colleagues, and hated by Dr. Appleton, the school's efficient, businesslike principal.[23] Sex confounds the lives of two teachers in the play "Tea and Sympathy"; malicious students accuse Tom Lee's English teacher, Mr. Harris, because he went swimming in the nude with Tom. Harris denies the rumors in an interview with the dean, but the students are not impressed and continue to associate the teacher and student as homosexual partners. Bill Reynolds, another teacher, posing as a great outdoor man, dislikes his wife's solicitude for Tom, a "fairy" who should be dismissed. But Bill himself has homosexual tendencies which his wife points out; his masculine bravado is merely a mask to conceal his true sexual feelings. Finally, after initiating young Tom into the pleasures of sex, she leaves Bill forever,[24] but Tom at least was eased into manhood by a gracious, compassionate, and suppressed woman who was wasted on a disturbed and dishonest husband.

IV   *Parochial School Teachers*

Public schools, private academies, and parochial schools all have their champions and detractors. James T. Farrell, for example, writes disparagingly of Chicago's parochial schools. St. Patrick's grammar school was a jailhouse to Studs Lonigan — forty to fifty squirming boys in a class were guarded by black-garbed sisters of Providence. Sister Carmel smacked students with a ruler's edge, and Battleship Bertha catechized the captives, taught them church history, mathematics, the Palmer method in handwriting, dull history lessons, and unintelligible grammar. Sister Bertha was old and crabby and "always hauling off on somebody," and Sister Magdalen was notorious for her "knuckling" of ill-mannered or unprepared boys.[25] Mary McCarthy was not charmed with her schooling at the Convent School of the Sacred Heart in Seattle. When the girl told her grandfather that Madame Barclay compared her to Byron, he angrily called the school for an explanation. Next day, Madame Barclay called to tell him that "Mary McCarthy did not resemble

Lord Byron in any particular; she was neither brilliant, loose-living, nor unsound."[26] Later, she was accused of reading heretical books by Father Dennis, who begs her to "give up reading that atheistic filth. Pray to God for faith and make a good confession." But Mary did not heed the admonition.[27] She had fun with the nuns as well. One of the sisters mistook blood on Mary's sheet for menstrual blood; actually, she had cut her foot and stained the sheet. Although Mary was only twelve years old, Motherly Slatterly thought that Mary required sex education. Perversely, Mary bled her leg every twenty-eight days to humor the sisters.[28]

V   *College Teaching*

The college inherits the products of the lower schools. Fearful students fill out as many as a dozen applications, burdening institutions with clerical costs that they can ill afford. Tens of thousands of students attend evening classes as part-timers because they lack full academic requirements for matriculation or because they must work full time. Since the aims of most college-bound students are vocational and social rather than intellectual, college professors have a great responsibility to teach their students that "man lives not for bread alone." Archibald MacLeish writes that "role of the teacher does not include proselytizing. Instead his function is to commit his charges to human experience, questioning, and selection."[29] But how is the teacher to avoid proselytism? How can the teacher dissociate what is happening around him from the course he professes to teach?

How can objectivity be maintained when scientists acquiesce in secrecy, as for example, in military and space research? Is not secrecy incompatible with science? asks Paul Goodman. Should teachers be the watchdogs of society?[30] In *Purely Academic*, Professor Schneider, now a director of the Winthrop Foundation, speaks sorrowfully of Professor Nast's ascension to a college presidency: "Undoubtedly the treason of the eggheads — not to their government, which they idolatrized, but to the truth, which exacts so much more loyalty than the most hysterical government dares demand — undoubtedly this treason of the eggheads was more painful to an egghead like himself than the treason of fatheads or boneheads could ever be."[31] Professor Nast believed that the economist's function was to inform the layman how wealth is made, not to reform society. In Bernard Malamud's novel *A New Life*, Chairman Fairchild exhorts his staff to avoid rocking the boat. Teach grammar, drill the students, and keep them busy with assignments was his advice. Bernstein, a militant Marxist in Farrrell's *My Days of Anger*, offends his economics teacher by denying that capitalism is the best of all possible isms for the masses. The two cannot come to terms; each believes the other is biased.[32] Similarly, George Willet, a conserver of traditionalism in *The Department*, hates young idealistic instructors who return from missions in Somaliland or Alabama as bearded world-savers convinced that the American political and educational way of life is stupid. They demonstrate, "sit-in," carry placards, and are probably mad. They are, to boot, creative writers, damnable evidence of their subversion.[33]

VI   *Teaching Requisites*

What qualifications should the teacher have besides a vague intuition that he should teach? Today's society inhibits him from emulating Chaucer's famed, impoverished clerk. Teachers like to eat well, dress well, travel, entertain, and own livable homes. But to be hired at a salary that vindicates Ricardo's Theory of the Iron Law of Wages, a teacher must indulge in self-praise that may twinge his conscience. When Theodore Roethke applied to President William Mather Lewis of Lafayette University in 1934 for re-employment, he stated four reasons to support his stand: (1) "The personality of the teacher . . . provides the leavening which makes a pedagogue, using the word in its popular and somewhat invidious sense, a genuine teacher." Roethke, of course, assured the president that he was a "genuine teacher." (2) He was widely published and acclaimed in literary circles. (3) He had written publicity for the college on athletics and general events. Save for the coaches, he knew more about the college than anyone else. (4) He had served as tennis coach, engaged in committee work, helped write the catalog, and visited secondary schools.[34]

A good teacher compensates for his ignorance by energy and enthusiasm. But he must close the gaps in his knowledge by reading widely in philosophy, history, and science.[35] In addition, writes Vardis Fisher, he should be "honest and forthright, with none of the clowning, none of the evasions and bluffing and theatrical gestures of many teachers whom he had known."[36] A man should love the subject he teaches,[37] and to be effective, recommends Ezra Pound, he should be a bit theatrical and imitative of the best professor he has known,[38] but he must also be a master of his discipline since "until the teacher wants to know all the facts, and to sort out all the roots from the branches, the branches from the twigs, and to grasp the *Main Structures* of his subject, and the relative weights and importances of its parts, he is just a lump of the dead clay in the system."[39] But will not his overspecialization narrow his vision? As Robert Sanderling regards his colleagues who are assembled to honor him on his resignation from Wyndham College, he muses: "They are all 'authorities.' Each one is presumed to know more about something than anyone else."[40]

What is the relationship between the Ph.D. degree and good teaching? Probably, administrators and scholars who support the doctoral degree view it as an expedient in the selection and advancement of personnel. Fortunately, some enlightened universities waive the Ph.D. requirement in appointing teachers who have proved themselves intellectually. On the other hand, self-conscious junior colleges have often sought Ph.D.'s to raise the status of their schools.

To most college chairmen, a promising teacher is one who intends to earn his doctorate. Instructor Levin learns from his colleagues at Cascadia that he will teach remedial grammar and composition until he gets his union card — the Ph.D. Professor Gilley warns him that in addition he had better shear off his beard — the president's wife dislikes bearded instructors.[41]

The frequently published teacher is hated by his less productive colleagues. At Benton College, article writers were frowned upon since most of the faculty did not care to publish.[42] Those who cannot write, review the books of their more fertile colleagues. Professor Spigliano, in Phillip Roth's *Letting Go*, is "a nuisance . . . to his more slothful colleagues, because he writes, as he will tell you, an article a month, and writes pathologically."[43]

VII   *The Inadequate Professor*

Because he deals with man's most precious possession — his child — the professor is vulnerable to many varieties of parental censure. Because his salary is paid by the state or partly by private donors, he is frequently the target of governmental or philanthropic censure. Since ancient times the teacher has been mocked, castigated, and harried as a timid and untalented soul, fit only, paradoxically, to teach the nation's young. Mencken is unkind to many teachers when he assumes that 95 percent "are of low mentality, else they would depart for more appetizing positions."[44] Willa Cather writes that: "America has long been the paradise for poor teachers." Commercialized education has made the ordinary professor utilitarian, political, and self-interested,[45] and to the dismay of America's students their teachers are for the most part unattractive and sexless.[46]

Bill Sanders, the college treasurer in *Purely Academic*, purportedly speaks for the nonteaching staff when he characterizes professors as "a special class of kept women" who compete fiercely with one another, insult students, snub nonteaching personnel, and clamor for higher wages.[47] Like Mencken, Ezra Pound accuses American professors of stupidity; they "lack curiosity, are ignorant of history, and their experts offer only bunk to an ignorant people."[48] They are naive, too, notes Vridar in *We Are Betrayed:* "Professors think students who sit before them and stare wide-eyed are listening," and they believe that those who ask many questions are interested.[49] The student plays his part well, better, perhaps, than his teacher. Professor Schneider in *Purely Academic* damns college teaching that "is uniquely organized for the destruction of conversation and the production of bores. In what other profession does a man expect a large audience of adolescents to write down whatever he says?" Often, the student cannot take notes because the teacher speaks over his head or lazily drones out to nodding students "the anemic and wordy bookishness" which he calls learning.

Teachers do not seem to work well collectively. Faculty meetings in *Purely Academic* are chaotic and usually the president controls the proceedings, although the faculty might block the president had it the will to oppose him. But how can a faculty that "can't change ideas — either in a formal meeting or at a cocktail party" unify to challenge administrative dogmatism?[50] Even a meeting to determine standards for grading papers leads to disaster. In *Letting Go*, Chairman John Spigliano astonishes the English department by giving a D to a paper that Paul Herz had awarded an A minus.[51]

VIII   *The Problem of Standards*

When teachers cannot cope with unsuccessful students, they frequently blame the students' poor secondary schooling. In *Purely Academic*, Professor Schneider resists administrative pressure to lower his standards, complaining that "I'm passing people now who can't write, can't spell, can't punctuate, can't think. It's shocking."[52] In *Time Out*, a novel attacking the emphasis upon football in American colleges, Joe Marks submits the well-known seashore scene from *David Copperfield* to Mr. Poodle, his English teacher, who gave him an E for the paper, his standard grade for anything turned in by Marks. Determined to teach Poodle a lesson, Marks states his case to the dean, a reasonable man, who has Marks submit a passage from his book on classical education to Poodle for his next theme. Amazing! Marks receives his inevitable E. The dean is disturbed, but he will not fire Poodle. Instead he transfers Marks to another class.[53] In *A New Life*, Levin tries to have a plagiarist in his class disciplined. His chairman, who dislikes Levin, transfers the accused student to another class, leaving the bewildered teacher feeling helpless and neglected.[54] Sex, too, sometimes influenced a teacher's grading. Gideon Planish at Kinnikinick College "looked at girl students who came to him prettily to raise their marks from C minus to C," and as he taught he was disturbed by the generous display of pulchritude as he swept the aisles with his voyeur eyes.[55]

IX   *Explaining the Inadequate Professor*

Critics of contemporary college teaching are blunt in their exposure of alleged shortcomings of the teacher. Riesman accuses many college professors of reading nothing weightier than *Life* or the *Saturday Evening Post*.[56] C. Wright Mills types the college teaching recruit as plebeian, narrow culturally, and handicapped by lower-middle class traditions.[57] Much earlier, Mencken had unreservedly classed Ph.D.s as imbeciles, epitomized in the person of Woodrow Wilson, the scholar-statesman who stupidly arrived at Paris before learning of secret peace treaties that would undermine his contemplated panaceas for world harmony.[58]

It is unfortunate but true that some teachers hate teaching. F. Scott Fitzgerald alleges that he fought with some of his English teachers at Princeton so vehemently that he had to drop English.[59] But it might be that his artistic spirit rebelled against their authority. Possibly, he achieved early success in writing because he unconsciously ached to vindicate himself in the eyes of these professors who "hated teaching." Hate for teaching may be sublimated into a professed love for learning. George Willet, a "varsity scholar" in *The Department*, attends all professional meetings, uses the terms scholarship and research with reverence, but never contributes anything to scholarship or research.[60]

X   *The Timid Scholar*

Can a teacher live happily with himself and others if he must diminish the truth to avoid offending his masters? Can a salaried man contractually hired assert himself in opposition to the educational aims of a state or private institution? Ludwig Lewisohn, who examined the teaching profession in 1923 in his autobiography, *Upstream,* asked, "Who and what are these American professors?" and answered his rhetorical question pessimistically:

They are not the servants of an idea or of a passion of the soul. Most of them could easily have been something else. They went into teaching either because they had a pleasant taste for learning and no particular taste for anything else; or because they were timid and of a retiring nature and didn't like the rough and tumble of the business world. Or because — in an appalling number of cases — they simply drifted into the academic life. Thus there is among them little intensity or power, little courage or independence, much pinch-beck dignity, and lust for administrative twaddle.[61]

In *American Inquisitors,* Walter Lippmann agrees with Lewisohn's strong indictment of timid teachers, adding that the profession "has not valued its own dignity sufficiently to command the respect of the community.[62] In times of crisis teachers tend to be ostriches, and if they are decent chaps, comments Ezra Pound, they will get nowhere because of their timidity.[63] Pound writes that servile professors "are worse than Jewspapers" — an elegant coinage — and "lie for hire and who continue to lie from sheer sloth and inertia and from dog-like contempt for the well-being of all mankind."[64] Rather than be taught by unmanly teachers, students would be better off out of college, Paul Goodman advises.[65] Of what benefit is learning ladled out by academics who avoid controversy, give tacit approval to authoritative commands, and impose self-censorship?[66] *In Take Her, She's Mine,* Sarah Walker, a coed, decides to cloister herself in college. She will take her master's, then her Ph.D., and ultimately teach since the real world is so wretched.[67]

Liberal teachers find it expedient to remain silent. In *The New Life,* Professor Fairchild dispraised President Roosevelt's socialism daily, but no one questioned him.[68] John Ciardi flayed liberal arts teachers for betraying their profession. In one instance, a liberal arts faculty actually begged corporation executives to define the type of graduate they preferred; in turn, the corporation continued supporting the college.[69]

XI   *Professional Ethics*

Teachers are their own severest critics. Would physicians ask of themselves what Bill Pinney in *The Spire* asked of his fellow teachers after he left an English department meeting — "Did you ever see so much assembled vanity, hypocrisy, affectation, and general masculine atrophy?"[70] Mary McCarthy exposes similar defects in her fictional backbiting dons in *The Groves of Academe*. Their academic lives seem to be wasted in endless factional disputes, idle debate, and demeaning polemics.[71] In Saul Bellow's *Herzog*, Sandor Himmelstein denounces intellectuals who are "sunshine patriots" but who refrain from visibly supporting a man pilloried by bigots.[72] President Engstrom advises Professor Sperry in Upton Sinclair's *CO-OP* to leave agitation to the young men, but Sperry rejects Engstrom's advice. The young teachers are too concerned with their own advancement to risk crusading for truth.[73] Professor Fabrican in *A New Life* does not support the Committee on Textbook Selection's choice of a new textbook for the English department, since he is up for promotion and does not want to jeopardize his chances by opposing the chairman.[74] Professor Gilley, who is attuned to community concern about obscenity, tells his staff that, although he too had read "Areopagitica," colleges have to be practical as well as idealistic. His concern is the story "Ten Indians" by Hemingway, which is viewed as dirty by several townsmen.

The genteel tradition emasculated many professors. Paul Shorey was upset because Santayana had satirized Harvard College in Europe. "It was not quite nice of him," complained Shorey in an address given before the august members of the National Academy of Letters.[75] To insure advancement in higher education, Gideon Planish converted to Episcopalianism, since New York or Washington progressives demanded that or atheism;[76] interestingly, Upton Sinclair charged in *The Goose-Step* that Nicholas Murray Butler had become an Episcopalian to ingratiate himself with the lords of Columbia when they were seeking a new president.[77]

XII   *The Low-Paid Professor*

In 1927 Abraham Flexner wrote about the economic serfdom of the professorial class: "I cannot overstress this statement: College and university teachers are part-timers. To their proper business of teaching and to the passion for research which inspires the best of them, they can devote only that time that is left after carrying on their academic routine and after earning through lectures, summer work, popular writing, translating, expert service, the sums which they need to balance the family budget and, worse still, to carry on their scholarly and scientific research."[78]

At Mary McCarthy's fictional Jocelyn college, the salary range for teachers was from three to five thousand dollars. Most of the teachers were young and unmarried. Since young couples would earn livable incomes as "husband and wife teams," salaries were deliberately kept low.[79] To supplement their marginal earnings some teachers engage in hackwork similar to the writing done by Gideon Planish's "intellectual commandos" for a quackish encyclopedia of which he was a sponsor.

XIII   The Good Teacher

But there is some balm in the educational Gilead. Teachers find themselves remembered by their successful students. For example, Walter Lippmann praised Professors Graham Wallas, William James, and George Santayana as profound influences on his thought. In his autobiography, A Mass for the Dead, William Gibson pays homage to his teacher of literature at City College, a little man, merely five feet tall, but an inspiring and honest critic. Gibson writes:

"I looked forward to each conference in his cubicle as to an assignation; there, knee to knee in a roomette jammed with small desk, two chairs, and noonday lamp, he dissected my manuscripts with respect, my first teacher, a childless Jew, whose buttony eyes on me achieved what the bishop's slap on my cheek had not, welcomed me to an act of communion."[80]

James T. Farrell's fictional professors Carlton and Darland in The Silence of History are also praiseworthy. Darland enjoyed ridiculing sundry gentlemen of means "who are possessed of the peculiar delusion that the stork brought Adam Smith, trailing clouds of wealth, only yesterday morning."[81] Edmund Wilson's Professor Grosbeake in I Thought of Daisy is a true teacher who was at home in literature, philosophy, and science. Fortunate was the student who heard him trace the consequences of discoveries in relativity and quantum physics for the concepts of general philosophy and construct a system to fit them.[82] James Michener's "Doc" Chisholm, a man who had doctored horses on a ranch, taught English at Dedham without the benefit of a Ph.D. His classes were delightful; unlike many English teachers who become narrowly addicted to their speciality, he ranged freely through numerous universes of discourse, bringing "the wind of freedom from all nations" to his worshipful students. He played the guitar, sang with his students and was loved as a friend and teacher.[83]

The enthusiasm of a student for his teachers is lovingly expressed by Vridar in *No Villain Need Be* by Vardis Fisher:

There was John Boardman, professor of physics: a militant and hard-headed scholar whose scorn for most of his colleagues was an unwavering brightness in his eyes. There was Abraham Haroldson, professor of philosophy: a giant of a man who had about him a weary astuteness, as if the political chicaneries here bored him to death. There was Miles Rowan, professor of biology, who ignored faculty meetings and stuck to his laboratory and his work. These men and a few others were not everlastingly jockeying for position and privileges; never, so far as Vridar knew, stooped to that underground gossip which was a disease in the school; and never played to their classes with clowning and faintly odorous jests.[84]

XIV   *Two Major Writers on Teaching*

A philosophy teacher usually cannot earn a livelihood away from the university, but a first-rate poet or a novelist can. Although Robert Frost taught at Amherst for some years, he was able to command a program that did not divert him unduly from his writing. Granted a full professorship by President Alexander Meiklejohn, Frost taught but two courses and had liberty to read his poetry elsewhere.[85] In a letter to Louis Untermeyer, Frost wrote: "I'm imperfectly academic, and no amount of association with the academic mind will make me perfect. It's too bad, for I like the academic in my way, and up to a certain point the academic likes me."[86] One academic in particular irked Frost to distraction. Unable to tolerate Stark Young, who he said "was a bad moral influence on the students," Frost asked President Meiklejohn to fire Young. The harried president appealed to Frost to be more reasonable; students, he said, needed a variety of views. But the impassioned poet resented Meiklejohn's imputation of anti-intellectualism and resigned.[87]

Frost disliked faculty meetings and faculty clubs, but he had warm sessions with his students at Amherst. He met with them in a beautiful room — an eclectic lot of philosophy, literature, economics, and science majors — to discuss literature and poetry.[88] In 1923 Frost discussed his teaching methods with Rose C. Feld, who wrote up the interview for *The New York Times*. Asked about his methodology, the poet said: "Well, I can't say you can call it teaching. I don't teach. I don't know how. I talk and have the boys talk. This year I'm going to have two courses, one in literature and one in philosophy. That's funny. I don't know much about either. That's the reason perhaps we get along so well."[89] A nonconformist in the classroom, Frost abhorred lectures, quizzes, grading, and busy work. He was especially kind to undergraduates thought queer by their fellows.[90] He describes his unusual thematic pedagogy in a letter to Louis Untermeyer: "After giving a class a chance to say if there was anything in the bunch of themes on my desk they wanted to keep and satisfied myself there wasn't, I threw them unread into the waste basket while the class looked on. If they didn't care enough for the themes to keep them I didn't care enough for the themes to read them. I wasn't going to be a perfunctory corrector of perfunctory writing."[91]

Perhaps it is fatal for a literary genius to teach undergraduates. How poor Thomas Wolfe tormented himself and his students at New York University because his creative urge was checked by his painful communication with students. How he brooded as he planned *Of Time and the River!* In a ruled notebook in the Houghton Library lie the frantic scrivenings of a man bursting with volcanic force: "My bewilderment and my despair — I close up suddenly — the lust for knowledge and recognition — the feeling of impotence — the books in the Widener Library — the hordes of people on the pavements — to know all things and try all places — the recourse to poetry — my enormous feats of reading — utter rebellion from the group — sullen resentment for the group."[92]

Wolfe rejected teaching early in life as inhibiting to the flow of genius, but as was — and still is — the case with unfound genius he had to become a teacher to live. He accepted an instructorship as Washington Square College, New York University, that earned him $1,800 for a seven-month year. At first the contract pleased him, for he was required to be in school only three hours daily, a schedule that would surely give him ample time for writing. But Wolfe was insecure in class. He expecially feared supervisors who "puritanically and haughtily" observed the chaos in his classes.[93] Wolfe invited a colleague to observe his teaching. Russell Kraus was unimpressed with Wolfe's drowsy and uninspired lessons, noting that the novelist was repetitious in teaching poetry.[94]

In *Of Time and the River* Wolfe, reveals his intense distaste for teaching. He corrected endless numbers of trivial themes — enervating drudgery — and was frustrated with brilliant Jewish students like Abraham Jones, who wrote flawless papers but who demanded individual consultation that he thought superfluous. A merciless grader, in his last semester he was unduly vindictive toward his perplexed students.[95] Wolfe showed his contempt for his students by returning their themes six weeks after collecting them. In class he lectured and read literary selections; he did not encourage class participation.

In *The Web and the Rock* he characterizes New York University as a "School for Utility Cultures," harboring a faculty of "venomous surly fools."[96] Two eminent and esteemed New York University professors, Thomas Clark Pollock and Oscar Cargill, ascribe Wolfe's hostility to the English department's alleged restrained reception of *Look Homeward Angel*. But Henry T. Volkening, a colleague of Wolfe, defended Wolfe's castigation of the department. Volkening noted that Wolfe was disgusted with his students, especially with his Jewish students whom he termed "tortured intellectuals." He struggled heroically to be patient with them and at times expressed sorrow for their painful expenditure of energy in their drive for knowledge.[97] But how could he keep them from sensing his contempt? In *Of Time and the River*, he describes his classroom teaching dramatically, but many of his contemporary colleagues and students do not believe that "he took those . . . swarming classes and looted his life clean for them: he bent over them, prayed, sweated, and exhorted like a prophet, a poet, and a priest — he poured upon them the whole deposit of his living, feeling, reading, the whole store of poetry, passion, and belief. . . ."[98] But this martyred tone cannot hold; finally, he cries out: "I have worked too hard, giving my brain and my heart to those stupid little fools; talking like an angel or a god in language too few of them will understand."[99] Here the maker and the teacher are at odds. The artist has too little time to spawn his mind-soul gifts; the teacher rarely sees his thought take root. The artist, scientist, and writer deal in tangible wares. To them are awarded Nobel laurels, but who has ever suggested that an unpublished teacher who has guided and inspired children to achieve meaningful lives be awarded international homage?

XV   *The Curriculum of the Lower Schools*

The teacher's learning, interest, skill, and compassion enable him to cope successfully with a reasonably motivated student. But can a brilliant teacher inspire dull pupils? Will he not usually just encourage bitterness? In *The Rector of Justin*, Professor Dahlgren advises an English teacher not to blame himself for failing to reach most of his students; only a handful of students will ever see the light. But his guilt-stricken colleague, Brian, feels obligated to save more than an elect few.[100]

Educational ax-grinders who long for the "good old days" have an excellent champion in Uncle Wadsworth, defender of Appleton's *Fifth Reader* and readin' and 'ritin' and 'rithmetic in Randall Jarrell's *A Sad Heart at the Supermarket*. His nephew Alvin objects. In the little, red schoolhouse there was no mention of civics, social studies, home economics, manual training, and extracurricular activities. Also, there were the hickory stick and its abominable applications.[101] But Uncle Wadsworth brushes aside Alvin's objections. He urges Alvin to scan the *Fifth Reader*. Alvin complies and is astounded. "L'Allegro" in the *Fifth Reader*? Why, he had read it as a sophomore in college. And worse yet, Appleton's *Fourth Reader* includes Gray's "Elegy" and selections from Wordsworth.[102] Uncle Wadsworth sees that he has Alvin on the run and strengthens his advantage by lecturing his nephew:

Alvin, about school-buildings, health, lunches, and responsibility, kindness, good humor, spontaneity, we have nothing to learn from the schools of the past, but about reading with pleasure and understanding, the best that has been thought and said in the world — about that we have much to learn. The child who reads and understands the Appleton's *Fifth Reader* is well on the way to becoming an educated, cultivated, human being — and if he has to do it sitting in a one-room schoolhouse, if he has to do it sitting on a hollow log, he's better off than sitting in the Pentagon reading *Days and Deeds.*[103]

There is a problem with Uncle Wadsworth's hypothesis. Who can test his assumptions? What evidence is there extant that fifth graders actually understood literature that today's college freshmen frequently find incomprehensible?

But Uncle Wadsworth has contemporary allies. Mark Van Doren questions the sincerity of schoolboys who tag a course as interesting. "Nothing that is not disciplined," he wrote, "can be interesting long."[104] In the same vein F. Scott Fitzgerald cautioned his daughter not to take courses that she could get an A in. "Take hard courses," he urged. "Those that are easy learn by yourself."[105] Accordingly, he recommended that she elect all mathematics courses, chemistry, and two languages. He himself had disliked English courses — "I learned about writing from doing something I had no taste for" — and insisted that she follow a scientific discipline even if it displeased her.[106]

Latin is Dan's nemesis in Farrell's *Father and Son*. Father Michael scolds the failing lad for his poor Latin grades, but Dan is not awed by his frocked mentor. "After all, Father, I'm a live guy and Latin's a dead language," he said.[107]

Conservatives and radicals alike attack the schools for turning out unreasoning students. Albert Jay Nock writes that: "By accepting what he reads in his schoolbooks as gospel, the student becomes an unthinking, prejudiced citizen."[108] Upton Sinclair has Vanzetti speak on education in *Boston*. Some people are interested in war he admits, but why? "Is it not teach in school? Who maka da school? Who maka giornale, da newspaper?" Vanzetti continues: "Sometimes I t'ink it mistake for teach istoria. People study tempo passato, make conservativo, timido. . . ."[109] An Italian workingman in Elmer Rice's *We the People* echoes Vanzetti's words. After being told by Miss Davis, his son's teacher, that Tony had spoken disloyally of the war, Louis Volterra sadly rebukes her: "In da school, too, you teacha da lettla kids war."[110]

Robert Frost strongly opposed watering down the high school curriculum. To prepare children for high school, he advised purposeful courses in reading, writing, and arithmetic. The high schools, he advised further, should give entrance examinations, not aptitude tests. Education should not be sped up; instead, it should be toned up.[111] In sharp contrast, Paul Goodman's experimentalism offers the elementary pupil an exciting format. Professor Mynheer in *The Empire City* sees the city as a classroom. In the subway students have living subjects for scrutiny. There they can study behavioral attitudes and learn to observe and record experiences. The street and sidewalks lend themselves to geometric study; the cornices of buildings illustrate architectural values. The handball courts — sometimes the walls of buildings — are arenas for the study of ethics. In the restaurants the young watch food prepared and perhaps taste the many preparations. Outside again, they observe the traffic lights — their timing and colors. Finally, students are encouraged to write letters — pro and con — of their impressions of the city.[112]

XVI   *The College Curriculum*

College students who cannot write effectively disturb their exasperated English teachers. English should be taught by Englishmen on the college level, and all students should be made to pass rigorous writing examinations.[113] So pontificates Edmund Wilson, and Ogden Nash supports him, especially in the case of education majors whose letters are "grammatical abominations."[114]

Humanist Moses Hadas acknowledges that English teachers have to teach spelling and punctuation and, at a more advanced level, "'creative writing,'" but he would prefer English teachers to dwell more on the literary legacy of the past and "with why and how it came to be what it is."[115] Unfortunately, Danny O'Brien in *My Days of Anger* is disheartened by Professor Donovan who represses students who dare discuss politics in a literature class. To Mr. Farrancini, who had initiated the political debate, Professor Donovan is a narrow martinet who cannot brook interdisciplinary communication.[116]. Danny sadly soliloquizes after Donovan's lecture: "He wanted everything, every kind of education. And look at what he was getting — one year of catch-as-can pre-legal work, and then the long, plodding study of law. He despaired of ever becoming truly educated."[117]

Danny's disillusionment has been experienced by legions of students. The reluctance of schools and teachers to present history honestly has, according to Albert Jay Nock, deprived young men of the ability to see through the political humbug and corruption of their times. Without a true sense of the past, a man is unprepared to cope with the present.[118] For example, in the thirties professors taught "the law of diminishing returns" as economic gospel without taking into account the technological advances in agriculture,[119] and other professors never explained why the market for foodstuffs had dropped and why the Federal Reserve Board "raised the discount rates for loans to farmers."[120] And how could students really appreciate history when teachers and talented students sold "ponies" to reluctant readers of the past?

Physical education, too, has its literary critics. Phillip Stong considered physical education wasteful and of doubtful benefit to youth. He could make more money beating carpets than waving his arms in the gymnasium.[121] Vardis Fisher painted physical education teachers as sly tyrants, seeking only to better their own fortunes. The faculty itself was partly to blame. One faculty meeting was particularly maddening to Fisher's autobiographical hero, Vridar. Why did reasonable men waste hours debating whether a student lacking three-tenths of an hour in physical education might graduate? Or whether physical education is better than all other courses?[122] Phillip Stong invented interesting metaphors to highlight his scorn for campus military courses. "You are sent to college a piece of academic catmeat," he wrote, "to develop whatever individual qualities you may chance to possess — then you deliberately spend two hours or so a day learning to act like the dumbest mechanized ballerina in the rear row of a troupe of trained fleas."[123]

In Ronald Forman's anti-football novel, *Time Out*, he has a football hero speak disparagingly of the college's uncultivated teachers, the administration's inordinate concern with money, and the inadequacy of the curriculum. Sex, social relations, and understanding of people are neglected courses; they are either omitted or glossed over in one or two cautious lectures.[124] Robert Benchley has his fun with the elective system; "French 1C, Exception to the verb *être*, and Botany 2A, the History of Flowers and Their Meanings." are examples of the watered-down courses that lulled him to sleep.[125] Shirley Jackson complements Benchley in *Hangsaman*. Natalie Waite attends a female college that encourages informality, drinking, and gambling. The elective system includes courses in modern dance and slang, but physical education is discouraged. Here the motto is, "theory is nothing, experience all."[126] Jacques Barzun warred against courses in "Cosmetology," "Advanced Ice-Cream Making," "Police Science," and "Fire Science."[127] Albert Jay Nock concurred; he felt that it was asinine to give degrees to majors in bricklaying and retail shoe merchandising.[128] Willa Cather considered the urgency of state legislatures to create university departments of business administration, experimental farming, dressmaking, and mechanics a threat to departments of science and humanities.[129]

Even the traditional curriculum is wanting. In *Fires of Spring*, David is disappointed in his college courses. English is dull, history pedantic, and French even sadder. In science, classification and drawing are the mainstays of a disgustingly taught subject. Phillip Stong reports similar frustration biographically; English is really advanced high school rhetoric; German is a continuation of high school language study, and Biblical Literature is no more than a discussion of familiar myths.[130] The college course could easily be completed in three years if properly administered. Southern Pacific, in Upton Sinclair's *Oil*, has similar problems. English is taught painfully by a bored young man; the Spanish teacher has a French accent; sociology is no more than a series of artificial abstractions; and history texts are scrupulously examined to preclude irking the feelings of Pete O'Reilley, the university's great endower.[131]

Departments of education are scored mercilessly. Mary Ellen Chase saw them as useless. Instead, she proposed that future teachers master their subject matter and look to good teachers to model themselves after.[132] H. L. Mencken callously derided the schools of education, especially those that specialized in learning situation, integration, challenges, emphasis, orthogenics, mind sets, differentia, and all the other fabulous fowl of the teachers college aviary. Jeeringly, he advocated that all candidates for the berths in the grade schools be exposed to the Simon-Binet Test and that all who revealed a mentality of more than fifteen years be rejected.[133] General education courses have also been attacked. Archibald MacLeish grants that these courses are pleasant, but since they are patronized by apprentices who rarely go back "to glimpse again the vistas they momentarily glimpsed" the apprentices will always remain apprentices.[134]

XVII   *The Classics*

To traditionalists like Albert Jay Nock, the classical curriculum will always be the bedrock of a good education. Greek, Latin, mathematics, metaphysics, and the history of the English language are invaluable courses.[135] T. S. Eliot deplored the neglect of Greek and Latin studies among linguists, historians, and writers. The American elective system has diminished the interest in classical studies: consequently, American culture has not attained its potential. But Eliot associates Latin and Greek with Catholicism — the arch foe of materialism — and damns an educational system that surrenders to materialism. A liberal society tolerates Latin and Greek. Radical societies replace Greek and Latin studies with science, an absolute rejection of religion and humanism. Since all education must be religious, a good society, that is, a Christian society, must have Greek and Latin roots.[136] Eliot, however, seems anachronistic in his medieval longings. He hopes for the expansion of monastic life to preserve Latin and Greek. Uncontaminated by worldly barbarism, the order would teach education for values unassociated with place-seeking, technical efficiency, or education for leisure. The secularization of the world makes it mandatory that Christian people develop an education "both for this world and for the life of prayer in this world."[137] But Eliot's hope for a renaissance in classical studies seems doomed; neither in cloister nor in school has there been a major movement to accord ancient glories to Greek and Latin.

XVIII   *Humanities and the Liberal Arts*

Concerned with the artistic and intellectual legacy of the race, the humanities find few sincere lovers in an age of business and technology. College students candidly report that their basic aim is to earn a substantial income. Moses Hadas correctly sees the humanities as informing and enriching the students' sensibilities, "not to prepare them for professional work in a given field."[138] Mark Van Doren almost deifies the liberal arts: "They involve memory, calculation, and measurement, and call for dexterity of both mind and hand. Without these powers no mind is free to be what it desires."[139] To give the young a sense of tradition they must be taught to revere and love the world's great books. But even where God and the humanities are emphasized, stockbrokers and snobs are manufactured in lots.[140] In Malamud's *A New Life*, Instructor Levin protests to his chairman that a college without liberal arts is heartless, but the practical-minded Gilley replies to naive Levin that neither the sudents, the practical farmers in the region, nor the conservative state legislature care for liberal arts.[141]

XIX   *The Curriculum and the Writer*

As a rule, college curricula do not affect the success or failure or professional writers. William Gibson hated his years at the College of the City of New York. Since his required courses left him no time for learning, he left the college to learn on his own.[142] F. Scott Fitzgerald admitted to his daughter that he had chosen his curriculum at Princeton on silly premises,[143] and James T. Farrell dropped out of the University of Chicago three times and finally decided that college was not suited to his aims.[144]

XX   *The Negro College Curriculum*

W. E. B. Du Bois fought diligently to broaden the scope of black college curricula. In *Mansart Builds a School*, unions and businessmen try to force the courageous Mansart to vocationalize his college. The unions, fearing black intrusion into their trades, order Mansart to limit the college's offerings to cooking and house serv-- ices. The poor whites who envy Mansart's education and position threaten him, but he is unflinching. Later, the white trustees of the college order Mansart to restrict his curriculum to cooking, cleaning, plowing, and harvesting, but he argues for the introduction of liberal arts courses instead. They compromise. For the present the college will have the curriculum of a modern high school, but eventually it would be permitted to train students for life and for matriculation at Northern graduate schools.[145] In 1941, at a convention of Negro Land Grant Colleges, Du Bois proposed that black colleges make a study of the needs of black communities and prepare educational programs to meet them. In addition, he resolved that a broad study be made of blacks' economic problems, including a census of blacks, their jobs, and their vocational potentials. Finally, he proposed a continuing study of the changing status of the Southern black. To facilitate such studies he recommended that social science departments in black colleges be strengthened; the colleges should include courses in world history, American history, African history, and local organization of black society.[146]

XXI   Student Attitudes Towards Learning

Can college be a meaningful experience to students who receive degrees but evade learning? Ezra Pound complained with reason "that young men are now lured into colleges and universities largely on false pretenses.[147] In *Judgment Day,* Studs Lonigan overhears college boys discuss their parents' "philanthropy." A workingman, Lonigan envies these unappreciative lads and regrets that he had neglected to attend high school and college and never "belonged to fraternities and had a good time."[148] Upton Sinclair's college students in *Mountain City* are in college either to please their parents or to acquire what they vaguely term a "broadening" education.[149] The matriculants in Stringfellow Barr's *Purely Academic* are a pathetic lot of rote learners taught by "tired, underpaid, repetitious, frustrated professors." The students studied just enough to get grades "that would add up with other grades to get them a diploma."[150]

Many students, who merely want to enter well paying professions, are academic misfits who should really be apprentices in the trades.[151] Pampering the reluctant learner will ruin him, wrote Robert Frost, who had two educational mottoes regarding students: "Those who will, may," and "those who won't, must." Fortunately, the free-born students will study independently and hate "an order to do what they were about to do of their own accord."[152] In illustration, Jesse Stuart's rural students at Winston High, a band of boys and girls whom he inspired, worked heroically to defeat a large urban high school in a curriculum match.[153] Stuart could hardly keep pace with his knowledge-hungry students; perhaps it was coincidence that brought his young intellectuals together, but it is doubtful that they would have risen to scholastic distinction without his guidance.

That much maligned student, "the greasy grind," generally surpasses his socially elevated peer after the sheepskin tournament is over. Even at women's colleges there is social scorn for the diligent student. Molly Michaelson complains in the play, *Take Her, She's Mine*, that the only way you can get honors at Hawthorn is by being an absolute grind. "You've got to work all the time and turn down dates. And if you do, people look at you as if you're absolutely queer or something."[154] In *Catch 22*, Major Major, a brilliant student, is regarded by his associates as possessing homosexual or communist tendencies.[155] Perhaps one of the best fictional representations of the greasy grind is Abe Jones, a son of Jewish immigrants, who is a student at New York University. Although Thomas Wolfe has praised the Jewish student as "burning in the night" to achieve intellectual and professional eminence, he disliked his Jewish students who were vulgar, malodorous, unkempt, and undisciplined.[156] In *Of Time and the River*, Abe Jones exasperated Eugene Gant with his blunt criticisms of his teacher's theme topics, his choice of bad texts, his proscription of Jewish authors, and his infrequent private conferences. Galled by Jones' carping, Gant loses his temper, calls the startled boy "a damned dull fellow" with a "damned Jew's face," and caps his tirade by shouting, "To hell with you. I never want to see your face again!" But Abe was not to be dismissed by this cossack of the classroom. Servile and in tears, he begged his tormentor for forgiveness: "I don't want to leave your class. Why that's the best class I've got! Honest it is. . . . All the fellows feel the same way about it."[157] The boy's misery touched a compassionate chord in Gant: "His gray ugly face as he stood there polishing his glasses had that curiously naked, inept, faded and tired wistful look that is common to people with weak eyes when they remove their spectacles; it was a good and ugly face, and suddenly Eugene began to like Abe very much."[158] According to Professor Pollock of New York University, Abe Jones had not asked unusual questions of his instructor; Wolfe, apparently, disliked criticism or questioning and he suppressed his students with his torrent of Southern rhetoric.[159]

How does a sensitive instructor deal with difficult students? Perhaps in "Of This Time of That Place," Dr. Joseph Howe should have immediately sensed that Ferdinand R. Tertan, was pathetically insane, but Howe was young, idealistic, and inclined to favor literary prodigies. Tertan was proud to be taught by Howe, a poet, critic, and lover of the arts. Howe also had to deal with Theodore Blackburn, Tertan's foil. A fawning, distasteful campus politico, Blackburn succeeded in conning teachers and deans into passing him, although he was a Philistine of the first order. Grading time tore at Howe's conscience. What grade could he give to the precocious but severely disturbed Tertan, author of novels, tracts, and philosophies never to be published? And how to divest himself of Blackburn, who fawned, threatened, and begged him for a passing grade which he could not earn. Blackburn's paper was a mess, but Howe weakly submitted to Blackburn's forceful rhetoric and gave the whimpering student another examination.[160] Unable to face Tertan, Howe avoided the poor lad's upraised arm in class, but his conscience dictated that he approve Tertan's candidacy for the Quill and Scroll Society. Meanwhile, he had given Blackburn's second paper a C to rid himself of further dealings with him, but Blackburn vindictively referred to a poor review that an eminent critic had written of Howe's latest book of poetry. Howe lost his patience and quickly changed the C to an F. But he relented once more and passed the now humble Blackburn, who thanked him for his kindness. Howe tried to justify his dishonest grade to an exultant Blackburn: "You didn't pass my course. I passed you out of my course . . . [because I] wanted to be sure that the college would be rid of you."[161] At commencement, the innocent dean links arms with Blackburn and Howe as Tertan, expelled because of his madness, surveys the respectable academic scene and utters "instruments of precision" — these three words epitomized the superficiality of the commencement, the faculty, the dean, and the students. Howe ran after Tertan but he was too late. The mad boy had disappeared. Despairingly, Howe faced the gowned assemblage and the clickings of well-aimed cameras.

Perhaps novelists delight in academic ills since utopias are rarely exciting. Are graduates of the Wharton School of Business actually as imbecilic as Joseph Heller claims in *Catch 22* — as dull as a girl "who couldn't count up to 28 each month without getting into trouble?"[162] On the other hand, are college curricula so dull that brilliant students cannot tolerate courses measured out in credits per unit? William Gibson, a brilliant writer, could not affect interest in his courses at the College of the City of New York. Because he refused to take examinations in any course but English he was expelled.[163] F. Scott Fitzgerald bought books in postcollege life to master subjects he had had difficulty in. In illustration, he possessed three hundred books on the Napoleonic era, a course which he had failed in college.[164]

Intelligent students who write themes for their lazy classmates cannot have much respect for their professors. Phillip Stong charged his clients $1.00 for an A paper, fifty cents for a B or C paper. Stong justified his encouragement of plagiarism since many architectural students for whom he had written C papers might have left college, depriving the world of great bridge and tunnel builders.[165]

Although modern students are curious to learn, they are under great pressure to conform to the seductions of pleasant affluency which, grieves William Faulkner, takes from them their individuality.[166] Too often, writes Morris Raphael Cohen, "college students are looked upon as children who are to be taken gently in hand by men of mellowed conformity and indoctrinated against radical ideas.[167] Robert Hutchins said his college classmates were "the most conservative race of people in the country."[168] But in 1917 John Reed boasted that "heresy has always been a Harvard and New England tradition." Had not Harvardians always criticized the faculty, mocked the fraternities, and attacked athleticism?[169] Students in recent decades have demonstrated that they are not easy dupes of a static, affluent, middle-class authoritarianism, but Art Buchwald attributes student protests to the absence of their teachers, a satirical hyperbolization that will astonish the majority of teachers who are not full professors lecturing abroad, writing books, or drafting presidential reports.[170] Buchwald, happily, does not neglect administrators in his academic diatribe. During student demonstrations at one college the chancellor was away on a fund-raising tour, the vice-chancellor was testifying at the state capital, the dean of men was attending a convention in Phoenix, the dean of women was addressing a garden club, and only the chief of campus police was "minding the store."[171]

In *The Man Who Stole a University*, the girls conduct a sleep-in, protesting rules abhorrent to them. They are hauled into paddy wagons after the security chief on campus charges that the militant girls turned water hoses on the police, hurled bottles at them, and threatened to burn down the dormitory.[172] A sympathetic professor briefs the president on the incident. Protest is the American way, he argues. Women have to demonstrate for their rights, since the old ways of seeking redress are useless. Besides, the girls have a right to a full sex life on the campus. Secretiveness induces guilt feelings and frigidity in women.[173] In a spoof of the female dissident, Phoebe and Henry Ephron tell in their play *Take Her, She's Mine* how a young woman pickets to free Bertrand Russell from jail two weeks after his release and dogmatically breaks her engagement with her fiancé because he supports Goldwater.[174] Some professors see student protests as battles against humanistic tradition. But the militants retort that the conservative humanists in the universities have rarely supported any movement to liberate man from spiritual or physical bondage. They point to mythic and historic beings that endured calumny and death for ideals. Of what value are the myth of Prometheus, the death of Antigone, the martyrdom of Socrates and Jesus, the heroism of Bruno, the prophetic pronouncements of Lovejoy, Garrison, and Wendell Phillips, if those who profess to know are silent in adversity?

In *The Groves of Academe*, Mary McCarthy catalogs a strange and forbidding student body — the eccentrics at Jocelyn College, repository for the unloved, the neglected, and the precocious. Jocelyn welcomed "angry only-children with inhibitions against the opposite sex — wild-haired progressive school rejects — remedial deposits by concerned parents, offspring of broken homes, sexually adventurous youth, fourteen-year-old mathematical Jewish prodigies with violin cases — peroxided blondes. . . ."[175] Theodore Morrison also composes a fictional catalog of student eccentrics in *The Stones of the House*. Dean John Abner of Rowley College sees his students as homesick, frightened products of divorced parents who coerced them into attending college. Among these unhappy scholars are cheaters, liars, pansies, and alcoholics for whom he can do little, since a jealous faculty inhibits him from participating in programs that might help the sorry misfits.[176]

Even among the "normal" students apathy and purposelessness reign. In *My Days of Anger*, Dan O'Neill sadly regards his bored classmates at the University of Chicago, most of them parsimonious readers who dislike discussion and expect passing grades for their mere presence in class.[177] At Jocelyn, students pass the hours dreamily, as if under a compelling hypnotic restraint.[178] The dullness of the Yale undergraduate whom John Trumbull had so amusingly satirized in 1770 is apparently a timeless characteristic of college students. In his introduction to the *Harvard Book*, William Bentinck-Smith includes this indictment of the undergraduate from a *Harvard Alumni Bulletin* of 1925: "The true enduring picture of the contemporary undergraduate will never be written, chiefly because his life, like that of any normal, average person, is hopelessly dull. We must have spice. We must peer over the escarpments of license and liberty if we are to look at all upon the young gentlemen who walk in the sequestered vale of the Academe."[179]

The American student is represented as apathetic, but he is not characterized as a social Walter Mitty. Smoking and drinking had been social hallmarks of high school students for many decades prior to their discovery of the more exhilarating stimulation of drugs. The initiation of youth into sports, cheerleading, and fraternity life in high school prepared them for similar frivolities in college. The private preparatory school, especially, introduced middle and upper class students to snobbishness, but Louis Auchincloss endows his fictional Justin with a puritanical tone. Headmaster Prescott favors manly pursuits for boys, but inhibits their natural instincts for laughter and exploration of life beyond the campus. Pure lads would shun drugstores, magazines, and girls. Two boys alone tempted the devil; therefore, he encouraged group recreational activities. Students both feared and respected him; all were touched by his histrionic flair.[180] He was a relentless judge . When a sadistic master found three cigarette butts in a hut, Prescott ordered all of the boys' huts demolished. When one of the boys protests, Prescott thunders, "We all share in original sin."[181] Julian, the young dissident, plots to lock the headmaster in his study, but he and his three fellow conspirators are discovered and brought before their inflexible judge. At first the quartet is silent, but after Prescott declares them dismissed Julian confesses his leading role in the plot. But Prescott will not backpedal; the boys were silent at a critical time. Angered Julian cries out: "I saw you weren't God. I saw that you don't believe in God. Even as yourself as God. I saw you were only a cardboard dragon."[182]

The American college student seeks status by joining fraternities, writing for the college paper or year book, singing in the glee club, running for student office, and having love affairs in the dormitories. Actually, his social life on campus is a copy in miniature of the world without; snobbery, competition, generalities, democracy, frivolities, and occasionally kindness are employed to meet the hectic demands of campus culture. The big man on campus resembles the business leader, banker, politician, and manufacturer who are his unprofessed go-getting idols.[183] For many students extracurricular bypaths are taken to render the scholarly regimen tolerable. Proms, May Day festivals, YMCA sessions, class get-togethers, cheering practice, chapel, class plays, and homecomings consume much of the student's educational time.[184] In Percy Marks' *Plastic Age*, Professor Hinley castigates his class for ostracizing truly cultured students, conforming to fashions in dress and grooming, scorning poetry lovers, adoring athletes who are actually professionals, worshiping mediocrity, supporting discriminative fraternities, and consciously practicing snobbery.[185] Seduced by the glamor of sports, they are blinded to the true purpose of a university; the renowned professor is hardly noticed.

The militant students of the sixties had their counterparts in the twenties. Despite prohibition alcoholism was rampant at Harvard. Students rioted less for ideology than for excitement, although newspaper accounts were probably exaggerated. At Drake University, according to Phillip Stong, sexual continence was unknown. The naive freshmen of one roistering fraternity all had sexual relations with a hired woman who unfortunately had gonorrhea. Each of the passionate freshmen learned, as Sophocles wrote, "that wisdom comes through suffering."[186]

Even female colleges conformed to this ritualistic nonsense. In *Hangsaman*, girls are initiated at night. Some are asked to reveal the status of their virginity; others are requested to tell dirty jokes.[187] In Mary McCarthy's bizarre Jocelyn College, students spike the punch at parties, carry hip-flasks on the dance floor, neck freely, and even smoke marijuana with impunity as their chaperons look away. The beer and convertible crowd at dances was comprised of the sons of ex-bootleggers, racketeers, movie agents, and advertising genuises who came to Jocelyn as a last resort.[188]

To Johnny O'Brien the fraternities at the University of Chicago compensate for the anti-Catholic professors — they believe in evolution — who dominate the school.[189] Usually, James T. Farrell's hard-working college boys, all Irish Catholics, dream of playing football and consorting with the good fellows of a fraternity, but in *My Days of Anger* his hero learns how snobbish fraternities are. And Michener's bookish David was ignored by fraternity scouts in *Fires of Spring*. They feared that a student who read too much might be a radical. Fraternities invariably practice racial or religious discrimination. In *We Are Betrayed*, David Roth rationalizes his allegiance to his fraternity: "Being in a frat makes it easier for me to get along. I can go to some social flings. . . . Now and then a Christian smiles at me. And that is quite a gift to a Jew."[190] Blacks have their fraternity problems too, even if they are straight A students and play on the freshman basketball team. Delta Gamma Rho, the oldest fraternity in *The Man Who Stole a University*, balances its clientele beautifully: There are the jock straps, the brain, and the bread in this ancient order.[191]

Eugene O'Neill was not fond of his campus experiences. In

Strange Interlude he mocks Sam Evans, a perennial undergraduate who wears the latest college fashions and is happiest when he is mistaken for a college man. But Stedman Harder in *The Moon for the Misbegotten* is even more affected in adult years by his undergraduate experiences. His greatest ecstasy in college came when he was tapped for an exclusive senior society to which his father had donated millions. Harder was a pleasant fellow, but he was immature, lethargic, and stupid.[192] F. Scott Fitzgerald was unhappy with his college club after he was suspended from its lordly numbers for indulging in fisticuffs. Although he termed the trial unctuous and hypocritical, seven years later he wrote a complimentary article about Princeton, tolerantly admitting that one bad week does not make a bad full session.[193]

Nelson Algren praised his college dean for opposing drinking and sexual license, practices that Albert Jay Nock had frowned on at his college. And Upton Sinclair, muckraker, radical, and foe of drinking and sexual excesses, contrasted the women's university in Yenan with American universities and found our schools inferior. One thousand girls lived in two hundred caves in this strange school. They paid no tuition, but they attended to all of the school's chores, including two hours of laundrying each morning. Here students came willingly to learn without the lure of football, jazz, petting parties, and fraternity politics. But American educators might chide him for praising colleges that are politically monolithic and subservient to the state.

XXII *Graduate Study*

Once past the winnowing scrutiny of a legion of dons the triumphant undergraduate may elect to continue his schooling. No longer an academic adolescent more or less attracted to the glamorous games of campus life, he hopes to find self-fulfillment in graduate or professional study. But writers are as critical of graduate schools as they are of the lower schools. Robert Hutchins, in illustration, chides professional schools for their failure to be self-critical. It is undoubtedly easier for the legal, medical, scientific, and business professions to police their specialized precincts than it is for the humanistic professions to supervise their uncertain territorial bounds, but it was Abraham Flexner, intrepid iconoclast sans the seal of Apollo, who goaded conscientious medicos to shut down the barns and lofts purporting to house medical schools.

After observing the antics of Harvard's graduate students, Thomas

Wolfe thought that a period of hard, manual labor should be a requisite for matriculation at a graduate school.[194] In *Of Time and the River*, he accuses the graduate students in Professor Hatcher's celebrated drama class of escapism, a charge frequently made by critics of the Ph.D. candidate.[195] But escapism is only one of many faults ascribed to graduate students. Too many graduate students are so intent on their majors they neglect the ideas of the greatest writers, scientists, and philosophers.[196] Stringfellow Barr accuses teachers of debasing the spirit of learning; in *Purely Academic*, Chairman Nast of the economics department will not grant degrees to graduate students unless they could get employment.[197] Du Bois scores the faculty of the University of Chicago for limiting the number of black Ph.D.s by grading their examinations unfairly.[198]

Irate because the University of Pennsylvania had not offered him a teaching position, Ezra Pound wrote a violent letter of protest in 1928 to a probably astounded secretary of the alumni:

The matter of keeping up one or more otiose institutions in a retrograde country seems to me to be the affair of those still bamboozled by mendicancy, rhetoric and circular letters. In other words what the Hell is the grad. school doing and what the Hell does it think it is there for and when the Hell did it do anything but try to perpetuate the routine and stupidity that it was already perpetuating in 1873?

P.S. All the U. of P. or your damn college or any other goddam college does or will do for a man of letters is to ask him to go away without breaking the silence.[199]

Pound's hatred is echoed by an unnamed educational critic cited by Jacques Barzun in *The American University*. Advising a novice professor, the aggrieved critic deplores the "everlasting angling for place and promotion . . . the emphasis upon specialization, minutiae, and trivia." Finally, the correspondent characterizes teaching "as one of the bitchiest professions in the world."[200] To Upton Sinclair, an inveterate foe of the business-oriented college, Harvard's Graduate School of Business Administration, founded by President Lowell, a millionaire, to put a "gloss on the crudities of commercialism," had grown with such speed "that it was turning matters about, and taking a lot of the gloss of Harvard."[201]

Although experience has shown that purposeful students who elect to write on controversial topics do not suffer appreciably from doctoral inquisitors, Ph.D. candidates tend to be politic, cautious, and neutral in writing and discussion. Frequently, the candidate is advised by his committee to get his degree and then write a book that expresses his point of view strongly.[202]

What happens to the older graduate student who for a variety of reasons cannot complete his studies? Theodore Solotaroff portrayed the depressing fate of this hapless course-wanderer in his painfully realistic article, "The Graduate Student: A Profile": "Exploited by a research or teaching job, subject to the dislocation of his inner and family life, disarmed by the genteel authoritarianism of the academic will, he has become habituated to the feeling that the deeper questions of personal purpose are not worth asking and that the risks of intellectual freedom, passion, and nonconformity are not worth taking.[203]

In Barth's *End of the Road,* Jacob Horner passes his orals but will never complete his thesis.[204] His doctor advises him to drop the project and teach prescriptive grammar at a little teacher's college in Wicomico — sensible therapy for the plodding Horner. Phillip Stong ridicules the thesis examination for the master's degree. The candidate who has paid "robotish" attention to the superficial lectures easily negotiates an examination that includes "the resources by which an uninspired, insensitive, unversed little mutt could wave an M.A. at some tiny cow-college or high school and make $100 a year more salary than a mere B.A. could."[205]

To unhappy graduate students, Robert Frost offered the following advice: "If you have piled up a great rubbish heap of oily rags in the basement for your doctor's thesis and it won't seem to burst into flame spontaneously, come away quickly and without declaring rebellion. It will cost you only your Ph.D. union card and the respect of the union. But it will hardly be noticed even to your credit in the world. All you have to do is to amount to something anyway."[206]

Perhaps Frost is right, but genius is limited and of what value are his words to the steady but mediocre scholar? Yet, Ph.D. dissertation debunkers enjoy unearthing weird, useless, and ludicrous theses. Jacques Barzun castigates the composers of the large numbers of "swollen compendiums of compacted knowledge";[207] H. L. Mencken discovers nothing worse than the Ph.D. thesis in "the literature of astrology, scientific salesmanship, and Christian Science"; Stringfellow Barr adds fictional humor to the catalog of thesis baiting in this unlikely title — "Prepacking in Chain Groceries Considered As Customer Stimulation Toward Slightly Deteriorated Fresh Vegetables";[208] and James T. Farrell writes jocosely in *My Days of Anger* of a girl who is preparing a thesis on dish washing.[209]

Thomas Wolfe earned the enmity of his Ph.D. colleagues at New York University by calling them small seekers after facts who talk of writing but never write. A poem in his notebook revealed his deep antipathy for his learned colleagues:

Epitaph on a Ph.D. Man

Here lies a noble scholar
More musty than his books.
A tireless grubber after facts
A layman overlooks;
Who sucked the words of dead men dry,
Of new ones a despiser:
He left the world a duller place
But not a whit the wiser [210]

Jacques Barzun opposes the emphasis upon research, postdoctoral publishing, and contractual writing in the university. Unfortunately this stress on specialized research diminishes the intellectual breadth of the university and inhibits the development of "well educated persons in the university faculties, in college teaching, and in the nation at large."[211] But there is a place for the gifted research scholar in the Institute for Advanced Study, for in this haven for great scholars there is no regimentation; free men pursue their specialties without being burdened with teaching or administrative responsibilities.[212] No department heads impede their investigations; only one faculty meeting in seven years was held at the Institute.[213]

CHAPTER 7

Educational Values, 1918 - 1970

The perforated acoustic tiling above his head seemed the lining of a huge tube that would go all the way: high school merging into college, college into graduate school, graduate school into teaching as a college-section man, assistant, associate, full professor, possessor of a dozen languages and a thousand books, a man brilliant in his forties, wise in his fifties, revered in his seventies, and then retired, sitting in a study lined with acoustical books until the last time for the last translation from silence to silence, and he would die, like Tennyson, with a copy of "Cymbeline" beside him on the moon-drenched bed.[1] — John Updike

I   *Academic Freedom in Nonfiction*

CAN scholars in universities endowed by wealthy donors or underwritten by state legislatures challenge the premises of orthodox social, economic, and political mores with impunity? Jacques Barzun piously avows that teachers who "indoctrinate captive audiences have no right to cry infringement of academic freedom if censured or fired."[2] But how precise is the demarcation between freedom of speech and indoctrination? In a sense, all teaching is indoctrination. To avoid backlash from sincere believers in the omniscience of the composers of the Constitution, a history teacher might refrain from introducing his students to Beard's *Economic Interpretation of the Constitution*. Such passive teaching is tantamount to indoctrination since the omission might induce unexamined acceptance of partial truths.

Archibald MacLeish writes that, "since schools and colleges have a particular responsibility for the individual mind, the support of academic freedom is a support of all freedom."[3] In clarifying the teacher's role in the classroom, MacLeish says that the objective teacher commits his students "to the human experience of the human mind and the human soul — in the profound and never questioning confidence that if they truly taste of that experience, if they truly see the choices of their lives, they — they themselves — will choose."[4]

Thorstein Veblen, Upton Sinclair, and H. L. Mencken denounced teachers as timid and impoverished sycophants, not materially elevated in purpose and status from Washington Irving's hapless Ichabod Crane. Mencken, untainted with Marxist viruses, nevertheless denounced many of the celebrated fortunates who were assailed earlier by Veblen and Sinclair. Mencken ridiculed college professors as rubber stamps, ignominiously yielding to the inanities of their masters. Those who dared stand up to their tormentors were unceremoniously dismissed, slandered, and blackballed.[5] Hutchins exaggerates perhaps when he charges that the Southern universities were largely responsible for the Civil War, since they consistently refused to examine arguments against slavery and secession; however, it is conceivable that academic debate on these issues might have influenced the politicians and voters.[6]

Ezra Pound, unhappy with his teaching post at Olivet College in Michigan, declared that there was more truth in Fascist states than in American universities,[7] a belief that prompted him to broadcast Axis propaganda during World War II. Theodore Roethke believed himself to be the victim of academic oppression for teaching what he thought to be the truth about World War II. In a letter to Stanley Kunitz, he attributed his inability to relocate to Hunter College to his outspoken lectures.[8] Joseph Wood Krutch was proud of his classmates at Columbia University; one of them, Emery Neff, was fired from a small denominational school for corrupting the youth with immoral readings from the satanic works of George Bernard Shaw.[9]

Paul Goodman, repeating Upton Sinclair's criticisms, wrote that the colleges have to be conformist because the spineless professors protect administrative policy, which is frequently antithetical to academic freedom.[10] In a college that is barren of innovation, boldness, and even dissent, there can be no education. Occasionally, a college president hires prestigious teachers who outshine the others, but ultimately there are three classes of professors: the gripers, the men, and the empty smirkers.[11]

Robert Hutchins, a humanist not particularly admired by the left, spoke up strongly against the "red-herring" crusade of Senator Joseph McCarthy. Alarmed by the imputation that the colleges were inundated with hordes of assorted pinks and reds, administrators patriotically eliminated courses tinged with crimson hues and views and substituted vague curricula on Americanism.[12] In 1954 the National Education Association, until recently wary of associating itself with suspect unions, announced that its study of 520 school systems uncovered great danger to American freedom in the political crusade to unearth subversives in the schools. To immunize themselves against censure, thousands of teachers discreetly avoided contact with the germs of ideas.[13] Hutchins warned that super-patriots were attempting to stifle "freedom of teaching, inquiry, and discussion."[14] C. Wright Mills listed in *White Collar* some of the agencies and laws that he said were eroding academic freedom, namely, the Hatch Acts, business and political associations, trade organizations, army training programs, and restrictive foundation grants.[15]

Following in the tradition of Washington, Jefferson, and Madison on the role of religion in public education, Archibald MacLeish opposes those who would include faith or religion in the curri-culum.[16] If the teacher is made to teach religion, can he be truly a free man? Furthermore, history does not show that compulsory teaching of religion has advanced mankind's lot. Are not corrupt politicians, dishonest businessmen, and gangsters who profess a belief in Christianity too conspicuous in our society? And would instituting religious instruction at Yale to counter materialism and Marxism actually improve the student's moral character?[17] William F. Buckley, Jr. survived the supposed libertarian regimen at Yale, but not many of Yale's undergraduates, Buckley fears, possess his will, learning, and inspiration to ward off the Marxist temptations of the devil in red.

In 1902, two decades before Upton Sinclair startled the academic world with his muckrake of the universities, John Dewey naively asked how could a man with money "interfere directly with freedom of inquiry?" Surely, "no respectable university administration would defy public and academic opinion."[18] But one is tempted to ask: "What if the administration is not respectable?" Sinclair's thesis, namely, that university boards are controlled by businessmen, was challenged by many of his socialist friends. Although Robert Morss Lovett wrote that "education to be meaningful must cease to flatter nationalistic and capitalistic ambitions, and lay aside its 'pomp and ceremonies' which conduce mainly to sycophancy and cant," he later lectured Sinclair for unduly demeaning the University of Chicago. Lovett's response to Sinclair's thesis is similar to many other rejoinders to *The Goose-Step:* "Sinclair's explanations are too simple. They are explained in the light of one motive. Not all cases of academic freedom are the results of the actions of the ruling classes — nor are they specifically the results of the present social order. Intolerance may transcend the bounds of economic selfishness or religious bigotry. A college situation may involve not only trustees and a president, but faculty, alumni, and students."[19]

According to Brooks Atkinson, Harvard University was a rock of tolerance and freedom when World War I broke out. When intolerance swept the nation in the name of war effort, one still had the precious right to think, speak, and dissent at Cambridge.[20] Archibald MacLeish praised Harvard's professors who preserved its heritage of academic freedom in periods of national crisis. At the funeral of Percy Bridgman, MacLeish spoke of Professor Bridgman's work and of the spirit of freedom that pervades the university: "One felt the passage of time and the passage of life, and the meaning of the passage of life and time in this place: the high commitment, the intellectual passion, the pure integrity. It was almost as though the life of the mind had been made palpable and one were in it."[21]

II *Academic Freedom in Fiction*

In fiction, as in nonfiction, the perils to academic freedom are numerous and disquieting. Vardis Fisher includes a well-stocked catalog of administrative sins in *No Villain Need Be*. Vridar, Fisher's autobiographical hero, fears for his instructorship at Wasatch College for allegedly teaching the nondivinity of Jesus. Unfortunately, his stupid and prejudiced students, who cannot understand his sophisticated exegesis, sacrifice him unremorsefully. But the same intolerance prevailed in the Deep South, in the Mormon schools, and in the North where Scott Nearing had been dismissed with thousands of other bold teachers. Unable to abandon Ferdinand Thomas, a radical who had been dismissed from four American universities, Vridar wrote a letter in Thomas' defense which in essence is an indictment of the American way of education. Since "education in a democracy, supported by public taxes, and directed by boards of businessmen, must defer in all important matters to the prejudices and superstitions of the community it is supposed to serve," wrote Vridar, "it is futile, then, and it is stupid, to deplore want of education in a country in 'which there is no demand for it. . . ."[22] Fortunately, Vridar found some relief at last at New York University, for here, after a hellish period at Utah, truth meant freedom and courage.

Upton Sinclair rarely had kind words for President Abbott Lawrence Lowell of Harvard, who "boasted of complete academic freedom at Harvard, qualifying his remark that this was possible only if you hired the right professors."[23] Yet in *The Goose-Step*, Sinclair pays grudging respect to Lowell for unequivocally supporting Professors Harold Laski and Felix Frankfurter against the attacks of irate trustees who resented the pair's "radicalism." Sinclair's college presidents are of one cloth; President Saybuck in *Mountain City* will not have his teachers of economics teach the Single Tax Theory of Henry George,[24] and in *CO-OP* President Engstrom fires Professor Sperry who had been subjected to attacks by a small group of vociferous reactionaries for his liberal utterances. Engstrom is fretful. He dislikes firing Sperry, but the teachers' opponents are powerful people who could harm the college if Sperry were to remain. After his dismissal, Professor Sperry is feted by The American Civil Liberties Union, but the teachers' agencies have no work for him.[25]

One of Sinclair Lewis' disagreeable characters, the hypocritical Gideon Planish, participates in the activities of the Citizen's Conference on Constitutional Crisis in the Commonwealth, an antilabor, anti-Semitic, know-nothing organization that encourages schoolboards to throw out "unpatriotic" textbooks and recommends right-thinking professors for college posts.[26] Planish advises that literature should oppose Bolsheviks like Emma Goldman, H. L. Mencken, and Clarence Darrow. He is opposed to suffrage for women, knows that Sacco and Vanzetti were guilty, blasts the Weimar Republic, and hell-fires smoking, drinking, evil dancing, and giggling in darkened cars.[27]

Fired for being outspoken, Professor Thorpe in *The Fires of Spring* speaks dramatically in his last class lecture:

If I had been willing to shut up and stifle my beliefs, turn my back on what the world knows, I could have been your teacher for a long time to come. You can be sure that the old men in politics or religion or art or even education will always hate to the death young men with new ideas. That's why, if you're young, you've got to fight so desperately for what you know to be true, because it won't be long before you're one of the old ones. Then all you can do is hate.[28]

Experience and history contradict Thorpe's generalization. The senior professor may envy youth without wishing harm to his aspiring colleague. Perhaps "crabb'd age and youth cannot live together," but generation gaps in learning need not preclude respect between old and young. In Gerald Warner Brace's college novel, *The Department,* Robert Sanderling, an English instructor, is never told what to teach, is never spied upon, and is never summoned by an investigating committee to explain his work or attitudes.[29] Yet there were aging men on the faculty who might have caused him grief had their hearts been bursting with hate for the young.

Ideology, not hate, is the motivation for the attempted suppression of academic freedom in *The Male Animal.* Professor Tommy Turner is resolved to read the last letter of Vanzetti in his English class, but the trustees will not tolerate this. When an editorial appears in the college newspaper defending Turner's stand, Ed Keller, a trustee, sees this as the deathblow to endowments and the loss of a new stadium. But Turner informs the angry trustee that "this is a university! It's our business to bring what light we can into this muddled world — to try to follow truth!" Even the dean warns Keller that the faculty will not tolerate forced teaching. Keller replies contemptuously: "Do you think that Bryson and Kressinger and I are afraid of a few dissatisfied book-worms who work for twenty-five hundred a year?"[30]

Socrates, Bruno, Servetus — how far will men go for truth? How guiltless are the innocent? Dwight Macdonald interviewed a Nazi death camp paymaster whom the Russians proposed to hang. He is bewildered. "Why should they? What have I done?" His innocence of guilt provoked Macdonald to write: "Only those whose are willing to resist authority themselves when it conflicts too intolerably with their personal moral code, only they have the right to condemn the death-camp paymaster."[31] In *The Days of Simon Stern* by Arthur A. Cohen, the Messianic Mr. Stern devotes his energies and his millions to save the swiftly disappearing Jews of the Holocaust. As the Allied armies plod on to victory, a scorecard vision appears to the anguished man. One million gone; two million gone; three million gone. In anger he blames all of mankind for the apathy with which they regard the searing spectacle. Four million gone, where are you O liberal Westerners and why can't you bargain with your doomed enemies for the pitiful remnants they still are decimating? We know of the fifth and sixth millions. Gone. And Jacques Barzun writes that the intellectual defeat in Germany "can be attributed to the misuse of the university for a combination of political ends and pure research." It is dangerous "when specialists usurp the ranks of philosophers and educators." One might ask of Germany in 1933, "Where had all the teachers gone?" And the preachers? And the philosophers? But Barzun is even more frightening. He quotes Frederick Lilge who "is not sure that the American professoriat would resist better than the German in a comparable situation."[32] Who is guiltier, the paymaster or the professor?

III   *The Athletic Scene*

Academic freedom is a morbid topic especially when it leads to questions of relative responsibility for war crimes. Athletics is a happier subject, particularly when the flamboyant Mencken tackles college football, a sport that "would be much more interesting if the faculty played instead of the students, and even more interesting if the trustees played. There would be a great increase in broken arms, legs, and necks, and simultaneously, an appreciable diminution in the loss of humanity."[33]

Phillip Stong who played against fifty athletic teams in high school and college saw little evidence of sportsmanship on the playing fields.[34] He speaks with tongue in cheek of Robert Maynard Hutchins' attack upon "the emphasis on athletics and social life that infects all colleges and universities"[35] and of his "queer notion that people should go to college to learn something of use, and not to sit around in the cold on Saturday afternoon yelling infantile choruses at a small band of expensive mercenaries engaged in thumping each other."[36] So strong is the hold of sports, especially football, on the college mind that not even college presidents dare do away with what most of their number deem a nuisance. The demand of the alumni and the public pressure the presidents to conform. Although the faculty secretly dislikes the apotheosis of coaches, few members are brave enough to oppose these sainted worthies. Included in the gospel of football culture was the dictum that all important athletes must pass. Judge Hemingway, dean of the Law School at Mississippi, passed all athletes, including several, no doubt, who bought policies from William Faulkner that insured them against failing.[37]

IV   *Athletics in Fiction*

Coaches are the villains in many fictional works. The need of a winning team leads many coaches to overemphasize the significance of victory. At Ithaca High in *The Human Comedy*, Coach Byfield shows favoritism to Hubert Ackley III by relieving him from detention ordered by Miss Hicks, the school's teacher of ancient history. She is irate. Byfield, one of her former students, worries her.

On the practice field he had called Terranova a wop, an indignity that Miss Hicks protested. In agreement with Miss Hicks, the principal lectures the disgruntled coach soundly: "This is America, and the only foreigners there are those who forget that this is America."[38]

J. D. Salinger is more cynical about secondary school sports. In *Catcher in the Rye*, Caulfield sees through the murky glamour of ritualistic body-breaking. He is not moved by the dramaturgy of the sacred game with Saxon Hall, the last of the year, that could drive Pencey's worshipers to suicide if their begrimed eleven lost. He disliked the "athletic bastards" who always stuck together, including the coaches who loaned their cars to favorite stars.[39] Even at Justin Martyn, known for the severity of its hoary headmaster, football players were not hounded for reading movie magazines, a lapse from virtue that would be fatal to a commoner.[40] Parents who dream of their sons scoring eighty-yard-run winning touchdowns are chided by Arthur Miller in *Death of a Salesman*. Studious Bernard, Willy Loman's nephew, warns his uncle that his son Biff will not graduate if he does not study to pass the Regents examinations. Enraged, Willy answers: "What're you talking about? With scholarships to three colleges they're gonna flunk him?" Furthermore, Bernard's marks will not be as valuable to him in the business world as Biff's athletic accomplishments.[41]

The college athlete is a more conceited swaggerer than his high school counterpart. In *A New Life*, the head football coach has a list of names of professors who are unsympathetic to athletes. He advises his players to avoid these disloyal dons.[42] In Upton Sinclair's *Oil*, the head coach of Southern Pacific University earns three times the salary of a professor. To maintain his football empire, he receives $50,000 from an oil king. Part of this endowment he reserves for the purchase of illiterate huskies "who passed farcical examinations prepared by frightened professors."[43] Occasionally a fictional college president follows Hutchins' philosophy on athletics. Acting President Aiken in *Stones of the House* tries to convince trustees and donors that scholarship and libraries come before gymnasiums and teams.[44] In *The Plastic Age*, Percy Marks succinctly expresses the intellectual's disdain for the disruptive influence of sports: "The football season lasted from the first of October to the latter part of November, and during those weeks little was talked about, or even thought about, on the campus but football. . . . Raleigh was

Sanford's ancient rival; to defeat her was of cosmic importance."[45]

Time Out, a novel by Ronald Forman (1931), is still a readable exposé of college football. As in *The Plastic Age* and in *The Catcher in the Rye,* victory at Elite College is of cosmic importance. The head coach sets the tone of the book in his first exhortation to his team for victory "Remember," he shouts, "the immediate aim of our lives is to lick Indigo, and lick them good. Nothing else matters." Byrne, an intelligent player, tries to fathom why he submits himself to "the drudgery, the torture, the loss of self-respect" inflicted upon him by dictatorial coaches?[46] And Tom Meeker, the eleven's captain, sees the Elite team as "nothing but a bunch of immature kids who perform every Saturday without exactly knowing why."[47] Another player, Peltzer, knows why. Some play because they like the game, others because they believe that a good athletic record is a good business asset. Basically, football is played to win; a coach needs a winning team.[48] But after the season is over and the wounds are healed, the players agree that Elite had given them something: harmony in Music 8, the use of a good library, and acquaintance with teachers who had known some great minds. And if one dares to agree with Robert Frost, even football is creative, for poets and athletes are creators.[49]

V   *The Alumni*

To the professional alumnus, a college without a football team is a dreary wasteland that deprives him of congenial comradery, perpetual youth, and the joys of hyperbolization. Robert Maynard Hutchins regards alumni as puerile parasites who attack the "very things which are desirable in education."[50] Howard Mumford Jones accords them more respect; alumni bodies should not be overbearing but they should not abdicate their paternal rights to restrain unruly students.[51] John P. Marquand views the alumni compassionately; although alumni include "intellectual wreckage that drifts back to Cambridge beach, there's some virtue in forgotten studies that vanish into our attitudes."[52]

But the poor alumnus cannot escape fictional censure. In *The Plastic Age,* Hugh Carver admires the chapel "willed to the college by an alumnus who had made millions selling rotten pork," and in *The Homecoming Game* the alumni crowd in Pittsburgh petition President Nagle to remove courses on pagan Greek from the curriculum.[53] Alumnus Badger Bratten of Rowley College in *The*

Stones of the House tells President Aiken that "the normal American kids gets more real education out of belonging to a good frat than he does out of this book and classroom stuff."[54]

VI *Honorary Degrees*

For financial, altruistic, and egotistical reasons, universities revel in awarding honorary degrees. In *The Goose-Step*, Upton Sinclair notes that Nicholas Murray Butler of Columbia received twenty-five honorary degrees. Abbott Lawrence Lowell of Harvard twenty, and William Arnold Shanklin of Wesleyan eleven. Herbert Hoover received twenty to Woodrow Wilson's ten, but how many awards had Louis D. Brandeis, Clarence Darrow, Robert M. LaFollette, and William Borah won? Not one to divide among them, scolds Sinclair. Men who struggle all their lives to advance democracy are neglected by the sycophant universities.[55] Sinclair complained of this partiality in 1923, but thirty-five years later Stringfellow Barr was just as critical of the honorary degree. In *Purely Academic* Larry MacDonald donates $75,000 to the college athletic fund. A baseball club owner, MacDonald has no academic background. How can the college award a baseball magnate an honorary degree? The problem was resolved expeditiously. The proud MacDonald was named Doctor of Physical Arts.[56]

Eugene O'Neill received an honorary degree from Yale University in 1933. Until then he had refused all others, but he longed to receive one from Princeton. He doubted that he would be honored by his alma mater, but he admitted that "a morbid sense of humor might lead me to go through with it" if old Nassau relented.[57] When he received an honorary degree from Bishop's College, Sherwood Anderson told the audience that he had wasted his time at Harvard and that young men should take advantage of college — "a God-given opportunity."[58] The administrators at Mississippi University voted down an honorary degree for William Faulkner before he won the Nobel Prize; later, the university authorities were too ashamed to award him honors.[59]

VII *The Values of Lower Education in Non-Fiction*

If the schools are reflections of the aims of society, the educational values are outgrowths of these aims. Of all of the institutions of the land, the schools are the most vulnerable to attack by any individual, association, or lobby. Although the schools reap the harvest of family failure, including hordes of disturbed children from divorced homes, they are often indicted for the antics of their maladjusted charges. To many students, school is a fearful habitation. James Baldwin always spoke of his experiences at Douglass Junior High School as unadulterated horror, although he had written in 1939 that it was "one of the greatest junior high schools in the country."[60] William Gibson, perhaps too precocious for an ordinary high school, said of his schooling that "I flunked nothing, understood little, and loved less. . . ."[61]

Albert Jay Nock remembered his small boarding school with pleasure. The school plant was inadequate, the dormitories bleak and bare, but the headmaster was kind, his crippled teacher inspirational. Discipline was maintained with a degree of intelligent permissiveness.[62] Ogden Nash had kind words for his boarding school too. At St. George in Newport he was taught self-reliance and discipline.[63] But C. Wright Mills sees boarding schools in another light, attributing one cause of the national unity of the upper social classes to the exclusive private schools which "mold a spirit of upper-self consciousness among the young of the rich."[64]

The disciplined private schools admired by Nock and Nash have little in common with the progressive schools that have, according to Max Lerner, learned to work responsibly and realistically.[65] Mark Van Doren's criticism of progressive schools — their denial of our classical past and their refusal to entertain fixed programs of studies requisite for the development of all children[66] — has been heeded to the extent that progressive education has fused in many instances with traditional educational philosophies to the betterment of both.

The Brimmer School of Boston, which Robert Lowell attended, is puzzling. A blend of the military and the feminine, the school reserved its eight superior grades for girls. Here young Lowell had to unlearn his standard writing patterns for the printing forms of the Dalton plan, give up formal grammar for modern grammar, and pay heed to the strange eclecticism of Mr. Newell, who taught ecstatically of the sewage consumption of the conger eel. There were games and drawing exercises, but oddly, although Miss Manice, the principal, said that women were unequal to men, she had the girls engage in sports and marches that were denied to the boys. For diversion, the children were treated to an exhibition of Venetian glass blowing, a tour of the Riverside Press, a session with Rudy Vallee, and a concert by the Hampton Institute Choir. It was a woman's world, wrote Lowell, but it seems that something of value went on at the Brimmer School from time to time.[67]

Two female writers, Katherine Anne Porter and Mary McCarthy, were not pleased with their convent education. Miss Porter dismissed her education as ornamental.[68] Mary McCarthy wrote bitterly of the injustices students suffered at St. Joseph's Convent in Minneapolis. Standards were not high, and a student might skip a grade by winning a spelling bee. She saw no use in Catholic training for future educators. At all Sacred Heart Schools the dress, techniques of teachers, the system of rewards and punishments and rituals were all alike. At the Forest Ridge Convent School "daughters of dentists and lawyers, grocers and realtors, heiresses of the Chevrolet Agency and of Riley and Finn, contractors" were "adjured against the sin of doubt, that curse of fine intellect," by the Mother Superior.[69]

VIII   *The Lower Schools in Fiction*

Jesse Stuart, novelist and educator, is an optimistic educational seer, both in fiction and in practice. His successes as a rural educator are part of the nation's educational folklore, and he seems to have few pedagogical axes to grind. But in *Mr. Gallion's School*, he regrets that our emulation of the Greeks in athletics has not been balanced by a love of learning and creativity. Some of the fault lies in our delight in ostentation, implies John Hersey in *The Child Buyer*. An educational hierarchy that chooses to call a spade an instrument for soil development cannot administrate learning wisely, says Mr. Jones, the child buyer.[70]

High school students are more concerned with social events than with learning at Beach City High School in *Oil*. The middle-class students revel in their athletic fields, tennis courts, dance floors and swimming pools. They join secret societies and clubs and dutifully absorb their cultural medicine in "properly measured doses."[71] Mary McCarthy, who complains of her convent education, has even sorrier criticisms of her public high school. The less-disciplined teaching almost cost her a passing grade in English, her best subject.[72] And of what value was a high school diploma to a poor boy, wonders Danny in *Father and Son*? Where would it get him? A menial job with his father in the express company? [73]

Holden Caulfied is unhappy at Pencey Prep. He reads an ad about the school in a genteel magazine: "Since 1888 we have been molding boys into splendid, clear-thinking young men." Holden is not impressed. "Strictly for the birds." Pencey molds no better than any other school.[74] Holden's debunking of Pencey to Sally is angry and uncompromising:

You ought to go to a boy's school sometime. . . . It's full of phonies, and all
you do is study enough to be able to buy a goddam Cadillac someday, and
you have to keep making believe that you give a damn if the football team
loses, and all you do is talk about liquor and sex all day, and everybody sticks
together, the Catholics stick together, the goddam intellectuals stick
together, the guys that play bridge stick together, even the guys that belong
to the goddam Book-of-the-Month stick together. . . .[75]

In *The Bulwark*, Theodore Dreiser describes the Friend's School
at Oakwold, a female boarding school, as too rigid and practical
educationally and too snobbish socially. The girls think only of
beauty, charm, and personality; most of them conform to the
standards set by a few leaders. Another girl's school, Chadd's Ford,
is more progressive. Here there are laughter and gossip, field trips,
and excursions.[76] But Dreiser has praise for the University of
Wisconsin, a real college where girls are treated as if they have
intellect.[77]

IX   *The Value of College in Nonfiction*

Why do young people go to college? To learn? Nonsense, says
Albert J. Nock. A few matriculants have sincere academic interests,
but most high school graduates see a college tour as an escape from
work, as a source of social contacts,[78] and, until recently, as an
alternative to military service. Phillip D. Stong alleges that three-
fifths of the girls at Drake University were there to acquire
husbands, but girls will deny the validity of his statistics.[79] H. L.
Mencken echoes the declaration of a student to Henry Adams that a
degree from Harvard guarantees success in Chicago or elsewhere.
"A Harvard diploma," said Mencken, "would help him [his son] a
great deal more in his later life, American ideals being what they are,
whether God cast him for the role of metaphysician or for that of
investment securities broker."[80] But John Tunis, a Harvard man,
disagrees with Mencken's optimism. In 1936, for example, the class
of 1911 reported that the average income of the alumnus was 4,445
dollars, that one-eighth of them was on charity, and that 50 percent
of their wives worked. Tunis concluded his survey disparagingly:
"We are a bunch of contented college cows whose chief ambitions
are to vote the Republican ticket, to keep out of the bread lines and
to break 100 at golf."[81]

How effective is college education? Does Upton Sinclair criticize
his teachers and peers excessively in his charge that not once in five
years of chapel at Columbia did he hear an oration that "was guilty

of the vulgarity of being alive?"[82] Ezra Pound was infuriated when he was turned down for a fellowship on the grounds "that the University is not here for the unusual man."[83] He castigated universities for refusing to innovate and for championing mediocrity.

Moses Hadas valiantly defends the liberal arts diploma against those who see its value limited to entitling its owner to pay dues to an alumni association and to accord him freedom "from ever having to read another book."[84] But who, Albert Jay Nock asks, among the legions of liberal arts graduates turned out annually can read their diplomas? Would not these spectacles have caused Jefferson to smile wryly? [85] The decline of the liberal arts college at the expense of vocationalism and scientism has not ennobled the American university that now "vacillates between the slack and the sterile."[86] But to expect too much of the college graduate is foolish, Marquand said at Harvard in 1953. He himself had forgotten much of what he had learned at Harvard, an overstatement to be sure for his novels point to the contrary, and he chided his listeners for having been comforted too seldom "by the rod and staff of the academic mind."[87] Robert Frost was unhappy with the inability of contemporary colleges to instill a love for literature and art, and a capacity for critical thinking in its practical-minded students. Students, he felt, were unable to differentiate between fact and propaganda in political campaigns.[88] Like Ezra Pound, David Riesman sees the colleges as uncreative and uncritical; lacking innovation, they will not play an important part in shaping the future. Provincialism among American scholars is a serious hindrance to America's role in advancing culture. The scholars at the American Academy of Arts and Letters offended Pearl Buck by excluding discussion of Chinese symbolists in their symposium on symbolism. Asked by her why there were no Asiatic books in the One Hundred Great Books series, a scholar replied that nobody knows about them. Astonished, Miss Buck rejoined: "Nobody? Only millions of people. Oh, well . . ."[89]

Professor Noam A. Chomsky, accuses American intellectuals of contributing "to the sorry picture of American will to power now drowned in fatuity,"[90] a criticism somewhat akin to Barzun's view that the new university is influenced by a society that favors vocationalism, scientism, and alliance with the corporate community.[91] Practical men, though, are the enemies of the scholar, Thomas Wolfe complained. On the one hand they encourage youth to get a college education; on the other hand they sneer at college men in high office, since they are mere professors and should be replaced by practical men of business.[92]

According to Langston Hughes, the black colleges were no better. Fearful administrators of black colleges did not protest the indictment and arrest of the Scottsboro youths in 1931,[93] nor did Hampton Institute intervene when Juliette Derricotte, dean of women at Fisk University, was injured in an automobile accident and refused admission to a nearby white hospital. She died enroute to a distant colored hospital. When the coach of the Alabama National College for Negroes was killed by a white mob, the elderly black and white heads of the college would not let the students hold a protest meeting.[94] Interestingly, William Faulkner disapproved of two separate systems of education for blacks and whites. Admitting that Mississippi's schools were so poor that white students were leaving the state to matriculate elsewhere, Faulkner agreed that the existing education for blacks was much worse than it was for whites.[95]

But not all was wrong with the colleges. Albert Jay Nock praised the small liberal arts college for fostering individualism. Students created their own recreation and extracurricular activities. Instructors were learned and aloof but gentlemen.[96] The larger colleges had many champions also. John P. Marquand spoke eloquently of the diversity of genius that had attended Harvard:

A Harvard man now lies buried in the precincts of the Kremlin. Another was the founder of the New Deal, and several are still economic royalists, in spite of everything. There are devout Catholics, pagans, and atheists in the ranks of Harvard men. . . . There are some very intellectually brilliant Harvard men and a great many more dumb ones, and yet the belief still persists that we have all been poured into a mold, and collectively, we are a part of American folklore.[97]

There is room for variety in American education. James Leo Herlihy praises the experimental Black Mountain College, staffed by thirty-five teachers serving ninety students. Black Mountain was not concerned with degrees, vocational aims, and athleticism. Here young people were trained to think, to absorb, and to reach out for ideas.[98]

Summing up his views on the role of the intellectual in our society, Howard Mumford Jones writes: "We have not achieved justice, virtue, and love on this planet, and perhaps we never shall, but to slacken in the search now, to abandon the age-long quest to followers of irrationalists and fantastical theories — this is, indeed, the treason of the intellectuals."[99] But can Mr. Jones be certain that those whom he calls fantastical and irrational are always void of truth or glimpses of the truth?

X *Values of College in Fiction*

Fictional critics of educational values are varied in their barbs. James Michener types most American colleges of the late 1920s as mere outposts of England, barren in culture, and snobbishly indifferent to American culture.[100] In *Purely Academic*, Professor Schneider describes his college as vocational, supervised by trustees whose goals are to prevent subversion and remain solvent, and managed by a fund-raising president. Department heads are academic pirates who raid one another's precincts for more students; professors publish frantically to earn promotion and pay their debts; students avoid study, join fraternities, and seek mates on the campus; and the alumni seek winning teams.[101] Things are not very different at the University of Winnemac, Sinclair Lewis' educational Ford Factory where Martin Arrowsmith studied. Here in this vast emporium of learning, students might elect courses in Sanskrit, navigation, spectacle-fitting, Provençal poetry, and store advertising. The president is a fine fund raiser, the best in the country, and his mill turns out moral citizens who play bridge, drive good cars, and mention books that they do not read.[102]

To Upton Sinclair, Vanzetti was a truly educated man, infinitely more cultured than the Harvard men who would not defend him in his hour of need. Bitter indeed is Sinclair's defense of Vanzetti's literary style: "There are ten thousand graduates of Harvard College, every one of whom knows better than to say 'onderstand' or 'joostice'; yet there is only a handful who understand justice and not one who will die for it."[103] But there are fictional defenders of justice in the colleges; Doc Chisholm in *The Fires of Spring* learns that the college library is deficient but is not unduly perturbed. "Colleges are not for education," he says. "Colleges merely tell yew what to do if yew honest-to God want an education." To his students he is a free man, "the only teacher I've had," says David, "who is willing to tell the whole truth."[104]

To withstand the leveling tendencies in contemporary universities is an act of courage if one sincerely believes in honest scholarship. Martin Luther Strindberg fears in *The Man Who Stole a University* that state aid would lower admission standards and make the school subservient to the state.[105] It is too early at this time to evaluate the effects of open enrollment upon academic achievement, especially at the College of the City of New York, which ranked among the nation's highest colleges academically before open enrollment was initiated. Whatever conclusions will be reached by studies of open enrollment at the college, it is highly probable that they will not please everyone, since sociological interpretations of the findings will be mingled with academic analyses, forming a mixture that can easily be separated into partisan components.

XI   *Writers on Writing*

Writers differ regarding the value of English courses, including creative writing courses, for apprentice authors. Those who deny the need of formal education for professional writers point to Whitman, Dickens, Twain, Hemingway, and scores of other self-made authors. But others attest to the inspiration that their English teachers gave them in high school and college. James Baldwin remembers his elementary schoolteacher who told him that he was a talented writer.[106] Gwendolyn Brooks is equally grateful to Janice West, her English teacher at Englewood High in Chicago, for encouraging her to write poetry.[107] Robert Penn Warren praises John Crowe Ransome, his freshman writing coach at Vanderbilt, for helping him to start writing professionally.[108]

On the other hand, Robert St. John was told that he couldn't write by the same teacher who told Hemingway to forget writing; and William Faulkner received a D in English at Mississippi.[109] Years later, Faulkner spoke on the relationship between writing and a college education, but he was not decisive in response to his questioner. Some writers need formal English courses, others do not; but the college should first produce a human being, then the writer. If a writer can acquire humanitarian traits outside of college, he does not need the college.[110] Leo Rosten temporized when asked the same question. Academic training is of some value to the writer, "but an author writes not because he is educated but because he is driven to communicate."[111] Can writing courses actually help the novice author? Are the creative writing courses, writers' workshops, and manuscript readings by literary agents likely to assist aspiring writers to ascend to literary stardom? The consensus of successful writers is that good writers are not made in the schools. Stephen Vincent Benét doubts that anyone can think up a course that will teach someone to write. Great writers, especially, are loath to teach the art of writing.[112] Faulkner said, "I don't think anybody can teach anything. A young writer will learn from almost any source he finds."[113] Katherine Anne Porter advises young writers to read the masters to learn standards of literary excellence. Course-taking is no substitute for intensive reading of literary geniuses.[114]

Should a writer teach? Will he give up too much of his energy and time that he might instead devote to writing? Freneau, Whitman, Longfellow, and Thomas Wolfe began to detest teaching when it consumed their time for writing. George Pierce Baker told Thomas Wolfe not to teach since teaching might harm his talent;[115] later, Wolfe saw the wisdom of his mentor, for he was miserable grading papers at New York University when he should have been writing exclusively.[116] Hundreds of English teachers would gladly leave the classroom were they honored as affluent novelists, poets, or dramatists, but uncertain of their talents, they accept teaching and dream of the day when they will have time and money enough to indulge in their literary fancies. For most teachers the dream ends in the classroom where they discuss the masters with their students. Occasionally, a great writer attributes his success to the encouragement of an unusually dedicated and perceptive teacher, but more often than not, the teacher's role in a writer's development is difficult to assess.

XII   *Some Projections on Educational Themes in Future Fiction*

The issues of the sixties — war in Southeast Asia, militancy of racial minorities, women's liberation, law and order, sexual liberation, political corruption, and disruption of the traditional ways of family life — have significantly affected the course of American education for the seventies and beyond. The disheartening Watergate scandals of the early seventies, our final departure from Indo-China, the emergence of an African-Asian block not unsympathetic to the Soviet Union and the gargantuan communist state of China, and the economic power of Arab nations once dominated by the West will inevitably affect American educatonal values. The serious economic recession of 1975 left great cities almost bankrupt and millions of Americans dependent upon unemployment compensation or relief. Tens of thousands of college graduates find the professions closed to them. Sensitive teachers fret as their gowned products receive academic and parental accolades, for on the morrow too many of these spirited young people will vainly attempt to convert the coveted B. A. into tangible productivity.

Young writers will blossom forth and question their paradoxical age and their seemingly perplexed leaders. Of what meaning are the academic and political orations on commencement day to youths who see their universities contracting, their leaders betraying the virtues they give lip service to, their friends and relatives vainly seeking honorable employment? City leaders castigate their state governments for depriving them of necessities, and both city and state officials lash out at the national government in common cause for more funding.

The literature of the late seventies and beyond will be both critical of our institutions as well as escapist. Undoubtedly, there will be utopian, muckraking, and radical novels and plays in abundance to memorialize our hectic era. Education will not escape the writer's censure since educators have not been overly candid in exposing the societal ills that afflict us. Perhaps it is not the function of the schools to change the social order, but if educators, who by definition should be elevators of the mind, choose to be mere hollow men seeking security and comfort, there can be no melioration of the dismal plight of mankind. For as Chaucer's good parson of a town preached;

> That if golde ruste, what shall iren do?
> For if a preest be foul, on whom we truste
> No wonder is a lewde man to ruste.[117]

Notes and References

Chapter One

1. Henry Adams, "The Gold Conspiracy," in *A Henry Adams Reader*, ed. Elizabeth Stevenson (Garden City: Doubleday, 1958), p. 85. This article first appeared in *The Westminster Review*, October, 1870.

2. Malcolm Townsend, *Handbook of United States Political History* (Boston: Lothrop, Lee, and Shepard, 1905), pp. 149 - 94 passim.

3. Henry B. Parkes, *The American People* (London: Eyre and Spottiswoode, 1949), p. 295.

4. Richard Hofstadter, *The American Political Tradition* (New York: Random House, 1955), p. 160.

5. Vernon L. Parrington, *The Beginnings of Critical Realism in America* (New York: Harcourt, Brace, 1927), p. 231.

6. Eric Goldman, *Rendezvous with Destiny* (New York: Random House, 1962), p. 10.

7. Irvin G. Wylie, *The Self-Made Man in America* (New York: The Free Press, 1966), p. 59.

8. Ibid., pp. 58 - 59.

9. *The Scrap Book* (New York: Frank A. Munsey Publisher, 1907), p. 5.

10. Scott Nearing, *The Making of a Radical* (New York: Harper and Row, 1972), p. 78.

11. Ibid., p. 79. In *The Goose-Step* (Pasadena, 1923) Upton Sinclair charged that Scott Nearing lost his professorship at the Wharton School of Finance because businessmen resented his talks on child labor and unions. Finally, after Nearing had attacked Billy Sunday in a newspaper article, he was fired by the trustees. Although students, alumni, and some of the faculty protested Nearing's dismissal, the trustees were adamant. But Nearing is popular on college campuses to this day; students flock to hear him talk on organic farming but few of them question him on academic freedom as it was before World War I.

12. Richard Hofstadter, *Social Darwinism in American Thought* (Boston: Beacon Press, 1955), p. 106.

13. Charles Howard Hopkins, *The Rise of the Social Gospel in American Protestantism* (New Haven: Yale University Press, 1940), p. 326.

14. Eric Goldman, p. 83.

15. Ibid., p. 84.

16. Walter Rauschenbusch, *Christianizing the Social Order* (New York: Macmillan, 1913), p. 34.

17. Eric Goldman, p. 85.

18. Ibid., p. 86.

19. *The Scrap Book*, p. 2.

20. Eric Goldman, p. 43.

21. *The Scrap Book*, p. 485. Vernon Louis Parrington attributed the decline of muckraking to the influence of the rich and respectable citizens who resented the journalistic attacks upon their business ethics. Tycoons and moguls found it unpleasant to be arraigned in sensationalist columns by enthusiastic reporters whom they could not buy. But when the muckraking press went too far, the tormented industrial giants went after their pesty gadflies: "And so quietly, and as speedily as could be done decently, the movement was brought to a stop by pressure put on the magazines that lent themselves to such harmful disclosures. Then followed a campaign of education. Responding to judicious instruction, conducted in the columns of the most respectable newspapers, the American public was soon brought to understand that it was not the muck that was harmful, but the indiscretion of those who commented in print on the bad smells" (Parrington, p. 407).

22. "Final Report of the Commission on Human Relations, 1915," in *Documents of American History*, ed. Henry Steele Commager (New York: Appleton-Century-Crofts, 1968), II, 108.

23. Rod W. Horton and Herbert W. Edwards, *Backgrounds of American Literary Thought* (New York: Appleton-Century-Crofts, 1967), p. 267.

24. Julius W. Pratt, *Expansionists of 1898* (Chicago: Quadrangle Paperbacks, 1964), p. 7.

25. Ibid., p. 9.

26. Ibid., p. 11.

27. Horton and Edwards, p. 265.

28. Julius W. Pratt, p. 282.

29. Ibid., p. 286.

30. "Platform of the American Anti-Imperialist League, October 18, 1865," in *Documents of American History*, II, 12.

31. Horton and Edwards, p. 267.

32. Frederick Mayer, *American Ideas and Education* (Columbus: Charles E. Merrill, 1964), p. 254. Earlier in his life, Whitman had espoused the principles of manifest destiny, probably inspired by the notion that a democratic America would sincerely bring its blessings to the entire world. In *Democratic Vistas* he lamented the postwar hollowness of spirit in the hearts of men, the corruption of business, the decline of religious and

literary excellence, the apathy toward culture and education, and the general falling off in democratic faith.

33. Albert Bushnell Hart, ed., *American History Told by Contemporaries* (New York: Macmillan, 1964), IV, 608 - 9.

34. Richard Hofstadter, *The American Political Tradition*, p. 270.

35. Henry Adams, *The Education of Henry Adams* (New York: Modern Library, 1931), p. 505.

36. Irvin G. Wylie, p. 206.

37. Brooks Adams, "From the Theory of Social Revolution," in *American Thought from the Civil War to World War I*, ed. Perry Miller (New York: Holt, Rinehart, and Winston, 1954), p. 269.

38. Brooks Adams, "Introduction to the New Empire," in *American Thought from the Civil War to World War I*, pp. 256 - 57.

39. Henry B. Parkes, p. 231; Eric Goldman, p. 71; Richard Hofstadter, *The Age of Reform*, p. 145.

40. Henry B. Parkes, p. 256.

41. Henry Demarest Lloyd, *Wealth Against Commonwealth* (Englewood Cliffs, N.J.: Prentice-Hall, 1963), p. 181. Lloyd's thesis of university control by big business was followed in detail by Thorstein Veblen in *The Higher Learning in America* and by Upton Sinclair in *The Goose-Step.*

42. Frederick Mayer, pp. 321 - 27 passim.

43. William Graham Sumner, "The Absurd Effort to Make the World Over," in *American Thought from the Civil War to World War I*, p. 103.

44. Ibid., pp. 95, 98.

45. Lawrence A. Cremin, *The Transformation of the School* (New York: Knopf, 1962), p. 154.

46. Ibid., p. 19.

47. Frederick Mayer, p. 84.

48. Eric Goldman, p. 111.

49. Richard Hofstadter, *The Age of Reform* (New York: Knopf, 1966), p. 154.

50. Charles Beard in *The Dial* 64 (April 11, 1918), 335 - 36. For the account of Butler's unsigned editorial in *The New York Times* see Eric Goldman, p. 119.

51. Richard Hofstadter, *The Age of Reform*, p. 60.

52. Henry B. Parkes, p. 287.

53. "Resolution of Springfield, Illinois, Farmer's Convention, April 2, 1873," in *Documents of American History*, II, 528.

54. "Preamble of the Knights of Labor, January 1, 1878," in Ibid., p. 547.

55. "Populist Party Platform," in Ibid., p. 593.

56. Richard Hofstadter, *The Age of Reform*, p. 91.

57. Ibid., p. 131.

58. Ibid., p. 144.

59. Henry B. Parkes, p. 299.

60. Richard Hofstadter, *American Political Tradition*, p. 258.

61. Stewart Holbrook, *Dreamers of the American Dream* (Garden City: Doubleday, 1957), p. 349. I am indebted to Stewart Holbrook for the information I have used from his lively rendering of the doings of America's visionaires, idealists, and eccentrics. His book should be part of the readings assigned in American history courses for his catalog of little-known Americans is an excellent primer of a significant but neglected portion of the nation's history.

62. Irvin G. Wylie, p. 95.

63. Ibid., pp. 103, 112.

64. Francis Adams, "The Free School System of the United States," in *Turning Points in American Educational History*, ed. David Tyack (Waltham: Blaisdell, 1967), pp. 171 - 76.

65. Everett Dick, from "Sod House Frontier," in *The History of Education Through Readings*, ed. Carl H. Gross and Charles C. Chandler (Boston: D.C. Heath, 1964), p. 310.

66. Ibid., pp. 306, 312, 313.

67. Richard Grant White, "The Public School Failure," in *The History of Education Through Readings*, pp. 222 - 24.

68. Ibid., pp. 227, 229, 230 - 31.

69. John D. Philbrick, "The Success of the Free School System," an answer to Richard Grant White in *The History of Education Through Readings*, p. 233.

70. Lawrence A. Cremin, pp. 6 - 7.

71. Carl H. Gross and Charles C. Chandler, pp. 130, 195, 198.

72. Ellwood P. Cubberley, *The History of Education* (Boston: Houghton Mifflin Co., 1920), pp. 808 - 9, 811.

73. Lawrence A. Cremin, pp. 129 - 30.

74. Francis W. Parker, "An Account of the Cook County and the Chicago Normal School from 1883 to 1889," in *The History of Education Through Readings*, p. 265.

75. Ibid., p. 271.

76. Lawrence A. Cremin, p. 99.

77. Rod W. Horton and Herbert W. Edwards, p. 173.

78. Adolphe E. Meyer, *An Educational History of the American People* (New York: McGraw-Hill, 1967), p. 263.

79. Ibid., p. 262.

80. Ibid., p. 261.

81. *The Scrap-Book*, pp. 167 - 68.

82. Adolphe E. Meyer, p. 148.

83. James E. Russell, "The Function of the University in the Training of the Teacher," in *The History of Education Through Readings*, p. 318.

84. Ibid., p. 321.

85. Ellwood P. Cubberley, p. 835.

86. Ibid., p. 837.

87. Andrew Johnson, "Annual Message, December 3, 1867," in *Reconstruction in the South*, ed. Harvey Wish (New York: Farrar, Straus and Giroux, 1965), p. 1031.

88. George W. Williams, *The Negro in America: 1619 - 1880* (New York: Arno Press and *The New York Times*, 1968), pp. 378 - 79.

89. *Reconstruction in the South*, p. 34.

90. Carl Schurz, in *American History Told by Contemporaries*, ed. Albert Bushnell Hart, IV, 454.

91. David Tyack, p. 286.

92. *Reconstruction in the South*, p. 37.

93. Albert Bushnell Hart, ed. *American History Told by Contemporaries*, IV, 455.

94. George W. Williams, p. 382.

95. "Black Code of Louisiana," in *Documents of American History*, II, 455.

96. "Black Code of Mississippi," Ibid., p. 452.

97. Ibid., pp. 453 - 54.

98. Samuel A. Tilden, in Hart, IV, 475.

99. "Proclamations by Military Governments," in Hart, IV, 486 - 88.

100. Richard Hofstadter, *American Political Tradition*, p. 157.

101. John R. Lynch, *The Facts about Reconstruction* (New York: Arno Press and *The New York Times*, 1968), p. 116.

102. George W. Williams, p. 383.

103. Ibid., p. 415.

104. Ibid., p. 170.

105. Ibid., pp. 530 - 32.

106. "Highlights of Black History at Fort Monroe," A Casement Paper, Fort Monroe Casemate Museum, Fort Monroe, Virginia, p. 5.

107. Ibid. Interestingly, one fourth of the enlistments in the United States Navy in the Civil War was black, and 180,000 black troops served in the Union army.

108. David Tyack, p. 279.

109. Benjamin Griffith Brawley, *A Short History of the American Negro* (New York: The Macmillan Co., 1939), pp. 132 - 33.

110. Henry J. Perkinson, *The Imperfect Panacea: American Faith in Education* (New York: Random House, 1968), p. 29.

111. Benjamin Griffith Brawley, p. 147.

112. Henry J. Perkinson, p. 15.

113. Ibid., p. 17.

114. *Reconstruction in the South*, p. 60.

115. David Tyack, p. 269.

116. *Reconstruction in the South*, p. 273.

117. George W. Williams, p. 517.

118. George Washington Cable, "The Negro Question," in *Reconstruction in the South*, p. 219.

119. David Tyack, p. 191.

120. Albert Bushnell Hart, IV, 44.

121. George W. Williams, p. 443.

122. Eric Goldman, p. 63.

123. Ibid., p. 137.

124. David Tyack, p. 364.

125. Adolphe E. Meyer, p. 213.

126. Ellwood P. Cubberley, *Public Education in the United States* (Boston: Houghton Mifflin Co., 1919), p. 210.

127. Charles A. Beard and Mary R. Beard, *The Rise of American Civilization* (New York: Macmillan Co., 1937), II, 476.

128. Adolphe E. Meyer, p. 202.

129. Eric Goldman, p. 100.

130. Ibid., p. 204.

Chapter Two

1. *The Complete Poems of Robert Frost* (New York: Holt, Rinehart, and Winston, 1961), p. 222.

2. *George Santayana, The Last Puritan* (New York: Charles Scribner's Sons, 1935), p. 83.

3. Roy W. Meyer, *The Middle Western Farm Novel in the Twentieth Century* (Lincoln: The University of Nebraska Press, 1965), pp. 9 - 10.

4. Edna Ferber, *So Big* (Garden City: Doubleday and Co., 1924), p. 117.

5. F. Scott Fitzgerald, *This Side of Paradise* (New York: Charles Scribner's Sons, 1920), p. 27.

6. Jack London, *Martin Eden* (New York: Macmillan and Co., 1936), p. 75.

7. George Santayana, pp. 80 - 81.

8. Clarence Darrow, *The Story of My Life* (New York: Charles Scribner's Sons, 1960), p. 23.

9. Ernest Poole, *His Family* (New York: Macmillan Co., 1917), pp. 81 - 82.

10. Lawrance Thompson, *Robert Frost: The Early Years* (New York: Holt, Rinehart and Winston, 1966), p. 358. Frost wrote favorably of Henry Clinton Morrison, Superintendent of Public Instruction for the state of New Hampshire, Morrison, after observing young Frost teach at the Pinkerton School, was so impressed with the young teacher's performance that he invited him to address teachers on methodology (Ibid., p. 348).

11. Theodore Dreiser, *Dawn* (New York: Horace and Liveright, Inc., 1931), pp. 278 - 79.

12. Frank Dobie, *Some Part of Myself* (Boston: Little, Brown and Co., 1967), pp. 171, 173.

13. Dorothy Canfield Fisher, *Seasoned Timber* (New York: Harcourt, Brace and Co., 1939), pp. 151, 147.

14. Carl Sandburg, *Always the Young Strangers* (New York: Harcourt, Brace and Co., 1953), p. 127.

15. Owen M. Johnson, "The Prodigious Hickey," in *The Lawrenceville Stories* (New York: Simon and Schuster, 1967), p. 106.

16. Ibid., p. 169.

17. Myra Kelly, "Morris and the Honorable Tim," in *Candles in the Night*, ed. Joseph L. Baron (Philadelphia: Jewish Publication Society of America, 1945), pp. 294 - 308.

18. Theodore Dreiser, *Dawn*, p. 190.

19. Mary Ellen Chase, *A Goodly Fellowship* (New York: Macmillan Co., 1932), p. 53.

20. *Dawn*, p. 33. The immigrant Jew found Elysium in the public school. Barred from schooling in many of the eastern European lands, the immigrant rejoiced to find free public schools for his children in America. See Hutchins Hapgood's *The Spirit of the Ghetto* (New York: Funk and Wagnalls, 1965) for a sympathetic study of the immigrant Jew in New York City's East Side.

21. Lous Bromfield, *The Farm* (New York: Harper and Brothers, 1946), pp. 174 - 75.

22. W. E. B. Du Bois, *Autobiography* (New York: International Publishers, 1968), p. 77.

23. John Adam Moreau, *Randolphe Bourne: Legend and Reality* (Washington, D.C.: Public Affairs Press, 1966), p. 90.

24. Orrick Johns, *The Time of Our Lives* (New York: Stackpole Press, 1937), p. 118.

25. Ibid., p. 126.

26. William Allen White, *Autobiography* (New York: The Macmillan Co., 1946), pp. 37 - 38.

27. Mary Antin, *The Promised Land* (Boston: Houghton Mifflin Co., 1940), p. 293.

28. Albert J. Nock, *Memoirs of a Superfluous Man* (New York: Harper and Brothers, 1943), p. 293.

29. Noel Stock, *The Life of Ezra Pound* (New York: Pantheon Books, 1970), p. 9.

30. John Mason Brown, *The World of Robert Sherwood* (New York: Harper and Row, 1965), p. 65.

31. Louis Sheaffer, *Eugene A. O'Neill, Son and Playwright* (Boston: Little, Brown and Co., 1968), p. 93.

32. Edmund Wilson, *The Triple Thinkers* (New York: Oxford University Press, 1948), p. 239.

33. Ida Tarbell, *All in the Day's Work* (New York: The Macmillan Co., 1939), pp. 49 - 50.

34. Edgar Watson Howe, *The Story of A Country Town* (New York: New American Library, 1927), p. 37.

35. Edna Ferber, p. 50.

36. Frank Dobie, pp. 29, 26.

37. Clarence Darrow, *Farmington* (New York: Boni and Liveright, 1925), p. 51.

38. Edgar Lee Masters, *Skeeters Kirby* (New York: The Macmillan Co., 1923), p. 13.

39. Theodore Dreiser, *Dawn*, pp. 134, 129.

40. Louis Sheaffer, p. 64.

41. John Adam Moreau, p. 10.

42. Joseph Wood Krutch, *More Lives than One* (New York: William Sloane Associates, 1962), p. 15.

43. Ibid., p. 24.

44. Ernest Poole, *His Family*, p. 76.

45. Richard B. Hovey, *John Jay Chapman* (New York: Columbia University Press, 1962), p. 10. St. Paul's was founded by George C. Shattuck, Jr., an alumnus of George Bancroft's Round Hill School.

46. John Tunis, *A Measure of Independence* (New York: Atheneum, 1964), p. 80.

47. R. W. Stallman, *Stephan Crane* (New York: George Braziller, 1961), p. 24.

48. Mark Schorer, *Sinclair Lewis* (New York: McGraw-Hill Book Co., 1961), p. 48.

49. Charles A. Fenton, *Stephen Vincent Benét (New Haven: Yale University Press, 1958), p. 15.*

50. *Max Eastman, The Enjoyment of Living* (New York: Harper and Brothers, 1948), p. 19.

51. George Oppenheimer, *The View from the Sixties* (New York: David McKay, 1966), p. 19.

52. Booth Tarkington, *The Magnificent Ambersons* (Garden City: Doubleday, Page and Co., 1927), p. 28.

53. Winston Churchill, *A Far Country* (New York: The Macmillan Co., 1915), pp. 52 - 53.

54. Louis Auchincloss, *The Rector of Justin* (Boston: Houghton Mifflin Co., 1964), p. 61.

55. John P. Marquand, *H. M. Pulham, Esquire* (Garden City: Sun Dial Press, 1944), p. 69.

56. Upton Sinclair, *World's End* (New York: The Literary Guild, 1940), p. 74.

57. George Santayana, *The Last Puritan*, p. 298.

58. F. Scott Fitzgerald, *This Side of Paradise*, p. 29.

59. M. A. De Wolfe Howe, *Barrett Wendell and His Letters* (Boston: Atlantic Monthly Press, 1924), p. 223.

60. Max Eastman, p. 223.

61. Mary Antin, pp. 207, 208.

62. Carl Sandburg, pp. 138 - 39.

63. Frank J. Dobie, p. 135.

64. Louis Untermeyer, *Bygones* (Harcourt, Brace and World, 1965), p. 13.

65. E. K. Brown, *Willa Cather* (New York: Alfred A. Knopf, 1967), p. 32.

66. H. L. Mencken, *Heathen Days* (New York: Alfred A. Knopf, 1943), p. 39.

67. John Mason Brown, p. 66.

68. Owen Wister, "Dr. Coit of St. Paul," in *The Teacher's Treasure Chest*, ed. Leo Deuel (Englewood Cliffs, N.J.: Prentice-Hall, 1956), pp. 251 - 55 passim.

69. Edmund Wilson, *The Triple Thinker*, p. 236.

70. John Tunis, p. 76.

71. Ralph D. Gardner, *Horatio Alger* (Mendota, Calif.: Wayside Press, 1964), p. 80.

72. George Santayana, *The Last Puritan*, p. 94.

73. Edgar Watson Howe, p. 73.

74. Mary E. Wilkins, *The Portion of Labor* (New York: Harper and Brothers, 1901), pp. 140 - 66.

75. Joseph Calitri, *Father* (New York: Crown Publishers, 1962), p. 419.

76. Sherwood Anderson, "The Teacher," in *Winesburg, Ohio* (New York: Viking Press, 1965), p. 163.

77. Owen Johnson, "The Varmint," in *Lawrenceville Stories*, p. 231.

78. Ibid., p. 407.

79. Paul Sherman, *Edmund Wilson* (Urbana: University of Illinois Press, 1965), p. 13.

80. George Santayana, *Persons and Places* (New York: Charles Scribner's Sons, 1943), I, 157.

81. Elmer Rice, *Minority Report* (New York: Simon and Schuster, 1963), pp. 46, 53.

82. E. K. Brown, *Willa Cather*, p. 50.

83. Gertrude Atherton, *Adventures of a Novelist* (New York: Liveright and Co., 1932), p. 31.

84. Dale Kramer, *Chicago Renaissance* (New York: Appleton-Century-Crofts, 1966), pp. 69 - 70.

85. Mary Antin, p. 211.

86. Dale Kramer, p. 29.

87. Theodore Dreiser, *Dawn*, p. 195.

88. Orrick Johns, p. 37.

89. Mary Ellen Chase, p. 7.

90. Lawrance Thompson, *Robert Frost*, p. 149.

91. Joseph Wood Krutch, p. 15.

92. John Tunis, p. 59.

93. George Santayana, *Persons and Places*, I, 155.

94. Ernest Poole, *His Family*, p. 84.

95. George Santayana, *The Last Puritan*, p. 124.

96. Willa Cather, "The Professor's Commencement," in *Five Stories* (New York: Vintage Press, 1956), p. 285.

97. Sinclair Lewis, *The Trail of the Hawk* (New York: Harper and Brothers, 1915), p. 131.

98. Willa Cather, "Paul's Case," in *Five Stories*, p. 150.

99. Ibid., p. 152.

100. Ibid., p. 162.

101. Moses Maimonides, "Why All Men Cannot be Equal," in *The Wisdom of Israel*, ed. Lewis Browne (New York: Random House, 1945), p. 435.

102. Carlos Martyn, *Wendell Phillips* (New York: Funk and Wagnalls, 1890), p. 423.

103. H. L. Mencken, *Heathen Days*, p. 55.

104. King Hendricks and Irving Shepard, *Letters from Jack London* (New York: Odyssey Press, 1965), p. 87.

105. Louis Bromfield, *The Farm*, p. 56.

106. John Adam Moreau, p. 81.

107. Clarence Darrow, *The Story of My Life*, pp. 23, 26.

108. Louis Bromfield, p. 180.

109. Clarence Darrow, *Farmington*, p. 56.

110. Max Eastman, p. 98.

111. Louis Untermeyer, p. 12.

112. Mary Ellen Chase, p. 26.

113. Ibid., pp. 100 - 103 passim.

114. Ibid., p. 106.

115. Edmund Wilson, *The Triple Thinker*, pp. 253, 254.

116. Owen Johnson, "The Prodigious Hickey," in *Lawrenceville Stories*, pp. 145 - 46, 162 - 63.

117. Louis Untermeyer, ed., *The Letters of Robert Frost to Louis Untermeyer* (New York: Holt, Rinehart, and Winston, 1963), p. 289.

118. Edward C. Lathem, *Interviews with Robert Frost* (New York: Holt, Rinehart, and Winston, 1966), pp. 48 - 49.

119. Rosamond Gilder, ed., *Letters of Richard Watson Gilder* (Boston: Houghton Mifflin Co., 1916), p. 205.

120. Ernest Poole, *His Family*, pp. 83 - 84.

121. Elmer Ellis, ed., *Finley Peter Dunne: Mr. Dooley at His Best* (New York: Charles Scribner's Sons, 1938), p. 216.

122. George Santayana, *Persons and Places*, I, 154.

123. Mary Ellen Chase, pp. 188 - 89.

124. Theodore Dreiser, *Dawn*, p. 130.

125. Owen Johnson, "The Varmint," p. 343.

126. Owen Johnson, "The Prodigious Hickey," p. 19.

127. F. Scott Fitzgerald, *This Side of Paradise*, p. 9.

128. Edna Ferber, *So Big*, p. 180.

129. Ludwig Lewisohn, *The Island Within* (New York: Harper and Brothers, 1928), p. 114.

130. Owen Johnson, *The Lawrenceville Stories*, p. x.

131. H. L. Mencken, *A Mencken Chrestomathy* (New York: Alfred A. Knopf, 1956), p. 302.

132. H. L. Mencken, *Happy Days* (New York: Alfred A. Knopf, 1955), p. 29.

133. William Faulkner, *The Hamlet* (New York: Random House, 1959), p. 97.

134. Clarence Darrow, *Farmington*, p. 168.

135. George Santayana, *Persons and Places*, I, 168.

136. Mary Ellen Chase, p. 38.

137. Ellis, *Finley Peter Dunne*, p. 217.

138. John P. Marquand, *The Late George Apley* (Boston: Little, Brown and Co., 1956), p. 48.

139. Clarence Darrow, *Farmington*, p. 225.

140. Paul Sherman, *Edmund Wilson*, p. 12.

141. Ernest Jerome Hopkins, ed., *The Ambrose Bierce Satanic Reader* (Garden City: Doubleday and Co., 1968), p. 95.

142. Clarence A. Glassrud, *Hjalmar H. Boyesen* (Northfield, Minn.: The Norwegian-American Historical Society, 1963), p. 188.

143. Agnes Repplier, *Americans and Others* (Freeport, L.I.: Books for Libraries, 1971), pp. 117, 108.

144. M. A. De Wolfe Howe, *Barrett Wendell and His Letters*, pp. 87 - 88, 89.

145. Charlotte Perkins Gilman, *This Man-Made World* (New York: Charlton Co., 1911), pp. 149, 151, 162.

146. Ibid., p. 148.

147. George William Curtis, *Orations and Addresses of George William Curtis*, ed. Charles Eliot Norton (New York: Harper and Brothers, 1894), I, 417.

148. Ibid., p. 409.

149. Agnes Repplier, p. 112.

150. Pearl S. Buck, *My Several Worlds* (New York: John Day, 1954), p. 91.

151. Ida Tarbell, *All in the Day's Work*, pp. 44, 45.

152. William Faulkner, *The Hamlet*, p. 97.

153. Blair Rouse, *Ellen Glasgow* (New York: Twayne Publishers, 1962), pp. 78 - 79. Quoted by Mr. Rouse from Ellen Glasgow, *Virginia* (Garden City: Doubleday, 1913), p. 22.

154. Robert Herrick, *Chimes* (New York: The Macmillan Co., 1926), p. 59.

155. Mary Ellen Chase, pp. 291, 292.

156. Josephine Dodge Bacon, *Smith College Stories* (Freeport, L.I.: Books for Libraries, 1969), pp. 124 - 45, from the 1900 edition.

157. Sinclair Lewis, *Ann Vickers* (Garden City: Doubleday, Doran and Co., 1933), p. 42.

158. Ibid., p. 99

159. Ibid., p. 67.

160. Frank Marshall Davis, "Giles Johnson, Ph.D.," in *The Negro Caravan*, ed. Sterling Brown et al. (New York: The Arno Press, 1969), p. 397.

161. Carlos Martyn, *Wendell Phillips*, p. 581.

162. Albion W. Tourgée, *A Fool's Errand* (New York: Harper and Brothers, 1966), p. 387, from the 1879 edition.

163. Ibid., p. 388.

164. Thomas Dixon, *The Leopard's Spots* (Ridgewood, N.J.: Gregg Press, 1967, p. 387, from the original 1879 edition.

165. Ibid., p. 464.

166. Mark Twain, *The Gilded Age* (New York: The Trident Press, 1964), p. 142.

167. Bryant Morey French, *Mark Twain and the Gilded Age* (Dallas: Southern Methodist University Press, 1965), p. 128.

168. Ibid., p. 129.

169. Albion W. Tourgée, p. 50.

170. Ibid., p. 52.

171. Thomas Dixon, p. 44.

172. Ibid., p. 49.

173. Charles W. Chesnutt, "The Sheriff's Children," in *The Negro Caravan*, p. 38.

174. John Lloyd, *Stringtown on the Pike* (New York: Dodd, Mead and Co., 1900), p. 276.

175. Charles W. Chesnutt, *The House Behind the Cedars* (Ridgewood, N.J.: Gregg Press, 1968), pp. 200 - 206. (Reprinted from the 1900 edition.)

176. Ibid., p. 236.

177. Ibid., p. 246.

178. Cyrus Townsend Brady, *A Doctor of Philosophy* (New York: Charles Scribner's Sons, 1903), p. 93.

179. Ibid., p. 88.

180. Ibid., p. 97.

181. James Wendell Johnson, *The Autobiography of an Ex-Colored Man* (New York: Alfred A. Knopf, 1944), p. 10.

182. Ibid., p. 16.

183. Ibid., p. 19.

184. Ibid.

185. Langston Hughes, *A Langston Hughes Reader* (New York: George Braziller, 1969), pp. 334, 336.

186. W. E. B. Du Bois, *Autobiography*, pp. 108, 112, 114, 115.

187. Ibid., pp. 134 - 36. Du Bois charges that no black alumnus of Harvard was elected to membership to a Harvard Club (Ibid., p. 288).

188. Ibid., p. 140.

189. Ibid., p. 148.

190. Ibid., pp. 185 - 86.

191. Ibid., p. 199.

192. Ibid., pp. 217 - 18.

193. Gunnar Myrdal et al., *An American Dilemma* (New York: Harper and Brothers, 1944), II, 886.

194. Parke Godwin, *A Biography of William Cullen Bryant, with Extracts from His Private Correspondence* (New York: Russell and Russell, 1883), II, 331.

195. Adolphe E. Meyer, *An Educational History of the American People* (New York: McGraw-Hill, 1967), p. 222.

196. David B. Tyack, ed., *Turning Points in American Educational History* (Waltham: Blaisdell Publishing Co., 1967), p. 296.

197. Booker T. Washington in Tyack, *Turning Points*, p. 295.

198. Ibid., p. 299.

199. Ibid., p. 294.

200. W. E. B. Du Bois, pp. 225, 230.

201. Ibid., p. 231.

202. Ibid., p. 240.

203. Adolphe E. Meyer, p. 174.

204. Ellwood P. Cubberley, *Public Education in the United States* (Boston: Houghton Mifflin Co., 1919), pp. 252, 421.

205. Parke Godwin, *William Cullen Bryant*, II, 346.

206. Charles R. Anderson and Aubrey H. Starke, *The Letters of Sidney Lanier, 1878 - 1881* (Baltimore: John Hopkins Press, 1945), X, 69.

207. Ibid., p. 77.

208. Lucy Leffingwell Cable Biklé, *George Washington Cable: His Life and Letters* (New York: Russell and Russell, 1967), p. 188, from the 1928 edition.

209. Edward Bellamy, *Equality* (New York: Appleton and Century, 1897), p. 248.

210. Lucy L. C. Cable Biklé p. 1928.

211. Ernest Poole, *His Family*, p. 126.

212. Adolpe E. Meyer, p. 353.

213. Sinclair Lewis, *Babbitt* (New York: Harcourt, Brace and Co., 1922), pp. 84 - 85.

214. Ibid., p. 85.

215. James Harvey Robinson, *The Mind in the Making* (New York: Harper and Brothers, 1921), pp. 220 - 21.

216. Edward Bellamy, *Looking Backward* (Boston: Houghton Mifflin Co., 1929), pp. 221 - 22.

217. Ibid., p. 222.

218. Ibid., pp. 72, 73.

219. Ibid., p. 219.

220. Ibid., p. 66.

221. Edward Bellamy, *Equality*, p. 247.

222. Ibid., p. 249.

223. William D. Howells, *A Traveler from Altruria* (New York: The Sagamore Press, 1957), pp. 136, 144, 145.

224. E. Hudson Long, *Mark Twain Handbook* (New York: Hendricks House, 1957), p. 378.

225. Ibid., p. 379.

226. Charles Norman, *Ezra Pound* (New York: The Macmillan Co., 1960), pp. 156 - 57.

Chapter Three

1. Richard O'Connor, *Ambrose Bierce* (Boston: Little, Brown and Co., 1967), p. 16.

2. William James, "The True Harvard," in *The Harvard Book*, ed. William Bentinck-Smith (Cambridge, Mass.: Harvard University Press, 1961), p. 26.

3. Upton Sinclair, *The Jungle* (New York: Harper and Brothers, 1951), p. 301.

4. Elmer Ellis, ed., *Finley Peter Dunne: Mr. Dooley at His Best* (New York: Charles Scribner's Sons, 1938), p. 218. Compare Father Kelly's dictum with Randolph Bourne's educational shibboleth, "We must above all teach students to think," in *The History of a Literary Radical* (New York: S. A. Russell, 1965). p. 65, from the original 1919 edition.

5. John Jay Chapman, "Learning," in *The Collected Works of John Jay Chapman* (Western, Mass.: M and S Press, 1970), VI, 13 and 25 - 40 passim.

6. George William Curtis, "The Public Duty of Educated Men," in *Orations and Addresses of George W. Curtis*, ed. Charles E. Norton (New York: Harper and Brothers, 1894), I, 269.

7. John Jay Chapman, "Learning," I, 24.

8. William James, *Talks to Teachers* (New York: Henry Holt and Co., 1899), pp. 4 - 5.

9. Charles E. Fenton, *William Rose Benét* (New Haven: Yale University Press, 1958), p. 90.

10. E. Hudson Long, *Mark Twain Handbook* (New York: Hendricks House, 1957), p. 378.

11. Clarence H. Glassrud, *Hjalmar H. Boyesen* (Northfield, Minn.: The Norwegian-American Historical Association, 1963), p. 189.

12. William James, *Talks to Teachers*, p. 25.

13. Albert Jay Nock, *Memoirs of a Superfluous Man* (New York: Harper and Brothers, 1948), p. 89.

14. Abraham Flexner, *An Autobiography* (New York: Simon and Schuster, 1960), p. 67.

15. Elmer Ellis, *Finley Peter Dunne*, p. 22.

16. Ambrose Bierce, *The Collected Works of Ambrose Bierce* (New York: Gordian Press, 1966), VII, 80.

17. Ambrose Bierce, *The Devil's Dictionary* (New York: Dover Press, 1958), p. 9.

18. John Adam Moreau, *Randolph Bourne: Legend and Reality* (Washington D.C.: The Public Affairs Press, 1966), p. 21.

19. Mark Twain, *Letters from Earth*, ed. Bernard De Voto (New York: Crest Reprints, 1964), p. 21.

20. E. Hudson Long, 378.

21. Charles R. Anderson and Aubrey H. Stark, eds., *The Letters of Sidney Lanier 1878 - 1881* (Baltimore: Johns Hopkins Press, 1945), VII, 34.

22. Lincoln Steffens, *The Autobiography of Lincoln Steffens* (New York: Literary Guild, 1931), p. 644.

23. William James, "The True Harvard," p. 27.

24. Quoted by Harry Hartwick in *The Foreground of American Fiction* (New York: American Book Co., 1931), p. 348.

25. Randolph Bourne, "College," in *Youth and Life* (Freeport, N.Y.: Books for Libraries, 1967), from the original 1913 edition.

26. Sinclair Lewis, *Gideon Planish* (New York: Random House, 1943), pp. 8 - 9.

27. King Hendricks and Irving Shepard, *Letters from Jack London* (New York: Odyssey Press, 1965), p. 83.

28. Fred L. Pattee, *Tradition and Jazz* (Freeport, N.Y.: Books for Libraries, 1968), p. 178, from the original 1925 edition.

29. Sinclair Lewis, *Babbitt* (New York: Harcourt Brace and Co., 1922), p. 86.

30. Henry Seidel Canby, *Alma Mater* (New York: Farrar and Rinehart Co., 1936), p. 43.

31. William James, *Talks to Teachers*, p. 45.

32. Elmer Rice, *We the People* (New York: Coward McCann, 1933), pp. 137 - 38.

33. Ralph Barton Perry, *The Thought and Character of William James* (Cambridge: Harvard University Press, 1948), p. 389.

34. Wendell Phillips, "The Scholar in a Republic," in *Wendell Phillips*, by Carlos Martyn, (New York: Funk and Wagnalls, 1890), p. 575.

35. Joan London, *Jack London and His Times* (Seattle: University of Washington Press, 1937, p. 301.

36. Edward Cary, *George William Curtis* (Boston: Houghton Mifflin Co., 1894), p. 113.

37. Ibid., p. 112.

38. Lincoln Steffens, p. 131.

39. Wendell Phillips, "Phillipsiana," in *Wendell Phillips*, p. 527.

40. King Hendricks and Irving Shepard, p. 83.

41. Joseph Wood Krutch, *More Lives Than One* (New York: William Sloane Associates, 1962), p. 52.

42. Jack London, *Martin Eden* (London: Bodley Head, 1965), p. 103.

43. George Santayana, *Persons and Places* (New York: Charles Scribner's Sons, 1943), I, 192.

44. George Santayana, *The Last Puritan* (New York: Charles Scribner's Sons, 1946), p. 48.

45. Ralph Barton Perry, p. 151.

46. Pierrepont B. Noyes, *A Goodly Heritage* (New York: Rinehart and Co., 1958), p. 32.

47. Henry James, *Charles W. Eliot* (Boston: Houghton Mifflin Co., 1930), I, 219.

48. Lewis Gannett, "Opening Some Windows," in *College in a Yard*, ed. Brooks Atkinson (Cambridge, Mass.: Harvard University Press, 1957), p. 75.

49. Robert Herrick, *Chimes* (New York: The Macmillan Co., 1926), p. 208.

50. Clarence H. Glassrud, p. 123.

51. Albert J. Nock, p. 86.

52. Abraham Flexner, p. 32.

53. John Kendrick Bangs, *The Genial Idiot* (New York: Harper and Brothers, 1908), pp. 171 - 73.

54. Fred L. Pattee, *Tradition and Jazz*, p. 272.

55. Albert J. Nock, p. 84.

56. M. A. De Wolfe Howe, *Barrett Wendell and His Letters* (Boston: Atlantic Monthly Press, 1924), p. 53.

57. John Jay Chapman, "Learning," VI, 20.

58. E. K. Brown, *Willa Cather* (New York: Alfred A. Knopf, 1967), p. 34.

59 Ida M. Tarbell, *All in a Day's Work* (New York: Macmillan, 1939), p. 47.

60. Randolph Bourne, *History of a Literary Radical* (New York: S. A. Russell, 1956), p. 23.

61. James Russell Lowell, "Harvard Anniversary Address," in *James R. Lowell*, ed. H. Clark and Norman Foerster (New York: American Book Co., 1947), p. 442.

62. Henry Seidel Canby, p. 64.

63. Van Wyck Brooks, *New England Indian Summer*, (New York: E. P. Dutton and Co., 1940), p. 105.

64. Randolph Bourne, *The History of a Literary Radical*, p. 34.

65. William James, *Talks to Teachers*, p. 149.

66. Gay Wilson Allen, *William James* (New York: Viking Press, 1967), p. 203.

67. Clarence H. Glassrud, p. 41.

68. Woodrow Wilson, "My Ideal of the True University," in *Writers for Today*, ed. J. W. Cunliffe and Gerhard F. Lomer, 3rd ed. (New York: Century, 1923), p. 157.

69. Randolph Bourne, *The History of a Literary Radical*, p. 158.

70. B. A. Hinsdale, *Teaching the Language Arts* (New York: Appleton, 1897), p. x.

71. M. A. De Wolfe Howe, p. 193.

72. Ibid., p. 194.

73. William Lyon Phelps, *Teaching in School and College* (New York: Macmillan Co., 1912), p. 118.

74. Mildred R. Bennet, *Willa Cather's Short Fiction* (Lincoln: University of Nebraska Press, 1965), p. 210.

75. Fred L. Pattee, *Tradition and Jazz*, p. 215.

76. Albert J. Nock, p. 91.

77. Louis Sheaffer, *Eugene O'Neill, Son and Playwright*, (Boston: Little, Brown and Co., 1968), p. 114.

78. Frank Dobie, *Some Part of Myself* (Boston: Little, Brown and Co., 1967), p. 169.

79. Ibid., p. 217.

80. Ibid., p. 170.

81. Ibid.

82. Elmer Ellis, p. 218.

83. Ernest J. Hopkins, ed., *The Ambrose Bierce Satanic Reader*, p. 104.

84. Abraham Flexner, p. 45.

85. Ralph Barton Perry, *The Thought and Character of William James*, p. 236.

86. William James, *Talks to Teachers*, pp. 50, 222.

87. Robert Herrick, *Chimes*, p. 25.

88. Ibid., p. 18.

89. William James, *Talks to Teachers*, p. 104.

90. Willa Cather, *The Professor's House* (New York: Alfred A. Knopf, 1925), p. 28.

91. Gay Wilson Allen, *William James*, p. 197.

92. Mary Ellen Chase, *A Goodly Fellowship* (New York: The Macmillan Co., 1939), p. 268.

93. M. A. De Wolfe Howe, p. 14.

94. William James, *Talks to Teachers*, pp. 95 - 96.

95. Abraham Flexner, p. 50.

96. J. Frank Dobie, p. 150.

97. Sinclair Lewis, *The Trail of the Hawk* (New York: Harper and Brothers, 1915), pp. 67 - 69.

98. Winston Churchill, *A Far Country* (New York: The Macmillan Co., 1915), p. 88.

99. George William Curtis, *Orations and Addresses of George William Curtis*, p. 451.

100. Carl Van Doren, *Three Worlds* (New York: Harper and Brothers, 1936), p. 107.

101. Henry Seidel Canby, p. 181.

102. George Santayana, *Persons and Places*, I, 245.

103. Joseph Wood Krutch, p. 45.

104. John Dos Passos, "P. S. to Dean Briggs," in *College in a Yard*, ed. Brooks Atkinson (Cambridge, Mass.: Harvard University Press), p. 65.

105. William Allen White, *Autobiography* (New York: The Macmillan Co., 1946), p. 144.

106. Donald Pizer, *The Novels of Frank Norris* (Bloomington: University of Indiana Press, 1966), pp. 28 - 30.

107. Paul Sherman, *Edmund Wilson* (Urbana: University of Illinois Press, 1965), p. 27.

108. Bliss Perry, *And Gladly Teach* (Boston: Houghton Mifflin Co., 1938), p. 61.

109. Noel Stock, *The Life of Ezra Pound* (New York: Pantheon Books, 1970), pp. 22, 16.

110. Gay Wilson Allen, *William James*, p. 492.

111. Lawrence Thompson, *Robert Frost: The Early Years* (New York: Holt, Rinehart and Winston, 1966), p. 241.

112. Gertrude Stein, *Autobiography of Alice B. Toklas*, ed. Carl Van Vechten (New York: Random House, 1946), pp. 65 - 66.

113. Lincoln Steffens, p. 163.

114. M. A. De Wolfe Howe, *Barrett Wendell and His Letters*, pp. 27 - 28.

115. Martin Duberman, *James Russell Lowell* (Boston: Houghton Mifflin Co., 1966), p. 364.

116. Max Eastman, *Enjoyment of Living* (New York: Harper and Brothers, 1948), p. 224.

117. J. Frank Dobie, p. 144.

118. Randolph Bourne, *The History of a Literary Radical*, p. 29.

119. Leo Deuel, ed., *The Teacher's Treasure Chest* (Englewood Cliffs, N.J.: Prentice-Hall, 1956), pp. 162 - 63.

120. William H. Nolte, *H. L. Mencken's Smart Set Criticism* (Ithaca, N.Y.: Cornell University Press, 1968), p. 16.

121. Carl Van Doren, p. 81.

122. Dale Kramer, *Chicago Renaissance* (New York: Appleton-Century, 1966), p. 63.

123. J. Donald Adams, *Copey of Harvard* (Boston: Houghton Mifflin Co., 1966), p. 46.

124. Ibid., p. 101.

125. Granville Hicks, *John Reed* (New York: Benjamin Blom, 1968), p. 36.

126. John Tunis, *A Measure of Independence* (New York: Atheneum, 1964), p. 99.

127. J. Donald Adams, p. 172.

128. Ibid., pp. 154, 155.

129. Elizabeth Hardwick, ed., *The Selected Letters of William James* (New York: Farrar, Straus, and Cudahy, 1961), p. 200.

130. Ibid., p. 146.

131. Max Eastman, p. 268.

132. Ibid., p. 268.

133. Ibid., p. 282.

134. Anderson and Starke, V, xlviii.

135. Gay Wilson Allen, *William James*, p. 95.

136. Blake Nevius, *Robert Herrick, The Development of a Novelist* (Berkeley and Los Angeles, University of California Press, 1962), p. 288.

137. Carl Van Doren, p. 83.

138. Clarence H. Glassrud, p. 97; see also p. 47.

139. Ida M. Tarbell, pp. 53 - 54.

140. Noel Stock, p. 36.

141. Daniel Cory, ed., *The Letters of George Santayana* (New York: Charles Scribner's Sons, 1955), p. 119.

142. Ralph Barton Perry, p. 327.

143. Elizabeth Hardwick, p. 241.

144. Ibid., pp. 235 - 36.

145. Eleanor M. Tilton, *Amiable Autocrat* (New York: Henry Schuman, 1947), p. 371.

146. Ambrose Bierce, "Some Aspects of Education," in *The Collected Works of Ambrose Bierce*, IX, 128.

147. Henry Seidel Canby, p. 143.

148. Carl Van Doren, p. 81.

149. Clarence H. Glassrud, p. 88.

150. Henry Seidel Canby, p. 95.

151. George H. Fitch, *At Old Siwash* (New York: Grosset and Dunlap, 1911), p. 196.

152. Ludwig Lewisohn, *Upstream* (New York: Boni and Liveright, 1923), p. 171.

153. J. Frank Dobie, p. 168.

154. E. K. Brown, p. 53.

155. Lawrance Thompson, p. 235.

156. Mary Ellen Chase, pp. 208 - 9.

157. Sinclair Lewis, *Elmer Gantry* (New York: Harcourt, Brace and Co., 1927), p. 90.

158. Robert Herrick, *Chimes*, p. 67.

159. See my unpublished dissertation, "Upton Sinclair's Criticism of Higher Education in America" (New York University, 1963), for a detailed study of Sinclair's charge that big business dominated American higher education through the corporate trustees and donors who controlled the funding and administration of the nation's colleges and universities.

160. Upton Sinclair, *Love's Pilgrimage* (New York: Kennerley, 1911), pp. 437 - 38.

161. George H. Fitch, p. 198.

162. Robert Herrick, *Chimes*, pp. 64, 138.

163. George Santayana, *Persons and Places*, II, 162.

164. Charles A. Fenton, *William Rose Benét* (New Haven: Yale University Press, 1958), p. 90.

165. Henry Seidel Canby, p. 151.

166. Blake Nevius, p. 70.

167. Gay Wilson Allen, *William James*, p. 452.

168. Clarence H. Glassrud, p. 45.

169. John Erskine, *My Life As a Teacher* (Philadelphia: J. B. Lippincott, 1948), p. 17.

170. Robert Herrick, *Chimes*, p. 70.

171. Orrick Johns, *The Times of Our Lives* (New York: Stackpole and Sons, 1937), p. 127.

172. George Santayana, *The Last Puritan*, p. 430.

173. George Santayana, *Persons and Places*, II, 155.

174. John Tunis, p. 97.

175. Ralph Barton Perry, p. 327.

176. Charles W. Flandreau, "Harvard Episodes," in *The Harvard Book*, ed. William Bentinck-Smith (Cambridge, Mass.: Harvard University Press, 1961), pp. 243 - 48.

177. Henry Adams, *The Education of Henry Adams* (New York: The Modern Library, 1931), p. 307.

178. George Santayana, *Persons and Places*, II, 160 - 61.

179. Abraham Flexner, p. 34.

180. John Adam Moreau, p. 23.

181. Abraham Flexner, p. 33.

182. George H. Fitch, p. 104.

183. Carleton Putnam, *Theodore Roosevelt: The Formative Years* (New York: Charles Scribner's Sons, 1958), p. 139.

184. Henry James, *Charles W. Eliot*, II, 148.

185. Randolph Bourne, *The History of a Literary Radical*, p. 147.

186. Ludwig Lewisohn, p. 160.

187. James Russell Lowell, p. 439.

188. Henry Adams, p. 301.

189. Robert Herrick, *Chimes*, p. 62.

190. Ralph Barton Perry, p. 381.

191. D. D. Paige, ed., *The Letters of Ezra Pound, 1907 - 1941* (New York: Harcourt, Brace and Co., 1950), p. 99.

192. James Elliot Cabot, *A Memoir of Ralph Waldo Emerson* (Boston: Houghton Mifflin Co., 1887), II, 631.

193. Abraham Flexner, p. 34.

194. Henry Seidel Canby, pp. 130 - 31.

195. George Santayana, *The Last Puritan*, pp. 424 - 25.

196. Randolph Bourne, *The History of a Literary Radical*, p. 149.

197. Ibid., p. 35.

198. Randolph Bourne, *Youth and Life* (Freeport, N.Y.: Books for Libraries, 1967), p. 318, from the 1913 edition.

199. Henry Seidel Canby, p. 69.
200. William Allen White, p. 170.
201. Woodrow Wilson, p. 159.
202. John P. Marquand, *The Late George Apley* (Boston: Little, Brown and Co., 1956), pp. 78 - 81.
203. John Tunis, pp. 90, 260 - 61.
204. John Kendrick Bangs, *The Genial Idiot* (New York: Putnam, 1908), pp. 178 - 80.
205. George H. Fitch, p. 13.
206. Ibid., p. 14.
207. Ludwig Lewisohn, *Upstream*, p. 156.
208. John P. Marquand, *H. M. Pulham, Esquire* (Garden City: Sun Dial Press, 1944), pp. 96 - 97.
209. John P. Marquand, *The Late George Apley*, p. 74.
210. John P. Marquand, *H. M. Pulham, Esquire*, p. 87.
211. George Santayana, *Persons and Places*, I, 198.
212. F. Scott Fitzgerald, *This Side of Paradise* (New York: Charles Scribner's Sons, 1920), p. 47.
213. Henry Seidel Canby, p. 32.
214. George H. Fitch, p. 60.f
215. Sinclair Lewis, *The Trail of the Hawk*, p. 63.
216. Hjalamr Hjorth Boyesen, *The Mammon of Unrighteousness* (Upper Saddle River, N.J.: Literature House, 1970), p. 18, from the 1891 edition.
217. Pierrepont Noyes, *A Goodly Heritage*, pp. 25 - 26.
218. William Roscoe Thayer, *The Life and Letters of John Hay* (Boston: Houghton Mifflin Co., 1915), I, 47.
219. Frank Norris, *Vandover and the Brute* (Garden City: Doubleday, Doran and Co., 1928), pp. 14, 16 - 17.
220. Upton Sinclair, *Love's Pilgrimage*, p. 27.
221. Eugene O'Neill, "Abortion," in *Ten Lost Plays* (New York: Random House, 1964), pp. 159 - 65 passim.
222. George Santayana, *The Last Puritan*, pp. 48 - 49.
223. Max Lerner, *America As a Civilization* (New York: Simon and Schuster, 1957), pp. 507, 508.
224. Upton Sinclair, *The Goose-Step* (Pasadena: Published by the author, 1923), p. 361.
225. Ibid., chapter 72, passim.
226. George Santayana, *Persons and Places*, I, 226.
227. Granville Hicks, p. 29.
228. George Oppenheimer, *The View from the Sixties* (New York: David McKay, 1966), p. 24.
229. F. Scott Fitzgerald, *This Side of Paradise*, p. 52.
230. Robert Herrick, *Chimes*, p. 3.
231. Gay Wilson Allen, *William James*, p. 436.
232. Ralph Barton Perry, *William James*, p. 383.
233. Bliss Perry, *And Gladly Teach*, p. 113.

234. Charles H. Fenton, pp. 89 - 90.

235. Mark Schorer, *Sinclair Lewis* (New York: McGraw-Hill Book Co., 1961), p. 136.

236. John Erskine, p. 12.

237. Noel Stock, p. 54.

238. Robert Herrick, *Chimes*, pp. 65, 66.

239. Mary Ellen Chase, pp. 272 - 73.

240. Elmer Rice, *Minority Report* (New York: Simon and Schuster, 1963), p. 82.

241. Carleton Putnam, *Theodore Roosevelt: The Formative Years*, p. 218.

242. Upton Sinclair, *Love's Pilgrimage*, p. 44.

243. Archibald MacLeish, *A Continuing Journey* (Boston: Houghton Mifflin Co., 1968), p. 257.

244. Bliss Perry, p. 252.

245. John Tunis, p. 98.

246. Upton Sinclair, *Love's Pilgrimage*, p. 437.

247. Mary Ellen Chase, pp. 199, 215.

248. Ambrose Bierce, "Some Aspects of Education," in *The Collected Works of Ambrose Bierce*, IX, 124, 127.

249. Elizabeth Hardwick, p. 119.

250. Fred L. Pattee, *Tradition and Jazz*, p. 300.

251. Orrick Johns, pp. 39, 41.

252. Bliss Perry, p. 46.

253. Edmund Wilson, *A Prelude* (New York: Farrar, Straus, and Giroux, 1967), p. 120.

254. Henry James, *Charles W. Eliot*, I, 311.

255. M. A. De Wolfe Howe, *Barrett Wendell*, p. 37.

256. Ibid., p. 93.

257. George Santayana, *Persons and Places*, II, 159 - 60.

258. Granville Hicks, p. 39.

259. Randolph Bourne, *The History of a Literary Radical*, pp. 68 - 70, 72.

260. Abraham Flexner, p. 27.

261. Lincoln Steffens, p. 647.

262. Charles M. Sheldon, *In His Steps* (New York: John C. Winston, 1937), p. 103.

263. Sinclair Lewis, *The Trail of the Hawk*, p. 102.

264. Blake Nevius, p. 54.

265. Ibid., p. 64.

266. Robert Herrick, *Chimes*, p. 4.

267. Ibid., p. 23.

268. Ibid., pp. 155 - 56.

269. Ludwig Lewisohn, p. 147.

270. Ibid., p. 168.

271. Upton Sinclair, *Love's Pilgrimage*, p. 534.

272. Bliss Perry, p. 6.

273. Ibid., p. 257.

274. Edmund Wilson, *A Prelude*, p. 76.

275. Francis Hyde Bangs, *John Kendrick Bangs* (New York: Alfred A. Knopf, 1941), p. 41.

276. R. L. White ed., *Sherwood Anderson's Memoirs* (Chapel Hill: University of North Carolina Press, 1942), p. 198.

277. Mark Twain, *The Autobiography of Mark Twain*, ed. Charles Neider (New York: Harper and Brothers, 1959), pp. 348 - 49.

278. Thorstein Veblen, *The Higher Learning in America* (New York: Huebsch, 1918), pp. 48, 66.

279. Thorstein Veblen, *The Higher Learning in America*, in *The Viking Portable Veblen* (New York: Viking Press, 1950), p. 533.

280. Upton Sinclair, *Love's Pilgrimage*, p. 533. Veblen had written earlier: "Where the board chooses the academic head, the president is usually a counterpart of the board itself." Veblen, *The Higher Learning in America* (New York: Huebsch, 1918), p. 86.

281. Blake Nevius, p. 288.

282. Robert Herrick, *Chimes*, p. 48.

283. Ernest Jerome Hopkins, ed., *The Ambrose Bierce Satanic Reader*, pp. 101 - 2. Bierce recommended that it would be wiser to abolish the Board of Regents than to abolish the university (Hopkins, p. 110).

284. Willa Cather, *The Professor's House*, pp. 54 - 55.

285. William Allen White, p. 169.

286. Robert Herrick, *Chimes*, p. 163.

287. In *Great Thoughts by Great Americans*, ed. Constant Bridges Jones (New York: Thomas Y. Crowell Co., 1951), p. 102.

288. Edna Ferber, *So Big* (Garden City: Doubleday and Co., 1924), p. 179.

289. Upton Sinclair, *Samuel the Seeker* (New York: E. W. Dodge, 1910), pp. 70 - 71.

290. Robert Herrick, *Chimes*, p. 1.

291. Sinclair Lewis, *Elmer Gantry*, p. 398.

292. Clarence H. Glassrud, p. 41.

293. Hjalmar Hjorth Boyesen, *The Mammon of Unrighteousness*, p. 211.

294. Ibid., pp. 10, 12.

295. Ibid., pp. 378 - 79.

296. Ibid., p. 189.

297. C. Wright Mills, *The Power Elite* (New York: Oxford University Press, 1950), p. 71.

298. George William Curtis, *Orations and Addresses*, I, 318.

299. Clarence H. Glassrud, p. 89.

300. Charles H. Fenton, pp. 90 - 91.

301. Albert J. Nock, p. 96.

302. William H. Nolte, p. 20.

303. Thorstein Veblen, p. 252.

304. Quoted in *University Control*, ed. J. McKeen Cattell (New York: Science Press, 1913), p. 456.

305. Henry Seidel Canby, p. 154.

306. Blake Nevius, p. 292.

307. George Santayana, *Persons and Places*, II, 159 - 60.

308. Orrick Johns, p. 164.

309. Joseph Wood Krutch, p. 54.

310. Upton Sinclair, *American Outpost* (New York: Farrar and Rinehart, 1932), p. 82.

311. Lionel Trilling, "The Van Amringe and Keppel Eras," *A History of Columbia College on Morningside* (New York: Columbia University Press, 1932), p. 25.

312. John Adam Moreau, p. 36.

313. Noel Stock, p. 41.

314. Winston Churchill, *A Far Country*, p. 113.

315. John O. Lyons, *The College Novel in America* (Carbondale: Southern Illinois University Press, 1962), p. 21.

316. Upton Sinclair, *Samuel the Seeker*, p. 74.

317. Sinclair Lewis, *Babbitt*, p. 187.

318. Ibid., p. 188.

319. Robert Herrick, *Chimes*, p. 32.

320. Elmer Rice, *We the People*, p. 230.

321. Sinclair Lewis, *The Trail of the Hawk*, pp. 84 - 120.

322. Ibid., p. 96.

323. William James, *Talks to Teachers*, p. 293.

324. Ralph Barton Perry, p. 240.

325. William James, "The True Harvard," p. 28.

326. Sinclair Lewis, *Elmer Gantry*, p. 121.

327. Richard B. Hovey, *John Jay Chapman* (New York: Columbia University Press, 1959), p. 151.

328. Abraham Flexner, p. 68.

329. Richard Ruland, *The Rediscovery of American Literature* (Cambridge, Mass.; Harvard University Press, 1967), pp. 62 - 63.

330. Paul Goodman, *The Community of Scholars* (New York: Random House, 1962), p. 90.

331. Ralph Barton Perry, p. 144.

332. Henry James, *Charles W. Eliot*, II, 26.

333. Granville Hicks, p. 33.

334. John Reed, "Almost Thirty," *The New Republic Anthology* (New York: Dodge Publishing Co., 1936), p. 67. See also Steffens, pp. 646 - 47.

335. Henry Adams, *The Education of Henry Adams*, p. 304.

336. Pearl S. Buck, *My Several Worlds* (New York: John Day, 1954), p. 96.

337. John Mason Brown, *The World of Robert Sherwood* (New York: Harper and Row, 1965), p. 67.

338. John Tunis, p. 94.

339. Henry Adams, *The Education of Henry Adams*, p. 305.

340. Ibid., p. 306.

341. Carleton Putnam, pp. 177, 194.

342. Lincoln Steffens, p. 164.

343. Paul Sherman, *Edmund Wilson*, p. 19.

344. Lawrance Thompson, p. 146.

345. Bliss Perry, *And Gladly Teach*, p. 37.

346. William Allen White, p. 100.

347. Joseph Wood Krutch, p. 44.

348. Noel Stock, p. 422.

349. Henry James, *Hawthorne* (New York: Macmillan Co., 1879), p. 43.

350. Henry Seidel Canby, p. 55.

351. Ibid., p. 75.

352. John Adam Moreau, p. 86.

353. Abraham Flexner, p. 44.

354. Randolph Bourne, *The History of a Literary Radical*, p. 156.

355. Joseph Wood Krutch, p. 56.

356. Joan London, p. 288.

357. Larzer Ziff, *The American 1890s* (New York: Viking Press, 1968), pp. 254 - 55.

358. Lincoln Steffens, p. 119.

359. R. W. Stallman and Lilian Gilkes, eds., *The Letters of Stephen Crane* (New York: New York University Press, 1960), p. 8.

360. Theodore Dreiser, *Dawn*, p. 379.

361. J. Frank Dobie, p. 184.

362. Carlos Martyn, *Wendell Phillips*, p. 576.

363. Lincoln Steffens, p. 645.

364. Sinclair Lewis, *The Trail of the Hawk*, p. 58.

365. Ibid., p. 49.

366. Sinclair Lewis, *Elmer Gantry*, pp. 3 - 4.

367. George Santayana, *The Last Puritan*, p. 187.

368. George Ade, *Breaking into Society* (New York: Harper and Brothers, 1904), p. 22.

369. Ibid., p. 29.

370. John Kendrick Bangs, *Coffee and Repartee* (New York: Harper and Brothers, 1893), pp. 46, 44.

371. Ambrose Bierce, "Some Aspects of Education," *The Collected Works of Ambrose Bierce* (New York: Gordian Press, 1966), IX, 125.

372. John P. Marquand, *The Late George Apley*, p. 70.

373. Ibid., p. 69.

374. Samuel B. Ornitz, *Haunch, Paunch, and Jowl* (New York: Boni and Liveright, 1923), p. 72.

375. Mary Ellen Chase, p. 203.

376. Edmund Wilson, *A Prelude*, p. 117.

377. Richard Ruland, *The Rediscovery of American Literature*, p. 63.

378. Albert J. Nock, p. 75.

379. Clara Barrus, *The Heart of Burrough's Journals* (Port Washington, N.Y.: Kennikat Press, 1967), p. 163, from the 1928 edition.

380. Henry Seidel Canby, p. 59.

381. George William Curtis, p. 325.
382. Ludwig Lewisohn, *Upstream,* p. 161.
383. Henry Seidel Canby, p. 243.
384. Sinclair Lewis, *Babbitt,* pp. 191, 193.
385. Ibid., p. 193.
386. Henry Seidel Canby, p. 234.
387. Henry Seidel Canby, pp. 242 - 43.
388. Carlos Martyn, *Wendell Phillips,* p. 582.
389. Ibid.

Chapter Four

1. Harold Laski, *The American Democracy* (New York: Viking Press, 1948), p. 761.
2. Henry Adams, *The Education of Henry Adams* (New York: The Modern Library, 1931), p. 266.
3. Ibid., pp. 271 - 72.
4. Ibid., p. 504.
5. Henry B. Parkes, *The American People* (London: Eyre and Spottiswoode, 1949), p. 322.
6. Richard Hofstadter, *The American Political Tradition* (New York: Vintage Books, 1955), p. 272.
7. Merle Curti, *The Growth of American Thought* (New York: Harper and Brothers, 1943), p. 682.
8. Ibid., p. 684.
9. Arthur S. Link and William B. Colton, *American Epoch: A History of the United States Since the 1890s,* 3rd. ed. (New York: Alfred Knopf, 1967), p. 209.
10. Ibid., p. 212.
11. Richard Hofstadter, p. 275.
12. H. L. Mencken, "Meditation in E Minor," *The New Republic Anthology,* ed. Groff Conklin (New York: Dodge Publishing Co., 1936), p. 128.
13. Henry B. Parkes, p. 302.
14. James Harvey Robinson, *The Mind in the Making* (New York: Harper and Brothers, 1921), p. 173.
15. Kenneth Burke, "Waste — The Future of Prosperity," in *The New Republic Anthology,* p. 331.
16. Ibid., p. 334.
17. Preston William Slosson, *The Great Crusade and After* (New York: The Macmillan Co., 1969), p. 424.
18. Henry B. Parkes, p. 280.
19. Ibid., p. 303.
20. Preston William Slosson, p. 94.
21. Frank R. Kent, "On the Dayton Firing Line," in *The New Republic Anthology,* p. 230.

22. Preston William Slosson, p. 299.

23. Robert D. C. Ward, "Americanization and Immigration," in *Immigration As a Factor in American History*, ed. Oscar Handlin (Englewood Cliffs, N.J.: Prentice-Hall, 1959), pp. 190 - 92.

24. Ibid., p. 199.

25. Ibid., pp. 204, 205.

26. Henry B. Parkes, p. 305.

27. Richard Hofstadter, p. 352.

28. Louis Adamic, "Thirty Million New Americans," in *Essays of Three Decades*, ed. Arnold L. Bader and Carlton F. Wells (New York; Harper and Brothers, 1939), p. 222.

29. Arthur Krock, *In the Nation, 1932 - 1966* (New York: McGraw-Hill Book Co., 1966), p. 9.

30. Gerald W. Johnson, *Incredible Tale* (New York: Harper and Brothers, 1950), pp. 174 - 75.

31. Louis Mumford, "Faith for Living," in *The Democratic Spirit*, ed. Bernard Smith (New York: Alfred A. Knopf, 1943), p. 870.

32. Howard Zinn, *Post-War America, 1945 - 1971* (Indianapolis: Bobbs Merrill, 1973), p. 118.

33. Ibid., p. 119.

34. Henry B. Parkes, p. 304.

35. Arthur S. Link and William B. Colton, p. 654.

36. Howard Zinn, pp. 73, 116.

37. Henry Wadsworth Longfellow, "The Arsenal at Springfield," in *The American Tradition in Literature*, ed. Sculley Bradley et al. (New York: W. W. Norton and Co., 1967), I, 1504.

38. H. E. Newbranch, "Law and the Jungle," in *Writing for Today*, ed. Gerhard Lomer and J. W. Cunliffe, 3rd ed. (New York: Century Co., 1923), p. 154.

39. Arthur S. Link and William B. Colton, p. 241.

40. Preston William Slosson, p. 308.

41. Henry Steele Commager, *The Commonwealth of Learning* (New York: Harper and Row, 1968), p. 43.

42. Preston William Slosson, p. 266.

43. Quoted by David Riesman et al., in *The Lonely Crowd* (New Haven: Yale University Press, 1963), p. 196.

44. Howard Zinn, pp. 124 - 25.

45. William Faulkner, "Letter to the North," in *The Borzoi College Reader*, ed. Charles Muscatine and Marlene Griffith (New York: Alfred A. Knopf, 1966), p. 505.

46. Ibid., p. 503.

47. James Baldwin, "Faulkner and Desegregation," in *The Borzoi College Reader*, p. 510.

48. Martin Luther King, Jr., in "A Letter from Birmingham Jail," in *The Borzoi College Reader*, pp. 355 - 56.

49. Howard Zinn, p. 131.

50. Ibid.

51. Ibid., p. 147.

52. Preston William Slosson, p. 320.

53. Ibid., p. 322.

54. Ibid., p. 326.

55. Arthur S. Link and William B. Colton, p. 371.

56. Ibid., p. 653.

57. Arthur S. Link and William B. Colton, p. 565.

58. Lawrence A. Cremin, *The Transformation of the School* (New York: Alfred A. Knopf, 1962), p. 328.

59. Henry B. Parkes, p. 274.

60. Harold Laski, p. 389.

61. David Riesman, p. 63.

62. Arthur S. Link and William B. Colton, p. 656.

63. Ibid., p. 655.

64. Lawrence A. Cremin, p. 333.

65. Ibid., p. 340.

66. Ibid., p. 345.

67. Ibid., pp. 348 - 50.

68. Arthur S. Link and William B. Colton, p. 656.

69. Adolphe E. Meyer, *An Educational History of the American People* (New York: McGraw-Hill Co., 1967), p. 330.

70 Harold Laski, p. 351.

71. Porter Sargent, *Between Two Wars* (Boston: Porter Sargent, 1945), p. 328.

72. Henry Steele Commager, pp. 222 - 23.

73. Ibid., p. 276.

74. Preston William Slosson, p. 89.

75. Arthur S. Link and William B. Colton, p. 657.

76. Henry Steele Commager, p. 235.

77. Ibid., p. 232.

78. Ibid., p. 273.

79. Rod W. Norton and Herbert W. Edwards, *Backgrounds of American Literary Thought* (New York: Appleton-Century-Crofts, 1967), p. 318.

80. Ibid., p. 306.

81. Harold Laski, p. 337.

82. Ibid., p. 338.

83. John Tunis, *A Measure of Independence* (New York: Atheneum, 1964), p. 225.

Chapter Five

1. William H. Nolte, *H. L. Mencken's Smart Set* (Ithaca: Cornell University Press, 1968), p. 222.

2. James T. Farrell, *The League of Frightened Philistines* (New York; Vanguard, 1945), p. 87.

3. Ibid., p. 88.

4. John Dewey, *Democracy and Education* (New York: Macmillan Co., 1928), p. 22.

5. Thomas S. Eliot, "Modern Education and the Classics," in *Selected Essays* (New York: Harcourt, Brace and World, 1960), p. 452.

6. Richard S. Kennedy and Paschal Reeves, *The Notebooks of Thomas Wolfe* (Chapel Hill: University of North Carolina Press, 1970), I, 5.

7. John Dewey, pp. 118 - 19.

8. Ibid., p. 24.

9. Mark Van Doren, *Liberal Education* (New York: Henry Holt and Co., 1943), p. 94.

10. Robert M. Hutchins, *No Friendly Voice* (Chicago: University of Chicago Press, 1936), p. 8.

11. John Dewey, p. 92.

12. Frederick L. Gwynn and Joseph L. Blattner, *Faulkner in the University* (Charlottesville: University of Virginia Press, 1959), p. 212.

13. Theodore Dreiser, *Dawn* (New York: Horace Liveright, Inc., 1931), p. 589.

14. Albert J. Nock, *Memoirs of a Superfluous Man* (New York: Harper and Brothers, 1943), p. 272.

15. Paul Goodman, *Compulsory Mis-education* (New York: Horizon Press, 1964), p. 184.

16. Mark Van Doren, p. 15.

17. Paul Goodman, p. 20.

18. Paul Goodman, *The Empire City* (New York: Macmillan Co., 1959), p. 125.

19. Walter Lippman in *The Obligations of the University to the Social Order* (New York: New York University Press, 1933), p. 456.

20. Max Lerner, *America As a Civilization* (New York: Simon and Schuster, 1957), p. 733.

21. In response to a questionnaire I mailed to professors of education in 1961 on the usefulness of *The Goose-Step* as a criticism of American education, some of the younger professors stated that they had never heard of the book. Sinclair's thesis is still aired in academic circles; see Milton Fisk's chapter, "Academic Freedom in a Class Society," in *The Concept of Academic Freedom*, ed. Edmund L. Pincoffs (Austin, Texas, and London: University of Texas Press, 1975). For a full treatment of this subject see also my unpublished dissertation, "Upton Sinclair and Higher Education in America," New York University.

22. Hardly any of the standard histories of education mention Sinclair's two educational works: *The Goose-Step* (1923) and *The Goslings* (1924).

23. In the Sinclair collection, Lilly Library, University of Indiana. The letter is dated March 8, 1923.

24. Upton Sinclair, *My Lifetime in Letters* (Columbus, Missouri, University of Missouri Press, 1960), p. 289.

25. Lerner, p. 738.

26. Paul Goodman, *Compulsory Mis-education*, pp. 150 - 51.

27. John Dewey, p. 27.

28. Paul Goodman, *The Community of Scholars* (New York: Random House, 1962), p. ix.

29. James B. Conant, *Thomas Jefferson and the Development of American Public Education* (Berkeley: University of California Press, 1962), p. 61.

30. Paul Goodman, *The Community of Scholars*, p. 30.

31. Lerner, p. 743.

32. Albert J. Nock, p. 274.

33. Robert M. Hutchins, p. 103.

34. H. L. Mencken, *A Mencken Chrestomathy* (New York: Alfred A Knopf, 1956), p. 316.

35. Ibid.

36. Jacques Barzun, *The American University* (New York: Harper and Row, 1968), pp. 247 - 86 passim.

37. Thomas S. Eliot, p. 455.

38. Ibid., p. 454.

39. Albert J. Nock, p. 270.

40. Gwynn and Blattner, pp. 190 - 91.

41. James B. Meriwether, *Essays, Speeches, and Public Letters of William Faulkner* (New York: Random House, 1965), pp. 220 - 21.

42. Martin Luther King, "Letter from Birmingham Jail," in *The Borzoi College Reader*, ed. Charles Muscatine and Marlene Griffith (New York: Alfred Knopf, 1966), p. 349.

43. Mary McCarthy, *The Groves of Academe* (New York: Harcourt, Brace and Co., 1952), p. 12.

44. Stringfellow Barr, *Purely Academic* (New York: Simon and Schuster, 1958), pp. 214, 239.

45. Phoebe and Todhunter Ballard, *The Man Who Stole a University* (Garden City: Doubleday and Co., 1967), pp. 227, 232, 239, 244.

46. Howard Nemerov, *The Homecoming Game* (New York: Simon and Schuster, 1957), p. 118.

47. James Thurber and Elliot Nugent, *The Male Animal* (New York: Samuel French, 1941), p. 18.

48. W. E. B. Du Bois, *The Worlds of Color* (New York: Mainstream Pub., 1961), p. 266.

49. Elmer Rice, *We the People* (New York: Coward McCann, 1933), p. 202.

50. Ralph Ellison, *The Invisible Man* (New York: New American Library, 1952), pp. 38 - 39.

51. Ibid., p. 44.

52. Du Bois, *The Worlds of Color*, p. 14.

53. Jesse Stuart, *The Thread That Runs So True* (New York: Charles Scribner's Sons, 1951), pp. 284 - 85. Mr. Stuart excelled as a teacher, principal, and writer.

54. Max Lerner, p. 734.

55. Ibid., p. 735.

56. Upton Sinclair, *My Lifetime in Letters*, p. 289.

57. Percy Marks, *The Plastic Age* (New York: Grosset and Dunlap, 1924), p. 298.

58. Upton Sinclair, *Boston* (New York: Albert and Charles Boni, 1928), II, 419 - 20.

59. Upton Sinclair, *Oil* (New York: Grosset and Dunlap, 1927), p. 233.

60. Upton Sinclair, *Mountain City* (New York: Boni, 1930), p. 28.

61. Stringfellow Barr, p. 78

62. Ralph Ellison, p. 101.

63. Mary McCarthy, *The Groves of Academe*, p. 66.

64. Richard Wright, *Native Son* (Harper and Brothers, 1940), p. 57.

65. Phoebe and Todhunter Ballard, p. 41.

66. Stringfellow Barr, pp. 262 - 63.

67. Abraham Flexner, *An Autobiography* (New York: Simon and Schuster, 1960), p. 273.

68. Ibid., p. 126.

69. Sinclair Lewis, *Gideon Planish* (New York: Random House, 1943), p. 249.

70. Theodore Morrison, *To Make a World* (New York: Viking, 1957), p. 258.

71. Ezra Pound, *Polite Essays* (Freeport, N.Y.: Books for Libraries, 1966), p. 109, from the 1937 edition.

72. Adolphe E. Meyer, *An Educational History of the American People* (New York: McGraw-Hill Co., 1967), pp. 340 - 41. Adolphe E. Meyer writes textbooks with belletristic finesse. His educational histories include passages worthy of publication as models of literary wit and wisdom.

73. Paul Goodman, *The Community of Scholars*, p. 63.

74. John Hersey, *The Child Buyer* (New York: Alfred Knopf, 1960), p. 42.

75. Jesse Stuart, *Mr. Gallion's School* (New York: McGraw-Hill Co., 1967), pp. 14, 44.

76. Joshua M. Craig, *Tales Out of School* (Boston: Houghton Mifflin Co., 1961), p. 11.

77. Ibid., p. 68.

78. Ibid., pp. 110, 208.

79. Edward Chodorov, "Decision," in *The Best Plays of 1943 - 44*, ed. Burns Mantle (New York: Dodd, Mead, 1944), pp. 134, 147, 150.

80. William Saroyan, *The Human Comedy* (New York: Harcourt, Brace and Co., 1943), pp. 67 - 68.

81. Louis Auchincloss, *The Rector of Justin* (Boston: Houghton Mifflin Co., 1964), pp. 40, 149.

82. James Gould Cozzens, *Children and Others* (New York: Harcourt, Brace and Co., 1964), p. 108.

83. Ibid., pp. 111 - 12.

84. Ibid., pp. 118, 125, 127.

85. Jerome D. Salinger, *The Catcher in the Rye* (New York: Bantam Books, 1966), p. 168.

86. David Riesman, *Constraint and Variety in American Education* (Garden City: Doubleday Anchor Book, 1958), pp. 38 - 39.

87. Abraham Flexner, *Do Americans Really Value Education?* (Cambridge, Mass.: Harvard University Press, 1927), pp. 14 - 15.

88. John Ciardi, "To the Damnation of Deans," in *Issues in Education*, ed. Barnard Johnston (Boston: Houghton Mifflin Co., 1964), p. 29.

89. H. L. Mencken, *Prejudices, Third Series* (New York: Alfred Knopf, 1922), p. 255.

90. Ezra Pound, *Polite Essays*, p. 122.

91. Langston Hughes, *The Langston Hughes Reader* (New York: George Braziller, 1969), pp. 402 - 3.

92. Jacques Barzun, *The American University*, p. 7.

93. Randolph Bourne, Upton Sinclair, and James Wechsler saw Nicholas Murray Butler as an apologist for the established order - a man of inordinate conceit whose dream of political greatness was never realized.

94. H. L. Mencken, *Prejudices, Third Series*, pp. 213 - 14.

95. Heywood Hale Broun, *Collected Edition of Heywood Broun* (New York: Harcourt, Brace and Co., 1941), p. 233.

96. Ibid., p. 234.

97. Ludwig Lewisohn, *Upstream* (New York: Boni and Liveright, 1922), p. 158.

98. Upton Sinclair, *The Goose-Step* (Pasadena, California: Published by the author, 1923), p. 98.

99. Upton Sinclair, *CO-OP* (New York: Farrar and Rinehart, 1936), p. 320.

100. Shirley Jackson, *Hangsaman* (New York: Farrar, Straus, and Young, Inc., 1951), p. 320.

101. Sinclair Lewis, *Gideon Planish*, p. 54.

102. Upton Sinclair, *Boston*, I, 188.

103. Howard Fast, *The Passion of Sacco and Vanzetti* (New York: Blue Heron Press, 1953), p. 45.

104. Sidney Finklestein, *Existentialism and Alienation in American Literature* (New York: International Publishers, 1965), p. 237.

105. Randall Jarrell, *Pictures from an Institution* (New York: Alfred Knopf, 1955), pp. 22 - 23.

106. Ibid., p. 27.

107. Vardis Fisher, *We Are Betrayed* (Garden City: Doubleday and Doran, 1935), p. 202.

108. Gerald Warner Brace, *The Spire* (New York: W. W. Norton, 1952), pp. 3 - 4.

109. Ibid., p. 121.

110. Ibid., p. 100.

111. Ibid., p. 40.

112. Gerald Warner Brace, *The Department* (New York: W. W. Norton, 1968), p. 26.

113. Brace, *The Spire*, p. 307.

114. Ibid., p. 114.

115. Vardis Fisher, *No Villain Need Be* (Garden City: Doubleday and Doran, 1936), pp. 103 - 4.

116. Ibid., p. 169.

117. Theodore Morrison, *The Stones of the House* (New York: Viking, 1953), pp. 124 - 26.

118. Phoebe and Todhunter Ballard, *The Man Who Stole a University*, pp. 110 - 11.

119. Ibid., p. 104.

120. Ibid., p. 212.

121. Mary McCarthy, *The Groves of Academe*, p. 9.

122. Ibid., p. 11.

123. Ibid., p. 178.

124. Ibid., p. 179.

125. Ibid., p. 301.

126. Alvin Johnson, "Black Sheep," in *The New Republic Anthology* (New York: Dodge Pub. Co., 1936), p. 166.

127. Ibid., pp. 168 - 69.

128. W. E. B. Du Bois, *Mansart Builds a College* (New York: Mainstream Publishers, 1959), p. 153.

129. Ibid., p. 150.

130. Ibid., pp. 102 - 3.

131. Ralph Ellison, pp. 103 - 4.

132. Ibid., p. 105.

133. Ibid., p. 124.

134. Ibid., p. 126.

135. Ibid., p. 130.

136. Ibid., pp. 130 - 50 *passim*.

Chapter Six

1. Arthur Guiterman, "Education," *Death and General Putnam* (New York: E. P. Dutton, Inc., 1935), p. 75.

2. Jesse Stuart, *The Thread That Runs So True* (New York: Charles Scribner's Sons, 1970), p. 82.

3. Louis Auchincloss, *The Rector of Justin* (Boston: Houghton Mifflin Co., 1964), p. 139.

4. H. L. Mencken, *A Mencken Chrestomathy* (New York: Alfred Knopf, 1956), p. 302.

5. Ibid., p. 311.

6. Jesse Stuart, p. 9.

7. Ibid., pp. 14 - 15.

8. Louis Auchincloss, p. 26.

9. James Michener, *The Fires of Spring* (New York: Random House, 1949), p. 167.

10. Jesse Stuart, p. 54.

11. Ibid., p. 131.

12. Joshua M. Craig, *Tales Out of School* (Boston: Houghton Mifflin Co., 1961), p. 56.

13. Fern Marya Eckman, *The Furious Passage of James Baldwin* (New York: M. Evans and Co., 1966), p. 77.

14. James Gould Cozzens, "The Guns of the Enemy," in *Children and Others* (New York: Harcourt Brace, 1964), pp. 157 - 69 passim.

15. H. L. Mencken, *Prejudices, Third Series*, p. 238.

16. H. L. Mencken, *A Mencken Chrestomathy*, p. 364.

17. Louis Auchincloss, p. 14.

18. Frances Markham Briggs, *The Changing Concept of the Public School Teacher As Portrayed in American Novels* (Chapel Hill: University of North Carolina Press, 1962), p. 24.

19. John Updike, "A Sense of Shelter," in *Modern Short Stories*, ed. Arthur Mizener (New York: W. W. Norton Co., 1962), p. 187.

20. Upton Sinclair, *It Happened to Didymus* (New York: Sagamore Press, 1957), p. 7.

21. Jesse Stuart, *Mr. Gallion's School* (New York: McGraw-Hill Book Co., 1967), p. 64.

22. Randall Jarrell, *A Sad Heart at the Supermarket* (New York: Atheneum, 1962,) p. 42.

23. Sidney Finklestein, *Existentialism and Alienation in American Literature* (New York: International Pub., 1965), p. 246.

24. Robert Anderson, "Tea and Sympathy," in *Fifty Best Plays of the American Theater* (New York: Crown Pub., 1969), pp. 150, 152.

25. James T. Farrell, *Studs Lonigan* (New York: Vanguard, 1935), pp. 3, 5, 27.

26. Mary McCarthy, *Memories of a Catholic Girlhood* (New York: Harcourt, Brace, and World, 1957), p. 96.

27. Ibid., p. 121.

28. Ibid., p. 134.

29. Archibald MacLeish, *A Continuing Journey* (Boston: Houghton Mifflin Co., 1968), p. 140.

30. Paul Goodman, *The Community of Scholars* (New York: Random House, 1962), p. 141.

31. Stringfellow Barr, *Purely Academic* (New York: Simon and Schuster, 1958), pp. 300 - 301, 53.

32. James T. Farrell. *My Days of Anger* (New York: Vanguard, 1943), p. 144.

33. Gerald Warner Brace, *The Department* (New York: W. W. Norton Co., 1968), p. 40.

34. Ralph J. Mills, Jr., ed., *The Selected Letters of Theodore Roethke* (Seattle: University of Washington Press, 1968), pp. 26 - 27.

35. Ibid., p. 173.

36. Vardis Fisher, *We Are Betrayed* (Garden City: Doubleday and Doran, 1935), p. 203.

37. John Erskine, *My Life As a Teacher* (Philadelphia: J. B. Lippincott Co., 1948), p. 19.

38. D. D. Paige, ed., *Letters of Ezra Pound* (New York: Harcourt, Brace and Co., 1950), p. 247.

39. Ezra Pound, "The Teacher's Mission," in *Polite Essays* (Freeport, N.Y.: Books for Libraries, 1966), p. 118, from the 1937 edition.

40. Gerald Warner Brace, pp. 14 - 15.

41. Bernard Malamud, *A New Life* (New York: Farrar, Straus, and Cudahy, 1961), p. 21.

42. Randall Jarrell, *Pictures from An Institution* (New York: Alfred Knopf, 1955), p. 88.

43. Phillip Roth, *Letting Go* (New York: Random House, 1962), p. 63.

44. H. L. Mencken, *Prejudices, Third Series*, p. 247.

45. Edward A. Bloom and Lillian D. Bloom, *Gift of Sympathy* (Carbondale: Southern Illinois University Press, 1962), p. 104.

46. Frances Markham Briggs, p. 22.

47. Stringfellow Barr, p. 273.

48. Ezra Pound, *Polite Essays*, p. 113.

49. Vardis Fisher, *We Are Betrayed*, pp. 236 - 37.

50. Stringfellow Barr, pp. 69, 72, 83, 90.

51. Phillip Roth, p. 231.

52. Stringfellow Barr, p. 47.

53. Ronald Forman, *Time Out* (New York: The Macauley Co., 1931), pp. 96 - 98.

54. Bernard Malamud, p. 178.

55. Sinclair Lewis, *Gideon Planish* (New York: Random House, 1943), p. 46.

56. David Riesman, *Constraint and Variety in American Education* (Garden City: Doubleday Anchor Book, 1958), p. 48.

57. C. Wright Mills, *White Collar* (New York: The Oxford University Press, 1953), p. 129.

58. William H. Nolte, *H. L. Mencken's Smart Set Criticism* (Ithaca: Cornell University Press, 1968), p. 125.

59. F. Scott Fitzgerald, *Letters to His Daughter*, ed. Andrew Turnbull (New York: Charles Scribner's Sons, 1965), p. 142.

60. Gerald Warner Brace, *The Department*, pp. 35 - 36.

61. Ludwig Lewisohn, *Upstream* (Boni and Liveright, 1922), p. 170.

62. Walter Lippmann, *American Inquisitors* (New York: The Macmillan Co., 1928), p. 34.

63. Ezra Pound, "Abject and Utter Farce," in *Polite Essays*, p. 112.

64. Charles Norman, *Ezra Pound*, (New York: The Macmillan Co., 1960), p. 352.

65. Paul Goodman, *The Community of Scholars*, p. 48.

66. C. Wright Mills, *White Collar*, p. 152.

67. Phoebe and Henry Ephron, *Take Her, She's Mine* (New York: Random House, 1962), p. 100.

68. Bernard Malamud, p. 229.

69. John Ciardi, "To the Damnation of Deans," in *Issues in Education*, ed. Bernard Johnston (Boston: Houghton Mifflin Co., 1964), p. 69. Fictional, dramatic, and scholarly literature do not present a laudable image of the professoriat. From my study of Upton Sinclair's correspondence with professors (Sinclair Collection, Lilly Rare Book Library) I have found that many professors who had volunteered to supply Sinclair with cases of alleged violations of academic freedom, later requested him not to include their briefs in his book since such disclosures might jeopardize their tenure. See also Ezra Pound on the timid scholar in *Polite Essays*, p. 107.

70. Gerald Warner Brace, *The Spire* (New York: W. W. Norton Co., 1952), p. 82.

71. Mary McCarthy, *The Groves of Academe* (New York: Harcourt, Brace and Co., 1952), p. 82.

72. Saul Bellow, *Herzog* (New York: Viking Press, 1965), p. 81.

73. Upton Sinclair, *CO-OP* (New York: Farrar and Rinehart, 1936, p. 313.

74. Bernard Malamud, *A New Life*, p. 279.

75. Paul Shorey, "The Relations of American Literature and American Scholarship in Retrospect and Prospect," in *Four Addresses in Commemoration of the Twentieth Anniversary of the Founding of the American Academy of Arts and Letters* (Freeport, N. Y.: Books for Libraries, 1966), p. 28, from the 1928 edition. In the same address Professor Shorey complained that Jewish writers and scholars were cosmopolitans — a pejorative term to the genteel professor — who were tainting American letters by stressing foreign literature and scholarship in their books and lectures.

76. Sinclair Lewis, *Gideon Planish*, p. 141.

77. Upton Sinclair, *The Goose-Step* (Pasadena: Published by the author, 1923), p. 12.

78. Abraham Flexner, *Do Americans Really Value Education?* (Cambridge, Mass.: Harvard University Press, 1927), p. 32.

79. Mary McCarthy, *The Groves of Academe*, p. 83.

80. William Gibson, *A Mass for the Dead* (New York: Atheneum, 1969), p. 220.

81. James T. Farrell, *The Silence of History* (New York: Dell, 1964), p. 280.

82. Edmund Wilson, *I Thought of Daisy* (New York: Charles Scribner's Sons, 1929), p. 222.

83. James Michener, *The Fires of Spring* (New York: Random House, 1949), p. 228.

84. Vardis Fisher, *No Villain Need Be* (New York: Doubleday and Doran, 1936), p. 109.

85. Lawrance Thompson, *Robert Frost: The Years of Triumph* (New York: Holt, Rinehart, and Winston, 1970), p. 110.

86. Louis Untermeyer, ed., *The Letters of Robert Frost to Louis Untermeyer* (New York: Holt, Rinehart, and Winston, 1963), p. 277.

87. Lawrance Thompson, pp. 120 - 21. When Meiklejohn finally resigned Frost was elated. But fourteen faculty members left in protest, thirteen seniors refused to accept their diplomas, and three-fourths of the juniors decided against returning (ibid., p. 228).

88. Louis Untermeyer, p. 290.

89. Edward C. Lathem and Lawrance Thompson, *Robert Frost, Poetry and Prose* (New York: Holt, Rinehart, and Winston, 1972), p. 292.

90. Lawrance Thompson, *The Years of Triumph*, p. 271.

91. Louis Untermeyer, p. 289.

92. Thomas Wolfe, "Eugene Gant's Harvard," *The Harvard Book*, ed. William Bentinck-Smith (Cambridge, Mass.: Harvard Univ. Press, 1961), pp. 261 - 62.

93. Thomas Wolfe, *Of Time and the River* (New York: Charles Scribner's Sons, 1935), p. 420.

94. Thomas Clark Pollack and Oscar Cargill, *Thomas Wolfe at Washington Square* (London: Oxford Univ. Press, 1954), p. 149.

95. Thomas Wolfe, *Of Time and the River*, p. 441.

96. Thomas Clark Pollack and Oscar Cargill, p. 33.

97. Ibid., pp. 34, 110.

98. Ibid., p. 3.

99. Ibid., p. 30.

100. Louis Auchincloss, *The Rector of Justin* (Boston: Houghton Mifflin Co., 1964), p. 285.

101. Randall Jarrell, *A Sad Heart at the Supermarket* (New York: Atheneum, 1962), pp. 43 - 44.

102. Ibid., pp. 50 - 51.

103. Ibid., pp. 62 - 63.

104. Mark Van Doren, *Liberal Education* (New York: Henry Holt and Co., 1943), p. 135.

105. F. Scott Fitzgerald, *The Crack-Up*, ed. Edmund Wilson (New York: New Directions, 1945), p. 294.

106. F. Scott Fitzgerald, *Letters to His Daughter*, p. 18.

107. James T. Farrell, *Father and Son* (New York: Vanguard Press, 1940), p. 151.

108. Albert J. Nock, *Memoirs of a Superfluous Man* (New York: Harper and Brothers, 1943), p. 202.

109. Upton Sinclair, *Boston* (New York: Albert and Charles Boni, 1928), I., 54.

110. Elmer Rice, *We the People* (New York: Coward McCann, 1933), p. 7.

111. Edward C. Lathem and Lawrance Thompson, *Robert Frost, Poetry and Prose*, pp. 439 - 40.

112. Paul Goodman, *Empire City* (Indianapolis: Bobbs Merrill Co., 1959), pp. 126 - 27.

113. Edmund Wilson, *I Thought of Daisy*, p. 163.

114. Roy Newquist, *Conversations* (Chicago: Rand, McNally and Co., 1967), p. 273.

115. Moses Hadas, *Old Wine, New Bottles* (New York: Trident Press, 1962), p. 17.

116. James T. Farrell, *My Days of Anger*, p. 16.

117. Ibid., p. 117.

118. Albert J. Nock, "The Disadvantages of Being Educated," in *The Borzoi College Reader*, eds. Charles Muscatine and Marlene Griffith (New York: Alfred Knopf, 1966), p. 52.

119. Upton Sinclair, *The Book of Life* (Pasadena: Published by the author, 1922), I, 25.

120. Upton Sinclair, *Mountain City* (New York: Charles Boni, 1930), p. 37. In his essay, "Abject and Utter Farce," Ezra Pound writes that "until education welcomes any and every fact, it will remain what it now is, a farce." *Polite Essays*, p. 115.

121. Phillip D. Stong, *If School Keeps* (New York: Frederick A. Stokes, 1940), p. 104.

122. Vardis Fisher, *No Villain Need Be*, p, 101.

123. Phillip Stong, p. 163.

124. Ronald Forman, *Time Out* (New York: The Macauley Co., 1931), p. 306.

125. Robert Benchley, *Inside Benchley* (New York: Grosset and Dunlap, 1942), p. 213.

126. Shirley Jackson, *Hangsaman* (New York: Farrar, Strauss, and Young, 1951), pp. 60 - 61.

127. Jacques Barzun, *The American University* (New York: Harper and Row, 1968), p. 216.

128. Albert J. Nock, p. 90.

129. Edward A. Bloom and Lillian D. Bloom, *Gift of Sympathy* (Carbondale: Southern Illinois University Press, 1962), p. 102.

130. Phillip Stong, p. 152.

131. Upton Sinclair, *Oil* (New York: Grosset and Dunlap, 1927), p. 234.

132. Mary Ellen Chase, *A Goodly Fellowship* (New York: The Macmillan Co.), p. 59.

133. H. L. Mencken, *A Mencken Chrestomathy*, p. 132.

134. Archibald MacLeish, *A Continuing Journey* (Boston: Houghton Mifflin Co., 1968), p. 246.

135. Albert J. Nock, p. 79.

136. T. S. Eliot, "Modern Education and the Classics," *Selected Essays* (New York: Harcourt Brace, and World, 1960), pp. 457 - 59.

137. Ibid., p. 460.

138. Moses Hadas, p. 138.

139. Mark Van Doren, *Liberal Education* (New York: Henry Holt and Co., 1943), p. 79.

140. Louis Auchincloss, p. 44.

141. Bernard Malamud, p. 28.

142. William Gibson, pp. 200, 208.

143. F. Scott Fitzgerald, *Letters to His Daughter*, p. 49.

144. James T. Farrell, *The League of Frightened Philistines*, p. 82.

145. W. E. B. Du Bois, *Mansart Builds a School* (New York: Mainstream Pub., 1959), pp. 104, 138, 140.

146. W. E. B. Du Bois, *The Autobiography of W. E. B. Du Bois* (New York: International Pub. 1968), pp. 312 - 13.

147. Eustace Mullins, *The Difficult Individual, Ezra Pound* (New York: Fleet Pub. Corp., 1961), p. 185.

148. James T. Farrell, *Judgment Day* (New York: Vanguard Pub., 1935), p. 192.

149. Upton Sinclair, *Mountain City*, p. 36.

150. Stringfellow Barr, pp. 31 - 32.

151. Edward A. and Lillian D. Bloom, *The Gift of Sympathy*, p. 105.

152. Edward C. Lathem, *Interviews with Robert Frost*, p. 70.

153. Jesse Stuart, *The Thread That Runs So True*, p. 72.

154. Phoebe and Henry Ephron, *Take Her, She's Mine* (New York: Random House, 1962), p. 52.

155. Joseph Heller, *Catch 22* (New York: Dell Pub., 1969), p. 88.

156. Thomas Wolfe, *Of Time and the River*, p. 428.

157. Ibid., p. 446.

158. Ibid.

159. Thomas Clark Pollack and Oscar Cargill, p. 27.

160. Lionel Trilling, "Of This Time, Of That Place," *The Forms of Fiction*, ed. John Gardner and Lennis Dunlap (New York: Random House, 1966), pp. 417 - 18.

161. Ibid., p. 428.

162. Joseph Heller, p. 221.

163. William Gibson, p. 163.

164. F. Scott Fitzgerald, *The Crack-Up*, p. 301.

165. Phillip Stong, pp. 118 - 19.

166. Frederick L. Gwynn and Joseph L. Blattner, *Faulkner in the University* (Charlottesville: University of Virginia Press, 1959), pp. 187 - 88.

167. Morris Raphael Cohen, *American Thought* (Glencoe: The Free Press, 1954), p. 40.

168. Robert Maynard Hutchins, *No Friendly Voice* (Chicago: University of Chicago Press, 1936), p. 7.

169. John Reed, "Almost Thirty," in *The New Republic Anthology*, ed. Groof Conklin, p. 67.

170. Art Buchwald, *Son of the Great Society* (New York: G. P. Putnam Sons, 1966), p. 103.

171. Ibid., p. 194.

172. Phoebe and Todhunter Ballard, *The Man Who Stole a University* (Garden City: Doubleday and Co., 1967), p. 78.

173. Ibid., p. 89.

174. Phoebe and Henry Ephron, p. 73.

175. Mary McCarthy, *The Groves of Academe*, p. 65.

176. Theodore Morrison, *The Stones of the House* (New York: Viking Press, 1953), p. 82.

177. James T. Farrell, *My Days of Anger*, p. 140.

178. Mary McCarthy, *The Groves of Academe*, p. 64.

179. Quoted by William Bentinck-Smith from the *Harvard Alumni Bulletin* (1925). *The Harvard Book* (Cambridge: Harvard University Press, 1961), p. 15. Bernard De Voto feared that "the college novel is going to get worse on the average, not better; college has replaced the war as the natural subject for first novels, and the ads are going to be full of hurt sophomores and disenchanted seniors" (ibid).

180. Louis Auchincloss, pp. 163, 246 - 47.

181. Ibid., pp. 259 - 60.

182. Ibid., p. 263.

183. Howard Mumford Jones, *One Great Society* (New York: Harcourt, Brace, and Co.), p. 123.

184. Phillip Stong, p. 109.

185. Percy Marks, *The Plastic Age* (New York: Grosset and Dunlap, 1924), pp. 192 - 95.

186. Phillip Stong, p. 105.

187. Shirley Jackson, *Hangsaman*, p. 77.

188. Mary McCarthy, *The Groves of Academe*, p. 23.

189. James T. Farrell, *The Young Manhood of Studs Lonigan* (New York: Vanguard Press, 1935), p. 251.

190. Vardis Fisher, *We Are Betrayed*, p. 34.

191. Phoebe and Todhunter Ballard, *The Man Who Stole a University*, pp. 148, 150.

192. Louis Sheaffer, *Eugene O'Neill: Son and Playwright* (Boston: Little, Brown and Co., 1968), p. 115.

193. F. Scott Fitzgerald, *The Crack-Up*, pp. 89 - 90.

194. Thomas Clark Pollack and Oscar Cargill, p. 194.

195. Thomas Wolfe, *Of Time and the River*, p. 170.

196. Mark Van Doren, p. 101.

197. Stringfellow Barr, p. 51.

198. W. E. B. Du Bois, *Worlds of Color* (New York: Mainstream Pub., 1961), p. 11.

199. D. D. Paige, ed., *The Letters of Ezra Pound, 1907 - 1941* (New York: Harcourt Brace and Co., 1950), p. 225.

200. Jacques Barzun, *The American University* (New York: Harper and Row, 1968), p. 227.

201. Upton Sinclair, *Boston*, II, 407.

202. Theodore Solotaroff, "The Graduate Student: A Profile," *Commentary* (December, 1961), p. 490.

203. Ibid.

204. John Barth, *The End of the Road* (Garden City: Doubleday and Co., 1967), p. 4.

205. Phillip Stong, pp. 228 - 29.

206. Hyde Cox and Edward C. Lathem, *The Selected Prose of Robert Frost* (New York: Holt, Rinehart, and Winston, 1959), p. 116.

207. Jacques Barzun, *The American University*, p. 222.

208. Stringfellow Barr, p. 189.

209. James T. Farrell, *My Days of Anger*, p. 237.

210. Richard S. Kennedy and Paschal Reeves, *The Notebooks of Thomas Wolfe* (Chapel Hill: The University of North Carolina Press, 1970), I, 30.

211. Jacques Barzun, *The American University*, p. 225.

212. Abraham Flexner, *An Autobiography* (New York: Simon and Schuster, 1960), pp. 236 - 37.

213. Ibid., p. 253.

Chapter Seven

1. John Updike, "A Sense of Shelter," in *Moderate Short Stories*, ed. Arthur Mizener (New York: W. W. Norton, 1971), p. 185.

2. Jacques Barzun, *Teacher in America* (Boston, Little, Brown and Co., 1945), p. 184.

3. Archibald MacLeish, *Continuing Journey* (Boston: Houghton Mifflin Co., 1958), p. 131.

4. Ibid., p. 140.

5. William H. Nolte, *H. L. Mencken's Smart Set Criticism* (Ithaca: Cornell University Press, 1968), p. 222.

6. Robert Maynard Hutchins, *No Friendly Voice* (Chicago: University of Chicago Press, 1936), p. 9.

7. Noel Stock, *The Life of Ezra Pound* (New York: Pantheon, 1970), p. 349.

8. Ralph J. Mills, Jr., ed., *The Selected Letters of Theodore Roethke* (Seattle: University of Washington Press, 1968), p. 102.

9. Joseph Wood Krutch, *More Lives Than One* (New York: William Sloane Associates, 1962), p. 63.

10. Paul Goodman, *The Community of Scholars* (New York: Random House, 1962), p. 7.

11. Ibid., p. 45.

12. Robert Maynard Hutchins, *The Higher Learning in America* (New Haven: Yale University Press, 1948), p. 6.

13. Leo Rosten, *The Many Worlds of Leo Rosten* (New York: Harper and Row, 1964), p. 214.

14. Robert Maynard Hutchins, *No Friendly Voice*, p. 121.

15. C. Wright Mills, *White Collar* (New York: Oxford University Press, 1956), p. 152.

16. Archibald MacLeish, *A Continuing Journey*, pp. 134, 136.

17. Ibid., p. 133.

18. John Dewey, *Democracy and Education* (New York: The Macmillan Company, 1928), p. 10.

19. Robert Morss Lovett, "Upton Sinclair," *English Journal* 17 (November, 1928), 712.

20. Brooks Atkinson, ed., *College in a Yard* (Cambridge, Mass.: Harvard University Press, 1957), p. 5.

21. Archibald MacLeish, p. 265.

22. Vardis Fisher, *No Villain Need Be* (Garden City: Doubleday and Doran, 1936), pp. 89, 96, 184, 214.

23. Upton Sinclair, *Boston* (New York: Albert and Charles Boni, 1928), II, 678.

24. Upton Sinclair, *Mountain City* (New York: Boni, 1930), p. 57.

25. Upton Sinclair, *CO-OP* (New York: Farrar and Rinehart Co., 1936), p. 323.

26. Sinclair Lewis, *Gideon Planish* (New York: Random House, 1943), p. 272.

27. Ibid., p. 118.

28. James Michener, *The Fires of Spring* (New York: Random House, 1949), p. 250.

29. Gerald Warner Brace, *The Department* (New York: W. W. Norton Co., 1968), p. 270.

30. James Thurber and Elliot Nugent, *The Male Animal* (New York: Samuel French Co., 1941), pp. 15, 63, 129, 134.

31. Noam A. Chomsky, "The Responsibilities of Scholars," in *The Dissenting Academy*, ed. Theodore Roszak (New York: Pantheon Books, 1968), p. 291.

32. Jacques Barzun, *The American University* (New York: Harper and Row, 1968), p. 257.

33. H. L. Mencken, *Minority Report* (New York: Alfred Knopf, 1956), p. 135.

34. Phillip D. Stong, *If School Keeps* (New York: Frederick A. Stokes, 1941), p. 123.

35. Robert Maynard Hutchins, *The Higher Learning in America*, p. 11.

36. Phillip D. Stong, pp. 125 - 26.

37. John Faulkner, *My Brother Bill* (New York: The Trident Press, 1963), p. 144.

38. William Saroyan, *The Human Comedy* (New York: Harcourt, Brace, Co., 1943), pp. 61, 78.

39. Jerome D. Salinger, *The Catcher in the Rye* (New York: Random House, 1966), pp. 2, 43.

40. Louis Auchincloss, *The Rector of Justin* (Boston: Houghton Mifflin Co., 1964), p. 11.

41. Arthur Miller, *The Death of a Salesman* (New York: Viking Press, 1964), p. 33.

42. Bernard Malamud, *A New Life* (New York: Farrar, Straus and Cudahy, 1961), p. 277.

43. Upton Sinclair, *Oil* (New York: Grosset and Dunlap, 1927), p. 394.

44. Theodore Morrison, *The Stones of the House* (New York: Viking, 1953), p. 57.

45. Percy Marks, *The Plastic Age* (New York: Grosset and Dunlap, 1924), p. 77.

46. Ronald Forman, *Time Out* (New York: The Macauley Co., 1931), pp. 20, 48.

47. Ibid., p. 104.

48. Ibid., p. 139.

49. Edward C. Lathem and Lawrence Thompson, *Robert Frost, Prose and Poetry* (New York: Holt, Rinehart, and Winston, 1972), p. 375.

50. Robert Maynard Hutchins, *The Higher Learning in America*, p. 22.

51. Howard Mumford Jones, *Violence and Reason* (New York: Atheneum, 1969), p. 136.

52. John P. Marquand, *Thirty Years* (Boston: Little, Brown and Co., 1954), p. 75.

53. Howard Nemerov, *The Homecoming Game* (New York: Simon and Schuster, 1957), p. 36.

54. Theodore Morrison, *The Stones of the House*, p. 53.

55. Upton Sinclair, *The Goose-Step* (Pasadena: Published by the Author, 1923), pp. 366, 388 - 99.

56. Stringfellow Barr, *Purely Academic* (New York: Simon and Schuster, 1958), pp. 190 - 91.

57. Louis Sheaffer, *Eugene O'Neill, Son and Playwright* (Boston: Little, Brown and Co., 1968), p. 125.

58. John Mason Brown, *The Worlds of Robert Sherwood* (New York: Harper and Row, 1965), p. 96.

59. John Faulkner, p. 141.

60. Fern Marya Eckman, *The Furious Passage of James Baldwin* (New York: M. Evans and Co., 1966), p. 62.

61. William Gibson, *A Mass for the Dead* (New York: Atheneum, 1968), p. 192.

62. Albert J. Nock, *Memoirs of A Superfluous Man* (New York: Harper and Brothers, 1943), p. 65.

63. Roy Newquist, *Conversations* (Chicago: Rand, McNally and Co., 1967), p. 261.

64. C. Wright Mills, *White Collar* (New York: The Oxford University Press, 1953), p. 64.

65. Max Lerner, *America As a Civilization* (New York: Simon and Schuster, 1957), p. 741.

66. Mark Van Doren, *Liberal Education* (New York: Henry Holt and Co., 1943), p. 92.

67. Robert Lowell, *Life Studies* (New York: Farrar, Straus, and Giroux, 1959), p. 25.

68. Roy Newquist, *Conversations*, p. 303.

69. Mary McCarthy, *Memories of a Catholic Girlhood* (New York: Harcourt, Brace and Co., 1957), pp. 18, 25, 102, 104.

70. John Hersey, *The Child Buyer* (New York: Alfred Knopf, 1960), p. 26.

71. Upton Sinclair, *Oil* (New York: Grosset and Dunlap, 1927), p. 105.

72. Mary McCarthy, *Memories of a Catholic Girlhood*, p. 138.

73. James T. Farrell, *Father and Son* (New York: Vanguard Press, 1940), p. 85.

74. Jerome D. Salinger, *The Catcher in the Rye* (New York: Bantam Books, 1966), p. 74.

75. Ibid., p. 131.

76. Theodore Dreiser, *The Bulwark* (Garden City: Doubleday and Co., 1946), p. 152.

77. Ibid., pp. 159 - 62.

78. Albert J. Nock, p. 260.

79. Phillip D. Stong, *If School Keeps* (New York: Frederick A. Stokes, 1940), p. 113.

80. H. L. Mencken, *A Mencken Chrestomathy* (New York: Alfred Knopf, 1956), p. 315.

81. Porter Sargent, *Between Two Wars* (Boston: Porter Sargent, 1945), p. 376.

82. Upton Sinclair, *Money Writes* (Long Beach, California: Published by the author, 1927), p. 130.

83. D. D. Paige, ed., *Letters of Ezra Pound*. (New York: Harcourt, Brace and Co., 1950), p. 196.

84. Moses Hadas, *Old Wine, New Bottles* (New York: Trident Press, 1962), p. 56.

85. Albert J. Nock, p. 264.

86. Max Lerner, p. 748.

87. John P. Marquand, *Thirty Years* (Boston: Little, Brown and Co., 1954), p. 75.

88. Hyde Cox and Edward C. Lathem, *The Selected Prose of Robert Frost* (New York: Holt, Rinehart, and Winston, 1959), p. 35.

89. Pearl S. Buck, *My Several Worlds* (New York: John Day, 1954), p. 90.

90. Noam A. Chomsky, "The Responsibilities of Intellectuals," in *The Dissenting Academy*, ed. Theodore Roszak (New York: Pantheon Books, 1968), p. 264.

91. Jacques Barzun, *The American University*, p. 54. See also Max Lerner, *America As a Civilization*, p. 742.

92. Richard S. Kennedy and Paschal Reeves, *The Notebooks of Thomas Wolfe* (Chapel Hill: University of North Carolina Press, 1970), II, 838.

93. Langston Hughes, *The Langston Hughes Reader* (New York: George Braziller, 1969), pp. 403 - 4.

94. Ibid., p. 402 - 3.

95. James B. Meriwether, *Essays, Speeches, and Public Addresses of William Faulkner* (New York: Random House, 1965), pp. 215 - 16.

96. Albert J. Nock, p. 75.

97. John P. Marquand, *Thirty Years*, p. 44.

98. Roy Newquist, *Conversations*, p. 134.

99. Howard Mumford Jones, *Violence and Reason* (New York: Atheneum, 1969), p. 59.

100. James Michener, *Fires of Spring*, p. 227.

101. Stringfellow Barr, *Purely Academic*, pp. 34 - 35.

102. Sinclair Lewis, *Arrowsmith* (New York: Harcourt Brace and Co. 1925), p. 7.

103. Upton Sinclair, *Boston*, II, 617.

104. James Michener, *The Fires of Spring*, pp. 231 - 32.

105. Phoebe and Todhunter Ballard, *The Man Who Stole a University* (Garden City: Doubleday and Co., 1967), p. 8.

106. Fern Marya Eckman, *The Furious Passage of James Baldwin*, pp. 48 - 49.

107. Roy Newquist, p. 37.

108. Ibid., p. 83.

109. Ibid., p. 330.

110. Frederick L. Gwynn and Joseph L. Blattner, *Faulkner in The University* (Charlottesville: University of Virginia Press, 1959), pp. 11 - 12.

111. Leo Rosten, *The Many Worlds of Leo Rosten*, p. 83.

112. Charles A. Fenton, *Stephen Vincent Benét* (New Haven: Yale University Press, 1958), pp. 46 - 47.

113. Frederick L. Gwynn and Joseph L. Blattner, p. 19.

114. Roy' Newquist, p. 304.

115. Thomas Clark Pollack and Oscar Cargill, *Thomas Wolfe at Washington Square* (London: Oxford University Press, 1954), p. 9.

116. Ibid., p. 74.

117. F. N. Robinson, ed., *The Complete Works of Chaucer* (Boston: Houghton Mifflin Co., 1933), p. 24.

Selected Bibliography

1. Bibliographical Studies

BRIGGS, FRANCES MARKHAM. *The Changing Concept of the Public School Teacher As Portrayed in American Novels.* Chapel Hill: University of North Carolina Press, 1962.
CHARLES, DON. C. "The Stereotype of the Teacher in American Literature." *Educational Forum* 14: 299 - 305.
COLEY, JAMES WATSON. "The Schoolmaster in Some Works of American Literature." M. A. thesis, University of North Carolina, 1953.
FOFF, ARTHUR. "Teacher Stereotypes in the American Novel." Ph. D. thesis, Stanford University, 1957.
FOWLER, HERBERT E. "Criticism of Education in Twentieth Century Novels." Ph. D. thesis, School of Education, New York University, 1932.
FURNESS, EDNA. "The Image of the High School Teacher," *Educational Forum* 24: 457 - 464.
GREENE, MAXINE. *The Public School and the Private Vision.* New York: Random House, 1965.
LYONS, JOHN O. *The College Novel in America.* Carbondale: Southern Illinois University Press, 1962.
TIEDT, IRIS M., and TIEDT, SIDNEY W. *Unrequired Reading.* Corvallis: Oregon State University Press, 1967.

2. Social Sciences

BRAWLEY, BENJAMIN. *A Short History of the American Negro.* New York: Macmillan, 1939.
CURTI, MERLE. *The Growth of American Thought.* New York: Harper and Brothers, 1943.
GILMAN, CHARLOTTE PERKINS. *This Man-Made World.* New York: Charlton Co., 1911.
GOLDMAN, ERIC. *Rendezvous with Destiny.* New York: Vintage Books, 1962.
HART, ALBERT BUSHNELL. *American History Told by Contemporaries.* 5 vols. New York: Macmillan, 1964.

HOFSTADTER, RICHARD. *The Age of Reform.* New York: Alfred A. Knopf, 1966.

HOLBROOK, STEWART H. *Dreamers of the American Dream.* Garden City: Doubleday, 1957.

HORTON, ROD W., and EDWARDS, HERBERT W. *Background of American Literary Thought.* New York: Appleton-Century-Crofts, 1967.

LASKI, HAROLD. *The American Democracy.* New York: Viking, 1948.

LERNER, MAX. *America As a Civilization.* New York: Simon and Schuster, 1957.

LINK, ARTHUR S., and COLTON, WILLIAM B. *A History of the United States Since the 1890's.* New York: Alfred A. Knopf, 1967.

LLOYD, HENRY DEMAREST. *Wealth Against Commonwealth.* Englewood Cliffs, N.J.: Prentice-Hall, 1963.

MILLER, PERRY, ed. *American Thought from the Civil War to World War I.* New York: Holt, Rinehart, and Winston, 1954.

MYRDAL, GUNNAR et al. *An American Dilemma.* 2 vols. New York: Harper and Brothers, 1944.

PARRINGTON, VERNON L. *Main Currents in American Thought: An Interpretation of American Literature from the Beginnings to 1920.* 3 vols. New York: Harcourt, Brace. 1927.

TOWNSEND, MALCOLM. *Handbook of the United States Political History.* Boston: Lothrop, Lea, and Shepard, 1905.

WILLIAMS, GEORGE N. *History of the Negro Race in America.* 2 vols. New York: Arno Press and *The New York Times*, 1968.

WISH, HARVY, ed. *Reconstruction in the South.* New York: Farrar, Straus, and Giroux, 1965.

WYLIE, IRVING G. *The Self-Made Man in America.* New York: The Free Press, 1966.

ZIFF, LARZER. *The American 1890's.* New York: Viking, 1968.

ZINN, HOWARD. *Postwar America, 1945 - 1971.* Indianapolis: Bobbs-Merrill, 1973.

3. Literary Criticism

BLAIR, WALTER et. al. *The Literature of the United States.* Chicago: Scott, Foresman and Company, 1957.

BRAWLEY, BENJAMIN G. *Early Negro American Writers.* Freeport, N.Y.: Books for Libraries, 1968.

ECKMAN, FERN MARYA. *The Furious Passage of James Baldwin.* New York: M. Evans, 1966.

FINKELSTEIN, SIDNEY. *Existentialism and Alienation in American Literature.* New York: International, 1965.

FRENCH, BRYANT MORY. *Mark Twain and the Gilded Age.* Dallas: Southern Methodist Univ., 1965.

LEWISOHN LUDWIG. *The Story of American Literature.* New York: The Modern Library, 1939.

MEYER, ROY, W. *The Middle Western Farm Novel in the Twentieth Century.* Lincoln: University of Nebraska Press, 1965.

NEVIUS, BLAKE. *Robert Herrick: The Development of a Novelist.* Berkeley and Los Angeles: University of California Press, 1962.

NEWQUIST, ROY. *Conversations.* Chicago: Rand McNally and Co., 1967.

PIZER, DONALD. *The Novels of Frank Norris.* Bloomington: University of Indiana Press, 1966.

QUINN, ARTHUR HOBSON. *The Literature of the American People.* New York: Appleton-Century-Crofts, 1951.

SINCLAIR, UPTON, *Mammonart.* Pasadena: Published by the author, 1925.

SPILLER, ROBERT et al. *The Literary History of the United States.* New York: Macmillan, 1959.

4. Educational Sources

ATKINSON, BROOKS, ed. *College in a Yard.* Cambridge, Mass.: Harvard University Press, 1957.

BARZUN, JACQUES. *The American University.* New York: Harper and Row, 1968.

CANBY, HENRY SEIDEL. *Alma Mater.* New York: Farrar and Rinehart, 1946.

COMMAGER, HENRY STEELE, ed. *Documents of American History.* New York: Appleton-Century-Crofts, 1968.

———. *The Commonwealth of Learning.* New York: Harper and Row, 1968.

CUBBERLEY, ELLWOOD P. *Public Education in the United States.* Boston: Houghton Mifflin, 1919.

CURTI, MERLE. *The Social Ideas of American Educators.* Paterson, N.J.: Pageant, 1959.

DEUEL, LEO, ed. *The Teacher's Treasure Chest.* Englewood Cliffs, N.J.: Prentice-Hall, 1956.

DEWEY, JOHN. *Democracy and Education.* New York: Macmillan, 1928.

FLEXNER, ABRAHAM. *Do Americans Really Value Education?* Cambridge, Mass.: Harvard University Press, 1927.

GOODMAN, PAUL. *The Community of Scholars.* New York: Random House, 1962.

———. *Compulsory Mis-education.* New York: Horizon, 1964.

GROSS, CARL H., AND CHANDLER, CHARLES C. *The History of Education Through Readings.* Boston: D. C. Heath, 1964.

GWYNN, FREDERICK L., and BLATTNER, JOSEPH L. *Faulkner in the University.* Charlottesville: University of Virginia Press, 1959.

HADAS, MOSES. *Old Wine, New Bottles.* New York: Trident, 1962.

HUTCHINS, ROBERT MAYNARD. *No Friendly Voice.* Chicago: University of Chicago Press, 1938.

JAMES, WILLIAM. *Talks to Teachers on Psychology.* New York: Henry Holt, 1900.

JONES, HOWARD MUMFORD. *Violence and Reason.* New York: Atheneum, 1969.

MAYER FREDERICK. *American Ideas and Education.* Columbus, Ohio: Charles E. Merrill, 1964.

MEYER, ADOLPHE E. *An Educational History of the American People.* New York: McGraw-Hill, 1967.

PERRY, BLISS. *And Gladly Teach.* Boston: Houghton Mifflin, 1938.

RIESMAN, DAVID. *Constraint and Variety in American Education.* New York: Doubleday Anchor Books, 1958.

ROBINSON, JAMES HARVEY. *The Mind in the Making.* New York: Harper and Brothers, 1921.

SARGENT, PORTER. *Between Two Wars.* Boston: Porter Sargent, 1945.

SINCLAIR, UPTON. *The Goose-Step.* Pasadena: Published by the author, 1923.

———. *The Goslings.* Pasadena: Published by the author, 1924.

SLOSSON, EDWIN C. *The American Spirit in Education.* New Haven: Yale University Press, 1921.

SMITH-BENTINCK, WILLIAM. *The Harvard Book.* Cambridge, Mass.: Harvard University Press, 1961.

TYACK, DAVID B. ed. *Turning Points in American Educational History.* Waltham, Mass.: Blaisdell, 1967.

VAN DOREN, MARK. *Liberal Education.* New York: Henry Holt, 1943.

VEBLEN, THORSTEIN. *The Higher Learning in America.* New York: Heubsch, 1918.

5. Biographical Sources

ADAMS, HENRY. *The Education of Henry Adams.* New York: The Modern Library, 1931.

ADAMS, J. DONALD. *Copey of Harvard.* Boston: Houghton Mifflin, 1960.

ALLEN, GAY WILSON. *William James.* New York: Viking, 1967.

ANTIN, MARY. *The Promised Land.* Boston: Houghton Mifflin, 1940.

BOURNE, RANDOLPH. *The History of a Literary Radical.* New York: S. A. Russell, 1956.

BRAGDON, HENRY WILKINSON. *Woodrow Wilson, the Academic Years.* Cambridge, Mass.: The Belknap Press, 1968.

BUCK, PEARL. *My Several Worlds.* New York: John Day, 1954.

CHASE, MARY ELLEN. *A Goodly Fellowship.* New York: Macmillan, 1956.

COX, HYDE. and CONNERY, EDWARD. *The Selected Prose of Robert Frost* New York: Holt, Rinehart, and Winston, 1959.

DARROW, CLARENCE. *The Story of My Life.* New York: Charles Scribner's Sons, 1960.

DOBIE, FRANK. *Some Part of Myself.* Boston: Little, Brown, 1967.

DREISER, THEODORE. *Dawn.* New York: Horace Liveright, 1931.

DU BOIS, W. E. B. *The Autobiography of W. E. B. Du Bois.* New York: International, 1968.

FAULKNER, JOHN. *My Brother Bill.* New York: Trident, 1963.

FENTON, CHARLES A. *Stephen Vincent Benét*. New Haven: Yale University Press, 1958.

FLEXNER, ABRAHAM. *An Autobiography*. New York: Simon and Schuster, 1960.

GIBSON, WILLIAM. *A Mass for the Dead*. New York: Atheneum, 1968.

GLASSRUD, CLARENCE A. *Hjalmar Hjorth Boyesen*. Northfield, Minn.: The Norwegian-American Historical Assn., 1963.

HARDWICK. ELIZABETH, ed. *Selected Letters of William James*. New York: Farrar, Straus, and Cudahy, 1961.

HICKS, GRANVILLE. *John Reed*. New York: Benjamin Blom, 1968.

HOVEY, RICHARD B. *John Jay Chapman*. New York: Columbia University Press, 1959.

HOWE, MARK A. DE WOLFE. *Barrett Wendell and His Letters*. Boston: Atlantic Monthly Press. 1924.

HUGHES, LANGSTON. *The Langston Hughes Reader*. New York: George Braziller, 1959.

JAMES, HENRY. *Charles W. Eliot*. 2 vols. Boston: Houghton Mifflin, 1930.

JOHNS, ORRICK. *Time of Our Lives*. New York: Stackpole, 1937.

JOHNSON, JAMES, WELDON. *The Autobiography of an Ex-Colored Man*. New York: Alfred A. Knopf, 1944.

KENNEDY, RICHARD S. and REEVES, PASCHAL. *The Notebooks of Thomas Wolfe*. 2 vols. Chapel Hill: University of North Carolina Press, 1970.

KRUTCH, JOSEPH WOOD. *More Lives Than One*. New York: William Sloane, 1962.

LATHEM, EDWARD CONNERY. *Interviews with Robert Frost*. New York: Holt, Rinehart, and Winston, 1966.

LEWISOHN, LUDWIG. *Upstream*. New York: Boni and Liveright, 1922.

LOWELL, ROBERT. *Life Studies*. New York: Farrar, Straus, and Rinehart, 1959.

McCARTHY, MARY. *Memories of a Catholic Girlhood*. New York: Harcourt, Brace, 1957.

MacLEISH, ARCHIBALD. *A Continuing Journey*. Boston: Houghton Mifflin, 1968.

MARQUAND, JOHN P. *Thirty Years*. Boston: Little, Brown, 1954.

MARTYN, CARLOS. *Wendell Phillips*. New York: Funk and Wagnalls, 1890.

MENCKEN, H. L. *Happy Days*. New York: Alfred A. Knopf, 1955.

———. *Heathen Days*. New York: Alfred A. Knopf, 1955.

MILLS, RALPH. J., ed. *Selected Letters of Theodore Roethke*. Seattle: University of Washington Press, 1968.

MOREAU, JOHN ADAM. *Randolph Bourne: Legend and Reality*. Washington D. C.: Public Affairs Press. 1966.

NOCK, ALBERT JAY. *Memoirs of a Superfluous Man*. New York: Harper and Brothers, 1943.

NOLTE, WILLIAM H. *H. L. Mencken's Smart Set Criticism*. Ithaca, N.Y.: Cornell Univ. Press. 1968.

PAIGE, D. D. ed. *Letters of Ezra Pound,* 1907 - 1941. New York: Harcourt Brace. 1950.

PERRY, RALPH BARTON, *The Thought and Character of William James.* Cambridge, Mass.: Harvard University Press, 1948.

POLLACK, THOMAS CLARK, and CARGILL, OSCAR. *Thomas Wolfe at Washington Square.* London: Oxford University Press, 1954.

RICE, ELMER. *Minority Report.* New York: Simon and Schuster, 1963.

SANTAYANA, GEORGE. *Persons and Places.* 3 vols. New York: Charles Scribner's Sons, 1963.

SHEAFFER, LOUIS. *Eugene O'Neill, Son and Playwright.* Boston: Little, Brown, 1968.

SINCLAIR, UPTON, *My Lifetime in Letters.* Columbus: Univ. of Missouri Press. 1960.

STEFFENS, LINCOLN. *Autobiography of Lincoln Steffens.* New York: Literary Guild, 1931.

STOCK, NOEL. *The Life of Ezra Pound.* New York: Pantheon, 1970.

STONG, PHILLIP D. *If School Keeps.* New York: Frederick Stokes, 1940.

STUART, JESSE. *The Thread That Runs So True.* New York: Charles Scribner's Sons, 1951.

TARBELL, IDA. *All in the Day's Work.* New York: Macmillan, 1939.

THOMPSON, LAWRANCE. *Robert Frost: The Early Years.* New York: Holt, Rinehart, and Winston, 1966.

TUNIS, JOHN. *A Measure of Independence.* New York: Atheneum, 1964.

UNTERMEYER, LOUIS. *Bygones.* New York: Harcourt, Brace, 1965.

———. *The Letters of Robert Frost to Louis Untermeyer,* New York: Holt, Rinehart, and Winston, 1963.

WHITE, WILLIAM ALLEN. *Autobiography.* New York: Macmillan, 1946.

WOLFE, THOMAS. *The Letters of Thomas Wolfe.* Edited by Elizabeth Nowell. New York: Charles Scribner's Sons, 1956.

6. Novels, Plays, and Essays

ALBEE, EDWARD. *Who's Afraid of Virginia Woolf?* New York: Pocket Books, 1966.

ANDERSON, ROBERT. "Tea and Sympathy." In *Fifty Best Plays of the American Theater.* New York: Crown, 1969.

AUCHINCLOSS, LOUIS. *The Rector of Justin.* Boston: Houghton Mifflin, 1964.

BACON, JOSEPHINE DODGE. *Smith College Stories.* Freeport, N.Y.: Books for Libraries, 1969.

BALLARD, PHOEBE and TODHUNTER. *The Man Who Stole a University.* Garden City: Doubleday, 1967.

BARR, STRINGFELLOW. *Purely Academic.* New York: Simon and Schuster, 1958.

BELLAMY, EDWARD. *Looking Backward.* Boston: Houghton Mifflin, 1929.

BELLOW, SAUL. *Herzog.* New York: Viking, 1965.

BENNET, MILDRED R., ed. *Willa Cather's Short Fiction*. (Lincoln: University of Nebraska Press, 1965.

BIERCE, AMBROSE. *The Collected Works of Ambrose Bierce*. 12 vols. New York: Gordian Press, 1966.

BOYESEN, HJALMAR HJORTH. *The Mammon of Unrighteousness*. Upper Saddle River, N.J.: Literature House, 1970.

BRACE, GERALD WARNER. *The Department*. W. W. Norton, 1968.

———. *The Spire*. New York: W. W. Norton, 1952.

BRADY, CYRUS TOWNSEND. *A Doctor of Philosophy*. New York: Charles Scribner's Sons, 1903.

BROMFIELD, LOUIS. *The Farm*. New York, Harper, 1946.

BROWN, STERLING et al. eds. *The Negro Caravan*. New York: Arno Press and *The New York Times*, 1969.

CALITRI, CHARLES, *The Father*. New York: Crown, 1962.

CATHER, WILLA. *Five Stories*. New York: Vintage, 1956.

———. *The Professor's House*. New York: Alfred A. Knopf, 1925.

CHESNUTT, CHARLES. *The House Behind the Cedars*. Ridgewood, N.J.: The Gregg Press, 1968.

CHODOROV, EDWARD. "Decision." In *The Best Plays of 1943 - 1944*, ed. Burns Mantle. New York: Dodd, Mead, 1944.

CHURCHILL, WINSTON. *A Far Country*. New York: Macmillan, 1915.

COZZENS, JAMES GOULD. *Children and Others*. New York: Harcourt, Brace, 1964.

CRAIG, JOSHUA. *Tales Out of School*. Boston: Houghton Mifflin, 1961.

DIXON, THOMAS. *The Leopard's Spots*. Ridgefield, N.J.: The Gregg Press, 1967.

DREISER, THEODORE. *The Bulwark*. Garden City: Doubleday, 1946.

DU BOIS, W. E. B. *Mansart Builds a House*. New York: Mainstream, 1959.

ELIOT, T. S. *Selected Essays*. New York: Harcourt, Brace, 1960.

ELLIS, ELMER. *Finley Peter Dunne: Peter Dooley at His Best*. New York: Charles Scribner's Sons, 1938.

ELLISON, RALPH. *The Invisible Man*. New York: New American Library, 1952.

EPHRON, PHOEBE and HENRY. *Take Her, She's Mine*. New York: Random House, 1962.

FARRELL, JAMES T. *Father and Son*. New York: Vanguard, 1940.

———. *The League of Frightened Philistines*. New York: Vanguard, 1945.

———. *My Days of Anger*. New York: Vanguard, 1943.

———. *The Silence of History*. New York: Vanguard, 1964.

———. *Studs Lonigan*. 3 vols. in one. New York: Vanguard, 1935.

FAST, HOWARD. *The Passion of Sacco and Vanzetti*. New York: Blue Heron Press, 1953.

FERBER, EDNA. *So Big*. Garden City: Doubleday, 1924.

FISHER, DOROTHY CANFIELD. *Seasoned Timber*. New York: Harcourt, Brace, 1939.

FISHER, VARDIS. *No Villain Need Be*. Garden City: Doubleday, 1936.
———. *We Are Betrayed*. Garden City, Doubleday, 1935.
FITCH, GEORGE H. *At Good Old Siwash*. New York: Grosset and Dunlap, 1911.
FITZGERALD, F. SCOTT. *Letters to His Daughter*. Edited by Andrew Turnbull. New York: Charles Scribner's Sons, 1965.
———. *Tender is the Night*. New York: Charles Scribner's, 1934.
———. *This Side of Paradise*. New York: Charles Scribner's Sons, 1920.
FORMAN, RONALD. *Time Out*. New York: The Macauley Co., 1931.
GOODMAN, PAUL. *The Empire City*. Indianapolis: Bobbs-Merrill, 1959.
HERRICK, ROBERT. *Chimes*. New York: Macmillan, 1926.
HERSEY, JOHN. *The Child Buyer*. New York: Alfred A. Knopf, 1960.
HOWE, E. W. *The Story of a Country Town*. New York: Dodd, Mead, 1927.
JACKSON, SHIRLEY. *Hangsaman*. New York: Farrar, Straus, and Young, 1952.
JARRELL, RANDALL. *Pictures from an Institution*. New York: Alfred A. Knopf, 1955.
———. *A Sad Heart at the Supermarket*. New York: Atheneum, 1962.
JOHNSON, OWEN. *The Lawrenceville Stories*. New York: Simon and Schuster, 1967.
LEWIS, SINCLAIR. *Anne Vickers*. Garden City: Doubleday, 1933.
———. *Babbitt*. New York: Harcourt, Brace, 1925.
———. *Elmer Gantry*. New York: Harcourt, Brace, 1927.
———. *Gideon Planish*. New York: Random House, 1943.
———. *The Trail of the Hawk*. New York: Harper, 1915.
LEWISOHN, LUDWIG. *The Island Within*. New York: Harper, 1928.
LINDSEY, HOWARD, and CROUSE, RUSSELL. *Tall Story*. New York: Random House, 1959.
LLOYD, URI JOHN. *Stringtown on the Pike*. New York: Dodd, Mead, 1900.
LONDON, JACK. *Martin Eden*. London: Bodley Head, 1965.
MALAMUD, BERNARD. *A New Life*. New York: Farrar, Straus, and Cudahy, 1961.
MARKS, PERCY. *The Plastic Age*. New York: Grosset and Dunlap, 1924.
MARQUAND, JOHN P. *H. M. Pulham, Esquire*. Garden City: Sun Dial Press, 1944.
———. *The Late George Apley*. Boston: Little, Brown, 1956.
MASTERS, EDGAR LEE. *Skeeters Kirby*. New York: Macmillan, 1923.
MENCKEN, H. L. *A Mencken Chrestomathy*. New York: Albert A. Knopf, 1956.
———. *Prejudices, Third Series*. New York: Alfred A. Knopf, 1922.
MERIWETHER, JAMES B., ed. *Essays, Speeches, and Public Letters of William Faulkner*. New York: Random House, 1965.
MICHENER, JAMES. *The Fires of Spring*. New York: Random House, 1949.
MILLER, ARTHUR. *The Death of a Salesman*. New York: Viking, 1964.
MORRISON, THEODORE. *To Make a World*. New York: Viking, 1957.
———. *The Stones of the House*. New York: Viking, 1953.

NEMEROV, HOWARD. *The Homecoming Game*. New York: Simon and Schuster, 1957.

NORRIS, FRANK. *Vandover and the Brute*. Garden City: Doubleday, 1928.

NORTON, CHARLES ELIOT, ed. *Orations and Addresses of George William Curtis*. 2 vols. New York: Harper, 1894.

O'NEILL, EUGENE. *Ten Lost Plays*. New York: Random House, 1964.

POOLE, ERNEST. *His Family*. New York: Macmillan, 1917.

POUND, EZRA. *Polite Essays*. Freeport, N.Y.: Books for Libraries, 1966.

RICE, ELMER. *We the People*. New York: Coward, McCann, 1933.

SALINGER, JEROME D. *The Catcher in the Rye*. New York: Bantam Books, 1966.

SANTAYANA, GEORGE. *The Last Puritan*. New York: Charles Scribner's Sons, 1946.

SAROYAN, WILLIAM. *The Human Comedy*. New York: Harcourt, Brace, 1943.

SHELDON, CHARLES M. *In His Steps*. New York: Winston, 1937.

SINCLAIR, UPTON. *Boston*. 2 vols. New York: Albert and Charles Boni, 1928.

———. *CO-OP*. New York: Farrar and Rinehart, 1936.

———. *Love's Pilgrimage*. New York: M. Kennerley, 1911.

———. *Oil*. New York: Grosset and Dunlap, 1927.

———. *Samuel the Seeker*. New York: B. W. Dodge, 1910.

STUART, JESSE. *Mr. Gallion's School*. New York: McGraw-Hill, 1967.

TARKINGTON, BOOTH. *The Magnificent Ambersons*. Garden City: Doubleday, 1927.

THURBER, JAMES and NUGENT, ELLIOT. *The Male Animal*. New York: Samuel French, 1941.

TOURGÉE, ALBION W. *A Fool's Errand*. New York: Harper, 1966.

TWAIN, MARK, and WARNER, CHARLES DUDLEY. *The Gilded Age*. New York: Trident, 1964.

WILKINS, MARY E. *The Portion of Labor*. New York: Harper, 1901.

WILSON, EDMUND. *I Thought of Daisy*. New York: Charles Scribner's Sons, 1929.

WOLFE, THOMAS. *Of Time and the River*. New York: Charles Scribner's Sons, 1935.

Index

273